Praise for *Rogue*

'One of the most entertaining books I've read i
of work, it really is. If it didn't matter so muc. ̤ ̤ ̤ ̤ ̤ ̤ ̤ ̤ ̤ ̤ ̤ ̤ ̤ ̤.... but it does
matter, and that's the point that you make.'
— Bruce Whitfield, *The Money Show*, 702

'This is one of the most engaging accounts that I have read in a long, long time ...
If it were up to me, this book would be in every school in the country! ... A very
important and timeous book; read it and have fun.'
— Marianne Thamm, *Daily Maverick* webinar

'This is a well written, superbly researched and highly entertaining history of how
the pervasive, systemic corruption of the apartheid years elided into South Africa's
democratic era. The rogues' gallery of characters reads like a who's who of lowlife
hoodlums out of a B-grade movie. Sadly, the consequences of their brazen thievery are
devastating for those who most need an honest, accountable and competent government. Anyone who wants an incredulous belly laugh at the crookery of our rulers
from time immemorial, and all who care about our democracy and accountability,
should read this book.'   — Andrew Feinstein, author of *After the Party*

'It may just be time to toss the history setwork books ... So much of what is written
today is lifeless or devoid of the necessary context that the public quickly loses interest,
but when you have writers such as these who are able to single out the rotten apples
for the ridicule they so richly deserve, that is something worth investing in – as readers
should in this book.'   — John Harvey, *Daily Dispatch*

'As you're reading *'Rogues' Gallery*, you realise that our politicians are no more corrupt
now than those in the past, and that only brave, honest people with the guts to blow
the whistle have saved us. It reinforces the need for fearless investigative journalism,
which has been the downfall of corruption and looting for centuries.'
— Lesley Stones, *Business Day*

'*Rogues' Gallery* lees soos 'n geskiedenisboek van Suid-Afrikaanse korrupsie, maar die
aanslag is allesbehalwe styf en dooierig met brokkies mond-oophang-inligting, spot-
prente, koerantknipsels en voorheen ongepubliseerde foto's wat vindingryk gebruik
word ... 'n belangrike boek wat 'n mens móét lees as jy will saam gesels oor korrupsie.'
— Theunis Engelbrecht, *Rapport*

About the authors

Matthew Blackman has written as a journalist on corruption in South Africa, as well as on art, literature and history. He recently completed a PhD in Creative and Critical Writing at the University of East Anglia. He lives in Cape Town with a dog of nameless breed.

Nick Dall has an MA in Creative Writing from the University of Cape Town. As a journalist covering everything from cricket to chameleons, his favourite stories are always those about people – dead or alive, virtuous or villainous. He lives in Cape Town with his wife and three daughters.

ROGUES' GALLERY

An Irreverent History of Corruption in South Africa, from the VOC to the ANC

MATTHEW BLACKMAN AND NICK DALL

PENGUIN BOOKS

Published by Penguin Books
an imprint of Penguin Random House South Africa (Pty) Ltd
Reg. No. 1953/000441/07
The Estuaries No. 4, Oxbow Crescent, Century Avenue, Century City, 7441
PO Box 1144, Cape Town, 8000, South Africa
www.penguinrandomhouse.co.za

Penguin
Random House
South Africa

First published 2021
Reprinted in 2021 (three times)

5 7 9 10 8 6 4

Cover images
Lord Charles Somerset: Cape Town Archives Repository; **Paul Kruger:** Library of Parliament, South Africa; **Sir George Yonge:** Cape Town Archives Repository; **Nico Diederichs:** supplied; **Cecil John Rhodes:** public domain; **Kaiser Matanzima:** source unknown; **Lucas Mangope:** source unknown; **Jacob Zuma:** © World Economic Forum/Eric Miller, CC BY-SA 2.0 via Wikimedia Commons; **Eschel Rhoodie:** National Archives, Pretoria; **Magazine letters:** vsilvek/shutterstock.com

PUBLISHER: Marlene Fryer
MANAGING EDITOR: Robert Plummer
EDITOR: Alice Inggs
PROOFREADER: Lisa Compton
COVER DESIGNER: Ryan Africa
TYPESETTER: Monique van den Berg
INDEXER: Sanet le Roux

Set in 11 pt on 15 pt Minion

Printed by **novus print**, a division of Novus Holdings

MIX
Paper from
responsible sources
FSC
www.fsc.org   FSC® C022948

ISBN 978 1 77609 590 2 (print)
ISBN 978 1 77609 591 9 (ePub)

To Shelly

And in memory of Michael Blackman

CONTENTS

INTRODUCTION

'The problem began when Jan van Riebeeck came here.' – Jacob Zuma

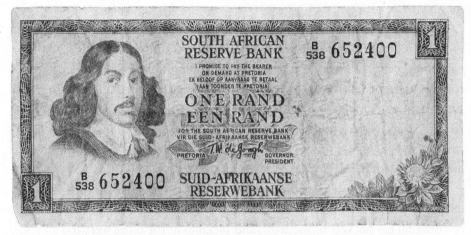

Jan van Riebeeck was considered too ugly to be the face of old
South African banknotes. A seventeenth-century Johnny Depp, by the
name of Bartholomeus Vermuyden, was chosen as his replacement

W HEN EXACTLY DID CORRUPTION START in South Africa? A lack of written records means we can't say for sure what went down prior to 1652. But we do know that Jan van Riebeeck, the once venerated founding father of colonial South Africa, ended up at the Cape because he'd been accused of graft at the Dutch East India Company's Tonkin trading post in Vietnam. That is, he was accused (although technically never found guilty – a common trend even today) of the very definition of corruption: utilising his 'official position' to, as Kempe Ronald Hope and Bornwell Chikulo put it, 'gain recognizable benefit for himself'.[1]

It is tempting to say that good old Jan brought with him to South Africa what some have termed 'the pandemic of corruption' and others refer to as 'our national sport'. The word 'corruption' does, after all, have its roots in Europe, coming from the Latin verb *rumpere*, which implies the breaking of something 'altogether' or 'completely'. In this there is the suggestion that it takes more than just one rogue to break something 'altogether'. And in South Africa, as you will discover in the pages that follow, corruption has in many ways been a multiracial, multicultural and multilingual endeavour.

The story of Van Riebeeck's corruption is, however, one of failure. Because, unlike the other men in this book (and they are all men), he resigned just before he could fill his pockets in Vietnam, and pickings at the Cape were too slim for him to make any real cash.

An up-and-coming employee of the Dutch East India Company (VOC), Van Riebeeck (who 'understood the Vietnamese language well and behaved civilly to the Vietnamese') was denied the top job in 'Nam after being accused of an illegal side hustle in 1648, and he hightailed it (in the seventeenth-century sense of the word) back to the Netherlands before he could be fired.[2]

As fate would have it, the ship that took him home stopped in Table Bay to pick up some men who'd spent almost a year living near what is today the Dolphin Beach Hotel after their vessel, the *Nieuw Haarlem*, had run aground the previous winter. Their descriptions of the Cape's fertile land, abundant fish and livestock, and relatively easy access to fresh water and firewood piqued Van Riebeeck's interest, so much so that he added his voice to their calls for the Company to establish a maritime replenishment service there.[3]

The *Haarlem* survivors submitted a 'remonstration' that went to great pains to convince the notoriously tight-fisted Company directors of how cheap it would be to establish a settlement. Their document also dismissed the popular conception that indigenous Africans were 'man-eating people' as 'nonsense', explaining that 'the killing of our people is caused more by revenge due to the stealing of their cattle, than because they want to eat us'. It would make sense, they argued, for the new settlement to have 'a good commander who treats the indigenous people politely and who pays for everything that is bartered from them, and to treat some of them with a bellyful of food'.[4]

They would not get their wish. In an attempt to climb back on the Company ladder, Van Riebeeck successfully petitioned to be the Cape's first commander. He was, according to Eric Walker, 'a thick-set, determined little man of thirty-three',[5] who, from the first day he set foot on South African soil, as he wrote in his

What Van Riebeeck really looked like: 'a thick-set, determined little man'

journal, saw the people of our 'wild nation [as] very bold, thievish, and not at all to be trusted'.[6]

As we've mentioned, the lack of written records means it's impossible to say with any certainty how virtuous or corrupt South Africans were before 1652. That said, one does get the impression from Van Riebeeck's journal (admittedly not an objective source) that knavery comes naturally to all members of the human race. It should come as no surprise that he had it in for the local population:

Hottentoos [Van Riebeeck used the term to refer to indigenous people of the Cape Peninsula] without cattle arrive at the fort, boldly stealing whatever they can lay their hands upon, not hesitating to deprive our people even under the fort, when unarmed, of their property, and coaxing the children aside to rob them of their brass buttons, though they are so well treated.[7]

His contempt for a man known to the Dutch as 'Herry' and by his own people as Autshumao, who acted as a go-between and interpreter, is a little more surprising:

All our cattle, 44 in number, stolen Sunday by the Watermen [known today as the Goringhaikona] during Divine service. The thieves have always been protected by us since our arrival, and we have shown them much kindness, especially the interpreter Herry, who daily dined at our table, and was clothed with Dutch clothes and adorned with a copper chain, a stick and plates. The others likewise were always well fed, and consequently always prepared to fetch water and fuel, to milk the cows and take charge of the calves. We were as kind to them as if they were our own people, and we believed that they were as favourably disposed towards us. We find that we have been deceived.[8]

The same goes for his own Company employees:

June 29th. Reported, that a soldier, Evert Barentz, of Groningen, had last night, during prayers, stolen some barley from the stores – denied it at first, but promised his liberty, he confessed that Hendrick Juriaensz, of Swartsluys, had urged him to do it. Various others had eaten of the barley, but all declared that they did not know whence it came, only that said Juriaensz had stated that he had obtained it from the *Tulp*. Being called he confessed everything and shewed the place where more had been hidden; consequently apprehended with Eldert Jansz, of Oost Friesland, who had mounted guard to do the deed.[9]

While Barentz managed to avoid punishment by ratting on his mates (plenty of that in the pages to follow), Juriaensz was keelhauled (and thrashed for good measure) and Jansz was made to fall three times from the yardarm, a punishment which involved being dropped from a ship's mast with your arms tied behind your back, generally resulting in two dislocated shoulders.

However comic the crimes and gruesome the punishments, this pilfering of cattle, brass buttons and barley is hardly worth writing home about when one considers the great feats of corruption that are to follow. The truth is, the Cape of the 1650s was not a sufficiently developed bureaucratic state for bona fide corruption as we know it to thrive. (Which is probably why Van Riebeeck spent much of his ten-year stay dreaming of a promotion to India.)

Certainly, Van Riebeeck did begin to *rumpere* many things in the Fairest Cape, setting in motion a process of land expropriation for the success of the service and the benefit of his employer, the legacy of which remains with us today.[10] But to see real 'abuse of public resources or public power for personal gain'[11] we would have to wait a few more years. By 1700, thanks to the ~~selfless nation-building~~ shameless self-enrichment of one Simon van der Stel, the stage was set for our nation's first home-grown corruptor. And given our status as a world leader in using family ties to 'break' the state 'altogether', it should come as no surprise that that honour should befall Simon's biological and ideological son – the (dis)Honourable Willem Adriaan.

PART ONE
OUTPOST AT THE CAPE

Colonial South Africa started off as little more than a victualling station for ships bound to or from the East. But it didn't take long for a succession of corrupt governors to rock the boat (and very nearly sink it too).

CHAPTER I

WILLEM ADRIAAN VAN DER STEL

At the Company's Expense
1699–1707

*'He was grossly immoral – to such a degree that he forbade the reading of the Ten Commandments at any service held in his presence.' – **Leo Fouché**[1]*

A replica of a painting (destroyed in a fire in Dublin in 1962)
which supposedly showed Willem Adriaan as a toddler with his father,
Simon van der Stel, who preceded him as governor of the Cape.
No verified portraits of either Van der Stel exist

Drinks on the governor!

February has always been Cape Town's hottest month, but for Governor Willem Adriaan van der Stel the February of 1706 was to prove the hottest of the lot. In his seven years in charge of the Dutch East India Company's newest and poorest colony, he had managed to make himself a very rich man – and hide this fact from the Company's directors back in the Netherlands. But now all of that was about to change.

The Cape outpost founded by Jan van Riebeeck in 1652 was never intended to be anything more than a maritime replenishment station for VOC ships bound to or from the East. A cure for scurvy would only be discovered a century later, but the Company had already worked out that stopping midway through the eight-month voyage to take on fresh provisions had a positive effect on the health of both its men and its balance sheet. The Company, which made all its money importing Asian goods like spices, textiles and ceramics to Europe, had no desire to establish a meaningful colony in 'dark', 'dangerous' and 'unprofit-able' Africa.

When the fleet from Batavia (present-day Jakarta, the VOC's administrative centre in the East) docked – bringing with it copies of documents which showed that an official complaint had been made about his behaviour – Willem Adriaan went into publicity overdrive. His actions would have made a modern-day repu-tation manager proud.

Before the fleet sailed on to Amsterdam, Willem Adriaan summoned all the male inhabitants of Cape Town to his official residence at the Castle of Good Hope. Whites, blacks, liberated slaves and ex-convicts mustered at the unpopu-lar governor's residence. Artisans and labourers of every description, fishermen and farmhands all gathered in the handsome courtyard overlooked by Table Mountain.

Imagine their surprise when, instead of receiving the *moering* they'd come to expect, they were plied with wine, beer and coffee. Even their pipes were stoked with the finest tobacco at the governor's expense. They should have known there was no such thing as a free lunch – not even in 1706.

Once sufficiently loosened up, the men were required to sign a certificate in which the governor was described as

[a] person of all honour and virtue in his whole conduct, government, inter-course, and treatment. That he always set, and always has set, a splendid

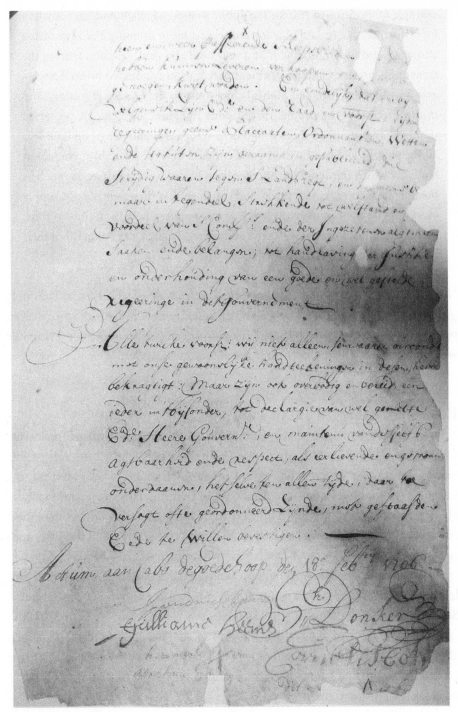

The 'certificate of good conduct' that Willem Adriaan coerced the burghers into signing

example of modesty, of zeal for the public welfare, of religion in the Christian form; further, that he is affable towards everyone, in listening and in granting audience, and finally, that he is of a very kind and gentle nature. During the time of his presence and government here, he has conducted himself always as a peace-loving, just, and faithful chief towards the Lords his masters, and in the interests of the people. He has done right and justice to all, protected the good, and punished the evil, and helped forwards and placed on their legs all the people who had by their good conduct deserved it ... by giving them lands on which they could properly earn a living; by taking care as much as possible of their corn, vineyards, and cattle, so that they were able to supply everything to the Company, as much as was required here from time to time, as well as to the passing ships' crews and others, selling and getting rid of their produce to their satisfaction.[2]

Not that the men who signed the document were aware of its contents. They only got to hear a few lines, read by a clerk in 'an extremely indistinct voice' before being politely 'requested'[3] by some heavies to put pen to paper – presumably while the governor leered over their shoulders.

Beelzebub comes to Satan's aid

A bit of free booze may have been enough to secure the signatures of the towns-folk on Van der Stel's certificate of good character; getting the burghers to sing his praises, on the other hand, would prove far trickier. It was, after all, the burghers – under the leadership of Adam Tas, Henning Hüsing, Jacobus van der Heiden and Pieter van der Bijl, who were more literate (and wealthier) than most of the other burghers – who had lodged an official complaint about the governor's corrupt practices.

In an effort to get the burghers on board, Willem Adriaan resorted to vio-lence, intimidation and torture. Or at least his henchman Jan Starrenburg, did. Starrenburg was the landdrost of Stellenbosch, a town that Willem Adriaan's father and predecessor as governor, Simon van der Stel, had founded and named after himself. Starrenburg, who'd only been landdrost a few months, had already earned himself the nickname Beelzebub among the burghers, thanks to his status as 'Satan's' right-hand man.

Burgher with an 'h'

To properly understand Willem Adriaan's crimes, you've got to know what a burgher is. For the first four years of Jan van Riebeeck's rule, Company employees were responsible for growing all the fruit and vegetables the ships needed and for bartering cattle from the Khoikhoin herders. That all changed in 1657, when, in an attempt to reduce their massive wage bill, the VOC decided to release some employees from their contracts in favour of giving them land to farm at their own expense. Anything these *vrye burghers* ('free citizens') produced could then be sold to the Company (at strictly regulated prices) for distribution to passing ships.

The free burgher experiment started small — the first nine burghers were given plots on the banks of the Liesbeek River in what is now suburban Cape Town (Observatory, Mowbray, Newlands) — but within a few years the Company had become dependent on the model, and scores of free burghers owned farms that reached far into the Boland. The economic market at the Cape was so tiny that for the burghers to be able to make a living, competition from Company officials had to be strictly prohibited. In 1668, aware that the free burghers needed all the encouragement they could get to stick it out at the Cape, the VOC directors in Amsterdam passed a law banning Company officials from having 'larger gardens or a greater number of cattle than they required for the use of their own households'. Over the decades that followed, senior officials at the Cape would be frequently reminded of this dictate. The burghers, however, were never made aware of its existence.[4]

Together with a band of armed ruffians, Beelzebub went from farm to farm trying to persuade the burghers to sign the document. His tactics, as per Adam Tas's diary, were not subtle.

> First the Landdrost tried to induce them to sign by promises, and afterwards with fierce threats. During the time he was so overcome with wrath that he became livid in the face and was shaking as he read out the document. A ruffian stood guard at the door, which he had locked.[5]

Similar scenes played out at farmhouses throughout the Boland. Beelzebub would sit at a table with his sword and pistols drawn while armed thugs stood guard at the door. There, he would induce the landowners to sign their names, trying 'every possible means; fair promises of favour and land, dire threats of how the governor should deal with all who refused to sign, how they would be stripped of every privilege, how they should be punished as rebels ...'[6] But still, as Tas recorded in his diary, many of the burghers refused to sign.

> This evening, the table being ready set for a mouthful of meat, there put in two Frenchmen, Etienne Niel and Jaques Malan. They told me that at Hercules du Pre's, Landdrost Beelzebub had made question of them, if they had aught to say against the Governor, and if they did not know him for an honest man, that did govern well, and was an upholder of religion. The same was read out to them in a letter, in order to their signing, but Mr. Niel declared to know nothing of it, and that he would not sign. Then come the Landdrost aboard him with harsh threatenings, but he give him for answer that he would not sign, no, not though Haman's gallows was building for him, and that he would make bold to affirm the same to the Governor his face, that he was dismayed of no man, and that rogues and robbers might be afeared, and more of like purport. The Landdrost declaring they should meet again, the man departed. Then Jaques Malan entered into the apartment, and received the same treatment, but give for answer that he would not sign, whereupon the Landdrost did call out. Then get you gone from here, and with that the man went off.[7]

Between the free lunch at the Castle and the strong-arm tactics of Beelzebub, Willem Adriaan was able to muster 240 signatures on the document attesting his good conduct. But it should be noted that around two dozen of these belonged to 'blacks, liberated slaves and convicts' (people whose opinions weren't normally canvassed in those days) in an attempt to bump up the numbers.[8] What's more, as one of the fathers of South African historiography, George McCall Theal, puts it:

> Not a few of the respectable names found on that extraordinary document are certainly not genuine, for they appear with a cross, though the men they professed to represent could write letters and sign other papers as well as the Governor himself could do.[9]

Considering the tactics used by Willem Adriaan, and the fact that the Cape's European population in 1705 numbered 526 adult men,[10] 240 signatures was actually a rather poor showing.

The next step in the reputation manager's playbook was for Willem Adriaan to turn his malevolent attentions towards his accusers, imprisoning many of the main conspirators and eventually physically or emotionally torturing several of them, including Tas, into recanting their accusations. But before we detail that tyranny, let's first examine the precise nature of the burghers' beef.

Nkandla version 1.0

When Dutch traveller and VOC chronicler Reverend François Valentijn visited in 1705, Vergelegen left an overwhelmingly positive impression on him:

> Next day I viewed this lovely homestead [with] an exceptionally lovely view in the direction of the False Cape, over the vineyards and other cultivation, as also towards the bay of the False Cape; and in addition there was a flower-garden on the other side, ornamentally laid out in four sections, and a fine river which divided into two branches.
>
> Asparagus and potatoes are not very common, though I ate of both on the estate Vergelegen of Heer Willem Adriaan van der Stel in Hottentots-Holland, as lovely and tasty as one could wish, and although the asparagus was only moderately large and barely as thick as an ordinary finger, it was so tender that all of it could be eaten; and the potatoes are exceptional both in flavour and scent, both red and white though for the most part oval ...[11]

There's much, much more where this came from, but you get the gist. Even today, Vergelegen stands head and shoulders above the competition as arguably the fairest Cape wine estate of them all. But don't let the noble proportions of the Cape Dutch architecture, the magnificent gardens and handsome camphor trees (even the trees are National Monuments!) fool you. Although no fire pools were seamlessly landscaped into Vergelegen's gorgeous grounds, it is the eighteenth-century equivalent of Nkandla.

The similarities between Vergelegen and Nkandla are buried in the document known as the Memorial, which was penned in 1705 by sixty-three burghers from Stellenbosch and Drakenstein. After years of maltreatment, they had finally plucked up the courage to put pen to paper – and to slip this catalogue of their grievances against Willem Adriaan onto a ship bound for Batavia. It was a very dangerous thing to do 'for if their names were to become known they knew that they would be made to feel the vengeance' of a governor who had the 'military power of the colony fully at his disposal'.[12]

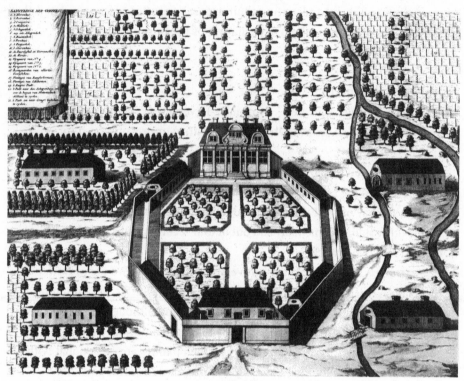

Vergelegen, as depicted by the complaining burghers in the Memorial

But still, they went ahead with their plan. The document starts thus:

> HON GENTLEMEN, Pressed by high necessity, we humbly take the liberty to lay our just complaints before you, especially because we are not only very much oppressed here by an unjust and haughty domination of the present governor, Willem Adriaan van der Stel, but treated worse than slaves. Bearing in mind we are free burghers and subjects of the States-General, it can easily be conceived that this unheard-of oppression must redouble our sorrows. What they are, we have decided in all truth to communicate as briefly as possible to your Honours as the unshakeable maintainers of right and fairness.[13]

It then goes on to list thirty-eight specific grievances, although, thanks to Tas's elegant penmanship, the nub of their complaint is contained in grievance number one.

> You are informed that the Governor has built, about twelve hours distant from the Cape, a country seat, large beyond measure, and of such broad dimensions, as if it were a whole town. Besides that, he possesses very many lands on whose area at least 50 farmers would be able to earn their living. He sows on that place annually an immense quantity of corn and has also planted a vineyard there of more than 400,000 vines. He possesses fully 800 head of cattle and 10,000 sheep. On that farm there are more than 60 Company's servants, subalterns, sailors and soldiers. All these people draw their pay, salary and rations from the Company, but the Governor uses them for his own private purposes. He has besides, on the same place and in his private service, some of the best slaves of the Company – as much as 100. He also uses for his own service daily the Company's smiths and wagon makers, and has for his wagons, ploughs, and what further belongs to agriculture, made from the Company's iron, whilst the wood is cut for him in the Company's forests.[14]

Quite something, considering Willem Adriaan was forbidden to own 'larger gardens or a greater number of cattle than [he] required for the use of [his] own household'.

The document also accuses Willem Adriaan of obtaining a thousand head of cattle 'by violent means'; of compromising the Colony's defence by spending weeks on end away from the Castle; of buying wine 'from poor farmers at a very low price and selling it to foreign ships at an enormous profit'; of compelling bakers 'by threats of his displeasure … to buy his wheat at high prices'; of 'requiring to be bribed before he would issue title deeds'; of not allowing the burghers to fell trees for timber or fish in the best fishing spots; and of paying no tithes.[15]

The burghers' document focuses only on the governor's professional failings. But, off the record, they had plenty to say about his personal life too. Theal notes that 'in his domestic life he was said to follow closely the example of our Charles II'.[16] This may not mean much now, but at the time the roguish British monarch who fathered at least twelve illegitimate children was the talk of the town.

Continuing this theme, in his diary entry of 24 December 1705, Tas notes:

> They tell me that the Governor's wife had, in a fit of despondency, tried to drown herself by jumping into the fountain behind the house at the Cape; however Mrs Berg [Anna de Koning – more about her later] was on the spot and ran to help her, pulling her out of the water, to whom the Governor's wife lamented that her life had become one of terror for her on account of the many scandalous acts she must daily hear and witness.[17]

So wicked was Willem Adriaan that he ordered that the Ten Commandments could not be read out in any church where he was present. Luckily, the Company clergyman was also on the take, so this was easily arranged. In fact, Clause 5 of the document is dedicated entirely to this fine man of the cloth, who was 'one of the largest agriculturists' at the Cape.

> He makes no work whatever of religion, as he occupies himself much more with his lands than with the pulpit ... It has often happened that people from the country, living two or three hours away from the Cape, had arrived in order to have their children baptized, or to be united in wedlock, but they were obliged to return home disappointed, as the preacher, in order to mind his worldly interests, was away in the country ... To some members who live somewhat out of the way he sends a drunken sexton, to others a Hottentot with a note; whereas it was beyond contradiction, his own personal duty. However irregular these matters may be, he cares very little about them, as he has wormed himself into the favour of the Governor.[18]

Finally, in clauses 37 and 38, the document comes to an impassioned conclusion where Tas memorably describes Willem Adriaan as 'a scourge unto the people of the land':

> All the above are incontestable proofs that the Governor may justly be considered as a scourge unto the people of the land, because he not only envies them their prosperity, but as far as possible, endeavours to pump them dry, and expose them to the danger of ruin. He uses as his maxim – a poor community is easily governed. But this is not to be wondered at, as he is insensible to virtue, and has not the slightest respect for an honest man, but

coarse knaves who live by roguery and theft are his best friends, and stand in great favour with him, as they fill his pockets. He moreover lends his ears to insipid people and flatterers, being afraid of the truth.[19]

An unlikely friendship

Strangely, one man who spent a lot of time at Vergelegen was the Rajah of Tambora. The rajah and his family had been exiled to the Cape in 1697 for rebelling against the Dutch (he had apparently attempted to murder a puppet leader installed by the Company). He and Willem Adriaan enjoyed very cordial relations. (It is tempting to imagine them drinking tea together as they sat on the handsome stoep that overlooked Vergelegen's rolling vineyards.)

While at Vergelegen, the rajah took advantage of the ample free time amid comfortable surroundings to transcribe the entire Quran from memory. So much did he value the governor's friendship that he presented the volume – thought to be the first copy of the Muslim holy book written at the Cape – to him as a gift. It has never been seen since.

After Willem Adriaan's recall, the rajah petitioned persistently to be returned to his homeland, but this was not to be, and he died at the Cape in 1719. His five children stayed in South Africa and all eventually converted to Christianity – probably so that they could marry Christians and advance their careers. Some say that the Voortrekker leader Piet Retief is descended from this royal line.

It is probably a good thing for the rajah's descendants that his pleas to return to Tambora were ignored. In 1815, the island was devastated by the largest volcanic eruption ever recorded. The eruption, which was four times more powerful than that of Krakatoa, devastated the island's vegetation and killed somewhere between 50 000 and 120 000 people. The ash cloud it formed travelled as far as London, where, for several months in the summer of 1815, 'brilliantly coloured sunsets and twilights' were observed.

A portrait of the (con) artist as a young man

Willem Adriaan was born in Amsterdam in 1664, the eldest child of Simon van der Stel and the grandson of the first Dutch governor of Mauritius. In 1679, his father was put in charge of the relatively unimportant colony at the Cape. As a teen, Willem spent five years in South Africa before returning to Amsterdam, where he stayed until he took over from his dad in 1699.

To this day, Simon is seen as one of the most effective administrators ever to serve at the Cape. During his twenty years in charge, he ramped up agricultural production and is credited with being the father of the wine industry. But a closer examination of the facts shows that he was no saint. His private farm at Constantia (the wine estates now known as Groot Constantia and Klein Constantia, as well as the modern-day suburb of Bergvliet, belonged to him) flouted the same rules that would eventually ensnare his son.

When he got to the Cape in 1699, Willem Adriaan's first move was to buy wine from the burghers at the lowest price possible. As governor, he would then 'improve' this wine (i.e. do absolutely nothing – a trick that would be repeated with dynamite in Kruger's republic) before selling it to passing (non-Dutch) ships at triple-figure profit margins. The Cape's wine market, however, was disappointingly small. The opportunities for profit were too meagre to keep Willem Adriaan's sticky fingers satisfied.

He quickly sussed out that the only way to make any real money was to tap into other aspects of the Cape's agriculture industry. Other men might have been put off by the law which forbade Company employees from owning land, but not our Willem Adriaan. Instead, in mysterious circumstances in 1700, he obtained 400 morgen (around 350 hectares) of land in the Hottentots Holland region. Not long afterwards, he added to this by granting a further 117 morgen to one of his dependants and 'buying' this back to form Vergelegen.

The unique challenges of corrupting the Cape

When Willem Adriaan took up his post at the Cape, the VOC had been in existence for just over one hundred years. Its geographic footprint included the nations we now know as South Africa, Mauritius, Indonesia, India, Japan, Taiwan, Malaysia, Thailand and Vietnam. At these outposts, the Company employed thousands of surprisingly poorly paid (depending on rank) officials. The combination of low wages and loose top-down control prompted officials to rob the Company 'in every direction and in the most shameless manner ... Men came to the East to amass wealth in haste. Money must be scraped together no matter how.'[20]

For officials working at trading stations in the East, there was ample opportunity to take their bit on the side – by slipping a few diamonds into one's pocket, perhaps, or by releasing Company funds for a sack of pepper that didn't actually exist. But at the Cape there was, to put it bluntly, virtually nothing to steal. Making a quick fortune at the southern tip of Africa, Willem Adriaan quickly realised, would require some lateral thinking. Luckily, he was richly blessed in this regard ...

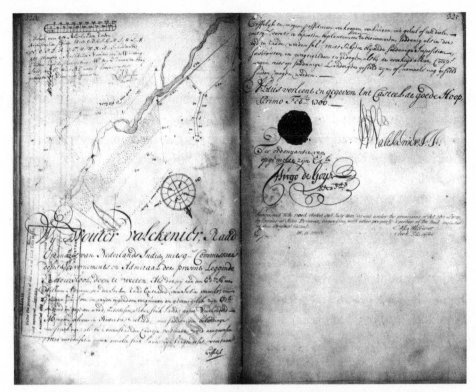

Visiting VOC commissioner Wouter Valckenier couldn't have known what
Willem Adriaan had planned for the land he granted him on 1 February 1700

Immediately, he set to work, laying out vineyards, groves, orchards, building work-
shops, granaries, blacksmith's forges, mills and slave quarters. Not to mention the
splendid manor house that left such an impression on both Reverend Valentijn
and the free burghers. Soon, Willem Adriaan had planted half a million vine stocks
– more than a quarter of the total number of vines in the Cape at the time. 'His
flocks and herds were on the same vast scale': 18 000 sheep and 1 000 head of
cattle roamed an immense swath of land to the east of Vergelegen which extended
as far as present-day Swellendam.[21]

Conjuring such a magnificent estate from next to nought – and in such a
short space of time – would require thousands upon thousands of hours of
manual labour and, in normal circumstances, would result in an enormous
wage bill. But Willem Adriaan simply had it all done for him by Company
employees. Sixty white employees (including the master gardener who was
supposed to be keeping the Company's Garden in Cape Town shipshape) and

hundreds of slaves (admittedly a handful of whom were owned by Willem Adriaan) were simply removed from their posts in Cape Town and seconded to Vergelegen.

As for the raw materials required to construct Vergelegen's many buildings, these were easily pillaged from Company storehouses. And to get around the potentially tricky problem of transporting so many tonnes of stuff to what was then a distant outpost, Willem Adriaan used his clout to commandeer the free burghers' wagons and oxen. 'As a rule, the farmer was much too afraid, much too well aware of his own dependence on the governor's favour, to make any substantial protest or resistance.'[22]

Soon, other VOC employees followed Willem Adriaan's shining example. The secunde (second in command), the commander of the garrison, the clergyman, the treasurer and the Company surgeon all had farms of their own and 'vied with one another in devotion to their new profession'. Willem Adriaan and his comrades 'soon became the formidable rivals of the regular farmer; everywhere, of course, they enjoyed preference, both in the disposal of their produce to the Company, and in the purchase of anything they required from the Company; moreover, unlike the farmer, they paid no tithes'.[23]

Willem Adriaan's brother Frans van der Stel, who *was* a burgher and thus legally allowed to own land, also benefited immensely from his important family connections. Frans 'was in the habit of requiring [the other burghers] to plough his land, to convey his produce to town, and perform other work for him, under threats that if they did not he would see that they should regret it'.[24] Among some quarters, Frans was even more unpopular than his *boet*, as you can see in Clause 9 of the burghers' complaint:

> Of the same doings is the Governor's brother, the so-called Squire Frans van der Stel, as full of them as an egg is full of milk. He treats his neighbours in the most unjust manner in the world, and depending on his brother the Governor, he does as much evil as his bile can suggest. He is a very dangerous instrument; yea! a pest to the Cape, who with pleasure annoys the freemen, considering it an art to cheat anyone; and if it were in his power to ruin the free burghers in one day, he would not take two days to do so.[25]

So, how did they manage to get away with it all for so long? With the utmost of ease, it turns out. For starters, most of the burghers knew absolutely nothing of the law that prohibited Company officials from owning land. Being so far from Company HQ in Amsterdam made it easy for Willem Adriaan (and his dad before him) to keep the burghers in the dark about their rights. Vergelegen's remote location was also extremely beneficial (and by no means accidental) as it allowed Willem Adriaan to conceal his excesses from both the residents of the Cape and the Company directors who occasionally visited Cape Town.

Willem Adriaan might have easily got away with it all, but instead he pushed things too far, squeezing the burghers out of every possible revenue stream and leaning on them for transport and other favours. Lodging an official complaint was a last resort.

'And carried away his writing desk'

Which brings us back to February 1706, in the weeks after our beloved governor had caught wind of the burghers' complaint …

Once he'd begged, bribed and bullied 240 men into signing the document proclaiming his bounteous virtues, Willem Adriaan went on the attack against his accusers. Not that he knew exactly who they were or what precisely they had accused him of. At this stage, he had only seen some of the initial complaints the burghers had forwarded to Batavia. But he was fairly certain something similar would be heading to Amsterdam soon.

In a quest to get to the bottom of the mystery – and hopefully prevent the burghers' gripes from reaching Amsterdam – he resolved to commit 'an act of extreme violence, contrary to all law and justice'. Before dawn on Sunday 28 February, Satan's right-hand man, Beelzebub, swooped on the home of Adam Tas

> … and without a warrant or any legal authority whatever, with a strong-armed party he surrounded the house of that burgher at early dawn in the morning of Sunday the 28th of February 1706, arrested him, sent him a prisoner to Cape Town, searched his house, and carried away his writing desk.[26]

Carrying away Tas's writing desk was the 1706 equivalent of confiscating his smartphone, forcing him to divulge his pin and then going through his WhatsApp chat history. Within the desk's drawers, Willem Adriaan found the smoking gun: an unsigned draft of the memorial the burghers had written to the Lords Seventeen, the VOC's all-powerful board of directors. Other documents in the desk gave away the identities of most of the people who had assisted in writing the memorial.

Tas immediately offered to tell his side of the story in a legitimate court of law. Instead, Willem Adriaan threw him into one of the Castle's mustier corners.

> There two soldiers, with drawn swords, kept guard over him day and night; the chimney of his cell was walled up; his meat and drink were examined, as well as any comforts that were sent him; paper and pen and ink were refused him; whilst his wife, who was unceasing in her prayers to have speech or sight of him, was but seldom admitted. There he lay for thirteen months and seventeen days ...[27]

When Tas's young son died, he wasn't allowed out of prison to see the corpse, let alone attend the funeral. The only time he saw the light of day was for his occasional appearances before a commission (led by Beelzebub) whose members were all hand-picked by Willem Adriaan. For appearance's sake, the governor refrained from actually sitting on the tribunal. Instead, he kept track of proceedings from behind a thin door through which 'it was possible to hear every word'.

> When any difficulty arose the commissioners and the prosecutor would step aside, with no attempt at concealment, to consult with the Governor! The Governor decided the point, and the commission would take action in terms of the decision given from behind the door. So that the commission, apart from its essential illegality, was nothing but a puppet show; it did nothing, it was the Governor who determined everything, and who directed the entire proceedings. Such being the character of the Court, van der Stel had succeeded in creating the following position: the burghers had impeached the Governor, but the Governor in his single person was at once prosecutor and judge in the case against himself.[28]

Many of the burghers refused point-blank to answer the questions put to them by such a heavily stacked jury. This meant that Beelzebub was, in his own words, 'obliged to use other means'. Take, for example, the case of Jacobus van der Heiden. At his first appearance before the tribunal on 9 March, he declined to answer the questions put to him, requesting instead that he be sent to Holland for a fair trial and demanding that Tas's writing desk be returned. One heated discussion culminated with Van der Heiden sarcastically calling Beelzebub 'a brave soldier … You will provoke me to fight now you have taken away my arms.'[29]

Once this had gone on for several hours, Beelzebub – in close consultation with his boss behind the door – threw Van der Heiden in jail. When hauled into the tribunal the following day, Van der Heiden again refused to testify. Day three – same story. By now, Beelzebub was so angered by the burgher who did 'persist with much obstinacy in his naughtiness' that he sought permission to place the prisoner 'in closer confinement, that by such means and other judicial threatenings he may be constrained unto obedience and his duty'.[30]

His duty, of course, being to take back all the nasty things he'd said about the governor.

Van der Heiden was moved to a darker dungeon under constant guard and without access to even 'the smallest comforts' for fifteen days. Suitably softened up – or so Beelzebub thought – he now appeared before the tribunal for a fourth time, where he once again refused to answer questions and complained strongly about his treatment, proclaiming that 'God would avenge' the violence he had suffered.

At this point, Beelzebub sent Van der Heiden to the Donker Gat: 'the most evil hole, from which no man hath ever emerged saving only to the scaffold [gallows]'.[31] There he spent twenty-seven days in the company of a murderer awaiting execution. (If you've been on a tour of the Castle, you'll remember the moment the tour guide cuts the lights and slams the door. The room is so petrifying that it's hard to imagine spending twenty-seven minutes there, let alone twenty-seven days.)

When Van der Heiden appeared before the tribunal for a fifth time, he was threatened with 'many terrifying threats', including rations of dry bread and water and an imminent date with the rack. After a five-hour examination, during which he nearly collapsed from physical exhaustion, he finally agreed to answer Beelzebub's questions and ultimately recanted his accusations against the governor. Once Van der Heiden's signature was in the bag, Willem Adriaan had the Company surgeon tend to the seriously ill prisoner. The death of a burgher in custody would not have been a good look.

Similar tactics were used against many of the other burghers – with some success. In total, thirteen burghers, including Tas himself, recanted their accusations:

The name of the defendant and place of birth? – Adam Tas of Amsterdam.

His age? – About 38 years.

Why he abuses so wickedly in his writings the Governor, his lawful chief, whom he owes every obedience, calling him a fellow lost to all honour, an accursed tyrant, a shameless slanderer, and false-hearted rogue? – He is sorry for it from the bottom of his heart that he wrote and put it down, and that it was done in a fit of mad passion.

Whether it is true, and he can show that 50 farmers can earn their living on the farm of the Governor? – He cannot prove it, but it has been suggested to him.

Whether he has ever been there, or seen that the size of it was as large as a whole town? – He had been there before the place had been completed, and can, therefore, not show that it is as large as a town.[32]

Luckily, when it came to passing judgment on the governor's case, the authorities in Amsterdam saw the recantations for what they were.

But now Willem Adriaan would make his big mistake. On the same ship that carried the sham certificate affirming the governor's good conduct and the thirteen recantations, he also allowed four of the burghers to return to Holland to present their cases in person. Not that he thought this would actually happen. Willem Adriaan had hoped that 'the groans and lamentings and tears of their womenfolk' would persuade the burghers to stay at the Cape. But the burgher men would not be swayed, setting the scene for one of the more hilarious episodes of this whole sorry story.

Accordingly, on the 4th April, when the fleet stood out to sea, the four colonists were still on board. At the last moment van der Stel appears to have realised the folly of allowing them to proceed to the Netherlands, there to give evidence against him. He leapt into a boat and attempted to overhaul the fleet, with the object of bringing the four burghers back again, or at all events Hüsing, the most important of them. Fortunately, the fleet was already out of hail, and the burghers, with their precious Memorial, were able to reach the Netherlands in safety.[33]

The man behind the brandy

Olof Bergh and Anna de Koning, as depicted by the
travelling artist Abraham Salm, who visited the Cape in 1685

Of all Willem Adriaan's lackeys, Olof Bergh, the commander of the garrison and
the name behind one of South Africa's ~~nastiest~~ favourite brandies, deserves special
mention. After arriving at the Cape from Sweden in 1676 aged only twenty-four years
old, Bergh quickly became one of Simon van der Stel's most trusted employees,
successfully leading several important missions into the interior. Soon after his
arrival, Olof married Anna de Koning, a liberated slave from Bengal whose immense
beauty made her the talk of the Cape. Before the decade was out, Bergh had been
appointed to the High Court of Justice.

His whole world came crashing down when he was put on trial for stealing
valuable goods from a shipwreck and concealing their existence from the Company.
Olof was duly banished to Robben Island, and later imprisoned at the Castle.
Once the furore had died down, Olof was demoted and redeployed to Ceylon.
After spending five years rebuilding his reputation in the East, he returned to the
Cape, where his old friend Simon appointed him Commander of the Garrison –
a position he continued to occupy when Willem Adriaan took over from his dad.

With all these friends in high places, and possibly the undeclared spoils of the
shipwrecks he'd plundered, Bergh became a very wealthy man. So wealthy that when
Simon van der Stel died in 1712, it was Bergh who bought Groot Constantia from

his estate. Bergh lived at Groot Constantia until his death in 1725, aged eighty-two. His wife, Anna, continued his legacy as the lady of the manor until 1734. Among the possessions listed in her last will and testament were twenty-seven slaves – including one from Bengal, the place of her birth.

The whistle-blowers' revenge

Even today, with the benefit of modern constitutions and instant communications, being a whistle-blower is a dangerous affair. But, incredibly, Tas and his fellow conspirators would have the last laugh. Granted, their success probably had more to do with the prevailing winds of global politics at the time than it did with their gripes being truly heard, but beggars can't be choosers.

At the very same time that Willem Adriaan's habit of spending weeks on end at his country paradise reached its peak, the Netherlands' involvement in the War of the Spanish Succession was approaching its crescendo. The Company bosses feared that French ships might attack the Cape at any moment, with the aim of seizing the Castle and the richly laden VOC fleets. Such an attack would be catastrophic for both Company and country.

> The great East Indiamen were the bulwarks of the Dutch republic, carrying as they did that wealth which alone enabled the Netherlands to maintain the contest against the most powerful monarch in the world. But van der Stel was deaf to the warnings and instructions of the Seventeen, who bade him 'day and night to be upon his guard' against the enemy. Vergelegen claimed all his time and attention.[34]

To use a modern analogy, it was like Donald Trump abandoning the White House during a crisis to play golf at Mar-a-Lago.

Adding to the directors' fears was the fact that many of the burghers who'd signed the official complaint about the governor's behaviour were French Huguenots, who, the theory went, could easily be persuaded to act as spies for France. None of this appeared to matter to our man Willem Adriaan – he just carried on living it up at Vergelegen, being a bastard to Dutchmen and Huguenots alike.

But history would prove that Willem Adriaan was not above the law. Having carefully considered all the arguments, counter-arguments and political ramifications, the members of the Chamber of Amsterdam signed and sealed a report in which they unanimously acquitted the burghers of 'sedition, conspiracy or treason', and which went on to declare the actions of the governor 'unjust'.[35]

Their report ordered that Willem Adriaan, the secunde Samuel Elsevier, clergyman Petrus Kalden and, of course, Beelzebub be recalled at once. (Like most of the rogues in this book, they retained their salaries and rank until they'd had a chance to defend themselves back home.) It also insisted that Frans van der Stel leave Company territory immediately.

Vergelegen, the report continued, should be returned to the Company. In a moment that seems strangely similar to aspects of the Nkandla debacle, the buildings – which by all accounts were also built using copious Company resources – were to be purchased back from Willem Adriaan at market value.

Turning to the burghers, the report recommended that all those who'd been banished from the Cape by Willem Adriaan be returned to their homes at the Company's expense and all those who had been imprisoned should be liberated immediately. It even proposed recompense for their suffering. The report reiterated the fact that Company officials could not own (or lease) land or trade in cattle, corn or wine 'either directly or indirectly'. Only the free burghers, the report concluded, were allowed to profit from farming at the Cape.

The long goodbye

It being 1706, the news would take some time to find its way to the Cape. A few days after the Chamber reached its decision, a sealed letter was entrusted to a ship's captain, who was on strict instructions to deliver it to the governor 'in the presence of witnesses'. After a nearly six-month voyage to the Cape, he finally got to deliver his important message on the morning of 17 April 1707.

In a formal meeting at the Castle, Willem Adriaan and his cronies were informed of their fate and ordered to return to Europe immediately. What's more, the governor was ordered to pay 'out of his own pocket for each of the woolled sheep he had acquired'.

As it turned out, Willem Adriaan managed to linger a year longer at the Cape, the appointment of one of his nephews as the new secunde having given him some wiggle room. On 23 April 1708, he sailed from the Cape for the last time. When he arrived in Amsterdam several months later, he was immediately dismissed from the Company's service.

Back at the Cape, Vergelegen was divided into four farms, which were sold by auction in October 1709. According to the Lords Seventeen, the manor house was to be broken down 'to avoid setting an example of ostentation'.[36]

Barend Gildenhuys, the new owner of the portion with the house on it, appears to have sidestepped these instructions by paying Willem Adriaan for the materials but neglecting to demolish much of the house. Renovations in the twentieth century showed that the majority of the building stood on its original foundations. Only the back third, including the three gables, had been knocked down, and the rubble was used in the renovation. In total, the sale of the four farms netted 24 400 guldens, of which 20 000 went to the Company and the rest to Willem Adriaan.

In attempting to calculate a current rand value for this transaction, we contacted Professor Johan Fourie from the Laboratory for Economics of Africa's Past, who advised comparing the amount against the value of cattle, the most traded commodity at the time. We'll leave it to Fourie to jump through the mathematical hoops: '1 gulden is equal to 16 stuivers, so 24 400 equals 390 400 stuivers. A cow was worth, on average, about 450 stuivers, so that converts to 868 cows. A cow today is about R8 500. So that converts to R7 378 000.'

If this seems low (the value of the four farms today would run into hundreds of millions), it is, as Fourie explains, 'exactly because land was pretty cheap back then, especially so early in the period when the entire area west of the first mountain ranges had not yet been fully settled'.[37] The fact that Willem Adriaan didn't pay a cent for it was also a factor.

But back to 1708. Without the support of state funds, Vergelegen was brought back down to earth. When Dutch sea captain Johan Splinter Stavorinus visited the home seventy years later, he noted that the fields, gardens and buildings 'all bore evident signs of the magnificence and wealth of the founder who had spent large sums of money on this spot; but everything is now much decayed, as the succeeding proprietors did not possess the same means as Mr van der Stel, to keep it in proper repair'.[38]

Speaking of decay, Willem would spend the rest of his life in the Netherlands, with no honour but plenty of cash. In a vain attempt to use the latter to buy the former, he published the *Korte Deductie* ('short explanation'), a 304-page propaganda rag designed to exonerate him of any wrongdoing. Amsterdam society, however, would not be conned that easily, and he carried the stain of corruption until his death in 1733, aged sixty-nine.

In his own words

Sketch of Vergelegen as contained in the *Korte Deductie*.
Note how much more austere it looks here than in the burghers' complaints

When it comes to shameless self-promotion, the *Korte Deductie* published by Willem Adriaan after his banishment is hard to beat. Here are some of the choicest titbits:

On the lower classes: The careful student of History will have observed that under all kinds of governments there are found men among the lower classes dissatisfied with those who hold the reins of Government ... In that manner it is often seen that the best men are contrary to their deserts, and without any reason, most violently accused and libelled.

On the charges: [The Governor] requests, and in the meanwhile hopes, that all those who were ere inclined to lend an ear to the calumnies uttered against him, will now also be willing to use their eyes, in order to read this short, simple, and true deduction. After that he trusts that every impartial and intelligent reader will be convinced of Van der Stel's innocence of all the charges mentioned.

On the declaration: More than 240 freemen resident at or near the Cape ... unanimously and fully bear testimony to the Governor in the best terms which can possibly be used in favour of a Governor, his conduct, and Government, but which his modesty forbids him to repeat here.

Of his accusers: Many of the same subscribers, when in a lawful, solemn, and orderly manner questioned before the Council regarding the general charges mentioned and heard on the same, had recalled their accusation and ... declared that they had been seduced or compelled to sign the abovementioned letter; that they had never been wronged or injured by the Governor; and that consequently they greatly repent of, and feel sorry for what they have done as vile and calumnious.[39]

A lasting legacy

There's a popular myth that after Adam Tas's release, he renamed his farm Libertas ('Tas is free', pun intended),[40] but historian Dan Sleigh points out that the farm had been given this name before Tas became its owner through marriage. This was remarked on by Willem Adriaan himself, who wrote that the 'canting Rogue [Tas]' who 'with those many years of idle living' had attained an 'unfamiliar affluency ... in a twinkling'.[41]

What is true, however, is that Tas's name adorns two of South Africa's most loved wines: Tassenberg and Oom Tas.

The burghers' bravery in standing up for what they believed in was later twisted into one of the founding myths of Afrikaner nationalism. But the contents of their testimonial make it pretty clear that their complaints were financial, not political. One thing should be clear, writes Kevin Davie, 'Tas was no working-class hero ... No great reforms flowed from this rebellion. The VOC remained in charge for another 100 years, slavery was only done away with after 140 years and democracy was a full 280 years distant.'[42]

Corruption, however, has lasted throughout.

CHAPTER 2

SIR GEORGE YONGE

The Lofty Twaddler
1799–1801

'He was decidedly the most incompetent man who has ever been at the head of affairs in the colony.' – George McCall Theal[1]

Sir George Yonge. The picture says it all

Doomed from the get-go

The signs were there from the start. Even before Sir George Yonge, the 5th Baronet of Colyton, arrived at the Cape, Lady Anne Barnard, wife of the incumbent colonial secretary, expressed her misgivings about him. In a letter to her lifelong pen pal and former suitor, British secretary of state for war Lord Henry Dundas, she wrote:

> Sir George Yonge's appointment was one that at first surprised people here. A successor to Lord Macartney was looked for in a more brilliant class of ability than that in which the world is apt to rank Sir George ... [2]

Macartney was said to be 'outraged' by the choice of his successor, and even the king, George III, was surprised by Sir George's appointment. Lord Bathurst commented that it seemed 'to promise so very ill'.[3]

History would (quite) soon prove them all (quite) right. Less than a month after Sir George's arrival at the Cape, Lady Anne was once again writing to Dundas:

> Dare I say it? – our new Governor, I fear, is a very, very weak old soul ... Sir George Yonge is for having every supposed improvement done at once, and I fear does not begin with the things most necessary, but with those most connected with his own domestic conveniency.[4]

Within weeks of his arrival, his domestic situation had indeed been 'dramatically convenienced'. He closed the Company's Garden to the public, converting 'the shady avenues which to the present day are among the chief charms of the city in the summer' into private grounds.[5] 'Fountains and fishponds' – the firepools of their day – 'were constructed by his order at the public expense and a high wall was built on the Parliament Street side.'[6] The wall, although not quite Trumpian in scale, did cost a whopping £6 000 (R10.8 million today*), emptying the entire contents of the treasury which had, according to commander-in-chief of the fleet at the Cape of Good Hope Roger Curtis, 'accumulated by means of the prudent line of economy adopted by his predecessors'.[7]

But Yonge's wall was much more than just a waste of money. The stunt he

---

* All conversions to modern currency are made for interest's sake only. Conversions were made by adjusting for GBP inflation and then converting to rands. Fluctuating inflation rates (the rate jumped from 12.5 per cent in 1799 to 36 per cent a year later, for example) mean that the conversions can vary wildly.

pulled by privatising the public gardens, notes Lady Anne, was a sure-fire way of making enemies with the locals, a decision rendered even more curious by Britain's tenuous hold on the Colony at the time.

> Had he torn the Magna Carta of the Cape into a thousand tatters he could not have put the Dutch into such an alarm. For 150 years they had enjoyed the privilege of walking under the shade of those oaks – 'tis the only public walk at the Cape – and all ranks of people, the women particularly, were furious.[8]

Andrew Barnard, Lady Anne's oft-overshadowed hubby, realised just how peeved Capetonians were and tried to convince Sir George to at least keep the main avenue open. Yonge eventually gave access to 'respectable people',[9] provided they signed their names in a register kept at the guardhouse at the lower end of the gardens. This 'foolish rule' didn't go down well with the townspeople, who some-times strolled the avenue 'a dozen of times in a day,' wrote Lady Anne. 'They think it a great trouble. This is a way of making private property of a public benefit.'[10] If there's a better definition of corruption out there, we have yet to come across it.

Sketch of Government Avenue by Lady Anne Barnard,
showing the guardhouse put up by Yonge in the bottom-left corner

But Sir George did not restrict his 'improvements' to the gardens. Barely a week after setting foot on African soil, he started doing up his official residence, De Tuynhuys. As Lady Anne told it, he spent his daytime

> at the Government House in overseeing reparations, improvements, and unpacking of furniture. The Governor has a great love of pretty things of that sort. I could have told him that less carving, and black morocco leather ... would have suited the Cape better; but it is needless to put people out of conceit with what they have got. If Sir George Yonge will superintend the reparation of the public buildings falling to decay (as they do here in a twelve month's time almost, if not attended to, so rapidly do the rains pierce and burst the clay walls), as well as he superintends the reparation of his own kitchen, he will be a treasure.[11]

Before long, Lady Anne had taken to referring to Sir George as 'The Lofty Twaddler' – both in conversation in Cape Town and in her frequent letters to Dundas and the other high-ranking officials, who would ultimately play a major role in his 'lofty tumble'.[12] Andrew Barnard, meanwhile, wrote to Lord Macartney to moan about the 'ridiculous schemes his Excellency [Yonge] hits upon to spend money' and 'the foul-fingeredness of the present Government'.[13]

Whose colony is it anyway?

The Colony under Sir George Yonge was 'as corrupt as in the days of the younger Van der Stel,' writes Theal. 'The history of one of these men is the history of the other. The colonists complained of both, and in each instance their complaints were well founded. Both were recalled, and both were dismissed by the supreme authorities and pronounced unworthy of being employed again.'[14]

But why did the Cape have a British governor?

By 1730 the VOC was struggling to turn a profit. One of several reasons for this was the corruption of its employees who, as we have already seen, found ways to supplement their low salaries. By the last decade of the eighteenth century, many jested the acronym VOC had come to stand for *Vergaan Onder Corruptie* ('perish under corruption'). On 31 December 1799, the VOC's charter from the Dutch government was quietly allowed to expire. At the same time, all of Europe had been thrust into a prolonged period of war by the political fallout that arose from the French Revolution of 1789. In the Netherlands, French-backed patriots overthrew the government in January 1795, causing the Prince of Orange to flee to England.

The arrival of a fleet of British naval ships in False Bay in 1795 posed something of a dilemma for the locals. The VOC officials supported the prince, but the vast majority of the burghers sided with revolutionary France. The burghers in Graaff-Reinet had even gone so far as to declare 'independence'.

Waving a document signed by the exiled Dutch prince, the captain of the British fleet announced that he'd come to protect the Cape from an attack by the French. While the VOC were inclined to welcome them ashore, they could not be seen to acquiesce to the orders of a fugitive prince. 'After exchanging letters for eight weeks to no purpose,' writes Theal, 'the English forces, having landed at Simonstown, marched along the shore of False Bay, and attacked the Dutch at Muizenberg. Colonel De Lille (no relation to Patricia, as far as we can tell), who was in command of the camp, fled without any attempt at defence, and the English took possession of the post.'[15] After a truly pathetic excuse for a battle in Cape Town proper, the Colony officially passed from VOC to British hands in September 1795.

The experienced administrator Earl Macartney became the Cape's first British governor. While being governed by a Brit must have been a bitter pill to swallow for the Dutch and Huguenot settlers, Macartney appeased the burghers by paying higher prices for their produce than the VOC ever had. Aware of the precarious nature of Britain's occupation of the Cape, he made a point of spending only what was vital. After a year and a half, Macartney returned to England to enjoy a well-earned retirement.

In the hiatus between Macartney's departure and Sir George Yonge's arrival, the Brits found themselves fighting a war with the Xhosa in the Eastern Cape, a conflict which would continue to smoulder for another eighty years.

In 1803, a truce agreed in Europe saw the Cape Colony being returned to the Dutch. The British soldiers and administrators duly returned to Blighty, but not for long. Three years later, the truce broke, and the Cape was given back to the Brits, who were only too happy to have control of the sea route to their vast interests in India.

'Gold was in his head'

Sir George Yonge represented the very worst of British aristocracy. Incompetent, entitled and totally unconcerned with the plight of his subjects, he spent much of his life running away from his creditors.[16] So it was only fitting that he should eventually be palmed off on the backwater that was the Cape Colony.

After finishing his schooling at Eton (where else?) and graduating from Leipzig

University, Sir George served as a member of Parliament for almost forty years. He also had a number of largely ceremonial (but always lucrative) side hustles. Over the years, he served as secretary of the embassy of Turin, vice treasurer of Ireland, lord commissioner of the Admiralty and finally secretary at war.

He was also a knight of the Order of the Bath, although the purifying process seems not to have worked on our Twaddler. According to one source,

> A man who was to be created a Knight was to first enter a bath to wash themselves and rid their bodies of any impurities, this washing has its basis in the idea of baptism to wash the sins of the soul away. Once they were bathed they were then carefully dried and dressed in a robe. They would then progress to the chapel to stay vigil overnight. Once dawn approached the future Knight would then hear mass and make his confessions ... Kneeling, the man would be presented with his Knight spurs, a belt for his waist and the King would then tap the man upon the head with his hand or a sword and thus the man was created a Knight of the Bath.[17]

On paper, Sir George's CV may have been impressive, but should anyone have contacted his references, this impression would have quickly fallen apart. As Theal put it, 'The grounds upon which the appointment was made are uncertain ... though he had filled important situations, had never displayed ability of a high order.'[18]

In 1794, given the turmoil in Europe, British prime minister William Pitt could no longer bear the liability of Sir George as secretary at war, so he found him a role as master of the mint. Pitt described the new job as 'an equivalent in point of income' to Yonge, who accepted the offer but had no shame in also asking for a peerage and a promise of 'a permanent provision for life' in the event of his 'being out of employment hereafter' (as it turned out, he'd be needing this sooner than expected). Pitt wasn't so foolish as to grant the Lofty Twaddler a peerage, but he was promised a yearly retirement pension of £1200 (that's R3.4 million today) 'to be extended for his wife's life after his death'.[19]

Barely a year after landing a job that quite literally entailed printing money, Sir George was once again hiding from his creditors and, according to the UK's parliamentary historians, unable to leave 'the precincts of the palace for fear of being arrested'. In an attempt to remedy this unfortunate predicament, Yonge asked Pitt for the 'vacant wardenship of the Mint to supplement his income as master which, he complained, had fallen far below the £3 000 a year [R7.3 million today] he had been led to expect'.[20] Pitt, who was very much on to Yonge by now, refused this request, but did grant him a government loan which would allow him to leave the palace grounds and prance the streets without fear of reprisal.

(As an aside, Sir George's time at the mint resulted in one of Lady Anne's more memorable put-downs: 'It has been thought, as I told you, that gold was in his head, perhaps from being so long at the head of the Mint! But if his head had been made of gold, I think Lady Yonge would have tried to melt it before now.'[21])

In 1798, during an investigation into the goings-on at the mint, Pitt replaced 'the master's variable fees with a fixed salary' and relieved Sir George of his position. Following this debacle, the Lofty Twaddler moved to Edinburgh, where he lived in debtors' sanctuary.

When Lord Macartney asked to be relieved of his position as governor of the Cape, the job was offered to Yonge of all people (perhaps 'out of sight, out of mind' was the theory here). He even had the staggering audacity to refuse the Cape job, expressing 'a reluctance insuperable almost to quit my present situation'. But when he learnt that the gig would net him over £4 000 a year (more than R9 million today), he swiftly changed his mind.

Henry Addington, who would soon succeed Pitt as prime minister, described Sir George's appointment as governor as 'a disgraceful job which [he] had tried to prevent'.[22]

Who was Lady Anne Barnard?

Despite living in a world dominated by men and spending only five years at the Cape, Lady Anne Barnard had a disproportionate impact on colonial society, politics and attitudes.

Born in 1750 to a noble Scottish family, she grew up to be a talented artist and writer (one of her ballads was set to music by Joseph Haydn) and a fiercely independent woman. Disgruntled by the insular scene in Scotland, she moved to London where she got involved with high society, which loved her for being the life and soul of any party.

In 1791, at the height of the French Revolution, she went to Paris to see what all the fuss was about, before returning to London and continuing to turn down marriage proposals (including one from her pen pal Dundas in 1791). By the time she finally acquiesced to marrying Andrew Barnard, an undistinguished soldier

Lady Anne Barnard, 1782

twelve years her junior, Lady Anne was able to use her influence to find a position for Andrew in far-off Cape Town.

Within a few weeks of her arrival, she borrowed a pair of Andrew's trousers and climbed Table Mountain via Platteklip Gorge. She even spent a night camped at the summit. She and Andrew also adored spending time at Paradise, a tiny cottage in Newlands Forest which 'Lord Macartney has given us to be rural in'.

In 1798 the Barnards embarked on a 'tour into the interior', covering 700 miles by ox wagon. On the month-long trip, Lady Anne wrote and painted while eating flamingo at Saldanha Bay and marvelling at the sincerity of a church service at Genadendal. 'I doubt much whether I should have entered St. Peters at Rome ... with a more awed impression of the deity and his presence than I did this little Church of a few feet Square, where the simple disciples of Christianity dressed in the skins of animals knew no purple or fine linen, no pride ... no hypocrisy,' she wrote.

In 1800 the Barnards built The Vineyard, the first English country house in South Africa, and now part of a well-known Cape Town hotel, in what were then the rural farmlands of Newlands. They were forced to return to London in 1802, when the Dutch regained control of the Cape. When the Colony was passed back to Britain five years later, Andrew was on the first ship out to the Cape. Tragically, he died before Anne could join him.

Anne was devastated by his death and described it as a sorrow 'not to be soon got the better of'. When she discovered that he had had an illegitimate daughter (Christina) by a slave woman, she did the unthinkable and accepted responsibility for the child, bringing her to London to raise as her own. Before her death in 1825, Anne helped Christina to marry into a prominent farming family in Wiltshire.

'What Anne Barnard did with Christina was most extraordinary for the time and very brave,' her biographer, Stephen Taylor, told us over the phone. 'But that was who she was. She was a woman for our time, a one-off ... an aristocrat and a rebel, who wanted to live independently. Her values were so against the current of the day ...'[23]

Cape of Storms

But getting back to the events at Cape Town in 1800: Once the Lofty Twaddler had turned the Company's Garden into his own private playground and made the accommodations at De Tuynhuys fit for a man of his station, he turned his corrupt attentions to the Colony at large. A commission of inquiry conducted after Sir George had been kicked out of the Cape states that 'scandals without parallel at any previous period of the history of the colony [were] brought to light'.[24]

Among other things, the report produced by the commission noted that Yonge had swiftly made enemies with the burghers. He did this by

1. levying a charge of £10 a year (R28 000 today) on every public billiard table,
2. making each burgher pay £1 a year (nearly R3 000 today) for the right to shoot game and, perhaps most heinously of all,
3. doubling the government tax on brandy.

Yonge also dabbled in a bit of nepotism, paying a family member £200 (R360 000) per year for what must be one of the best jobs ever. Theal writes:

> His establishment of a winetaster's office was regarded ... as a grievous, oppressive, and vexatious measure. Mr. Richard Blake, his relative and private secretary, was appointed winetaster, and had power given to him to enter into and search any premises where wine was sold, to open casks, and to destroy on the spot all wine of an inferior quality. The use which Mr. Blake made of this power was shown by his proposal to Mr. Michael Hogan, that this merchant should obtain the monopoly for the sale of wine, when he would approve of any quality, and they would share the profit.[25]

He also made the decision to ban the private cutting of timber for almost a full year. This was disastrous for both woodcutters and the building industry, but turned out to be a blessing for one Cape Town company which was granted the monopoly for dealing in timber.

In this and other matters, Blake was 'well known to have received various bribes on different occasions, and to a large amount,' writes Roger Curtis, before posing a rhetorical question for the ages: 'Shall we say the patron is upright when his dependants deal so largely in corruption?'

Another 'channel of peculation [embezzlement] to the Governor's party,' notes Curtis, was 'thro' the means of Mr Duckitt, a person sent out ... to fill the situation of agriculturalist'. Duckitt, a long-time friend of Yonge's, 'immediately became connected with the Governor's family and some of the best government farms were put into his hands'. But he still wanted more.[26]

At the beginning of 1801, Sir George wrote to the Burgher Senate (a council of up to seven citizens responsible for civic affairs) expressing his intentions to make a further grant in Duckitt's favour, this one comprising several farms which had once belonged to the VOC and were considered 'among the most productive in the colony'. The burghers, however, were having none of it. Due to 'the unreasonableness of the requisition, they were induced to write a respectful tho' strong reply, begging his Excellency not to pursue his intention any further'.

Once it had become clear to Yonge that he wasn't going to slip this one past the burghers, in a shameless attempt to cover his tracks he asked that his letters on the topic be returned. The burghers – who, as we have seen, had dealt with his like before – informed him that 'copies of all or any of his letters were at his service [but] they felt it necessary to retain the originals'. Curtis reports that the deal the burghers had obstructed was later 'proved to be a lucrative one on the part of Sir George who, it was confidently said, was to have received from Mr Duckitt on his receiving the grant, the sum of seven thousand pounds [R11.3 million today]'.[27]

Sir George's newspaper

In July 1800, Sir George Yonge appointed Messrs Walker and Robertson as sole printers to the government and gave them permission to publish a weekly newspaper. The 'sole right to undertake commercial printing was granted to these monopolists, and notice given that no one else would be allowed to print under a penalty of one thousand rixdollars [£150] and the confiscation of all printing materials'.[28] (How H.F. Verwoerd, Nico Diederichs and Eschel Rhoodie of later chapters longed for such powers.)

On 16 August, the first issue of the *Cape Town Gazette and African Advertiser* appeared in English and Dutch. Despite the fact that 'very little information concerning South Africa [was] to be had from it ... and even its foreign intelligence [was] generally limited',[29] Sir George quickly became 'uneasy at the editing of what was, to all intents and purposes, an official gazette being in private hands'.[30]

Walker and Robertson were paid handsomely for the equipment and the press was duly installed in the Castle, where the gazette would be printed until the arrival of George Greig twenty-two years later (more about him in the next chapter).

Despite all he'd done to piss them off, the Twaddler considered himself popular among the burghers. As Theal memorably notes, 'In one of his despatches to the secretary of state he reported that the colonists termed him their father; but in truth those who used such language were only a few suppliants for mercy.'[31]

Having picked up on the Barnards' very low opinion of him, the Lofty Twaddler started signing government contracts behind the colonial secretary's (i.e. Andrew Barnard's) back, with 'public business of all kinds'[32] going through Blake and Major James Cockburn, the governor's principal aide-de-camp. On behalf of the government, these (dis)reputable gentlemen chartered vessels, entered into contracts for the repair of public buildings and arranged the supply of meat to the troops – always at exorbitant rates. 'On one contract for the supply of articles to the barracks it was proved that Cockburn ... received a gratuity of £2 000 [R5.5 million today] and that the governor had consented to the prices in the tender of Mr Hogan [him again] being raised by ten per cent, obviously for the purpose of covering this.'[33]

Yonge created numerous 'new and unnecessary civil and military offices' and also conjured up an additional title for Mr Blake, which landed him an extra £1 200 (R3.3 million today). After creating a barrack department at a staggering cost of £40 000 (R110 million today), Sir George appointed his buddy Cockburn as the deputy barrack master general and promoted him to the rank of lieutenant colonel. Yonge managed to do this all behind the back of the general in command of the troops at the Cape.

These were only some of the improprieties unearthed by the commission. Theal concludes that there was

[e]very reason to believe that these favourites of his Excellency had in like manner benefited by a great many other transactions concluded at government house, and though the commission could not obtain absolute proof, the presumptive evidence before them was strong that Sir George Yonge was indirectly concerned in exactions from individuals who had indulgences to solicit, and that he connived at the corrupt practices of those about him.[34]

Curtis, meanwhile, provides damning evidence of a different kind. At the end of 1800, Yonge had to 'draw on the British treasury for seventy thousand pounds [R125 million today] – in addition to the usual expenses of the colony ... This wasteful prodigality tended to accelerate the disgrace to which this iniquitous government was deservedly consigned.'[35]

The curious case of the false logbook

While there is some humour in Sir George's treatment of the burghers and their brandy, his attitude towards slavery was downright despicable – even by eighteenth-century standards. By 1800, thanks to the pioneering activism of William Wilberforce, the tide of British public opinion had turned against the slave trade. Attitudes in the colonies, however, were very different, and the burghers saw the importation of slaves as the only way of dealing with the shortage of labour. In an attempt to walk this tightrope, writes Michael Charles Reidy, 'British colonial governors were instructed by the British imperial government to moderate slave importation to the Cape' by only importing slaves when absolutely necessary.[36]

Macartney did just this, as evidenced by the letter he sent Dundas on 24 July 1797: 'Soon after my arrival here, I had, after mature consideration, granted a permission for the importation of Negros, without a certain proportion of whom, the extensive cultivation of this Country cannot be carried on.'[37] In total, Macartney granted three licences to import slaves during his governorship.

But the floodgates would open as soon as Sir George arrived. Instead of going through the proper channels and getting permission from Dundas, the new governor teamed up with Michael Hogan (the same upstanding gentleman who had been granted the wine monopoly) to exploit a loophole in the regulations. According to Reidy, 'Yonge was rumoured to have permitted Hogan the importation of at least 600 slaves into the colony during his first week as governor.'[38]

In February, a vessel owned by Hogan aptly named the *Collector* docked in Table Bay with a cargo of 164 'prize slaves', but curiously without an accompanying prize vessel. (Under the laws of the time, any slaves which were found aboard vessels captured in combat were considered 'fair prize' and could be sold for the benefit of the captors.) When challenged as to the origins of these 'prize slaves', the captain swore that they had been captured from 'a prize brig run ashore and burnt'.[39] He might well have been believed had a Danish ship (the *Holger Dansche*) not arrived from Mozambique at the same time. The Danish officers swore they had seen the slaves being captured on Mozambican soil and brought aboard the *Collector*.

Donald Campbell, the port captain of Table Bay at the time, wrote to Sir George to say that he had 'full proof' that the slaves were not fair prize. 'Since there was a possibility that Yonge was involved in this business', Campbell also wrote to Macartney about the matter. Yonge made 'veiled threats' in an attempt to get Campbell to drop the matter but, despite the governor's remonstrations, a commission of inquiry was set up and the so-called prize slaves were confiscated.[40] As Reidy records,

> At first, the *Collector*'s crew presented a confusing 'equipoise of evidence' before the Court of Justice. However, one of the officers aboard the *Collector* eventually testified that two logbooks had been kept during the boat's voyage.
>
> A strange series of events thus unfolded. Firstly, nine of the *Collector*'s crew – witnesses at the hearing of the Vice-Admiralty Court – vanished. Campbell found the boat's 'true' logbook in the chief mate's trunk and 'the Defence was given up'. Captain Smart, who had made an oath on the false logbook before the Vice-Admiralty Court, mysteriously disappeared the day after the authentic logbook's discovery ...[41]

The commission found that the slaves on board the *Collector*, as well as a further 450 slaves aboard another vessel owned by Hogan (the *Joaquim*) and another sixty-four slaves purportedly captured as 'prize' by the *Collector* the previous year, had all been illegally brought to the Colony. The commission heard that Hogan had bribed Sir George to the tune of £5 000 (R13 million today), although this was never definitively proven.

While the court's findings were clearly damaging to Sir George, Lady Anne's recounting of the dodgy slave dealings described above seems to have contributed more to the Lofty Twaddler's downfall than any official correspondence. She wrote about the fiasco to both Dundas and Marquess Wellesley, the governor general of India, 'lament[ing] the discreditable shade which some events have lately thrown over Sir George Yonge's administration ... What has been here loudly whispered (and what has been too frequently corroborated by a blush that tinged the poor Governor's cheek when pressed by Mr. Barnard), that in some late transactions the hands of Government have not been so clean as they ought to have been.'

Sir George Yonge, she explained, had made 'so strong an exertion of power' that he gave a merchant not only the liberty to import slaves but also 'to land

Sketch of Cape Town by Lady Anne Barnard: front view from the Castle
showing the gallows and the barracks with Lion's Head in the background

here a supposed cargo afterwards proved by Captain Campbell in the Court of
Justice to be a smuggling transaction'. It was, she explained, 'generally believed
that a *douceur* [sweetener] of no small magnitude was given to effect what, had
it passed, would have put from £10,000 to £15,000 [between R27 million and
R41 million today] in the merchant's pocket'.

She then went on to defend her husband's role in the matter:

> You will naturally say, how happened it that Mr. Barnard, who knew how
> opposite this was to the ideas of our Government at home, permitted a slave
> traffic to go on at the Cape, and omitted to state its impropriety to the
> Governor? Mr Barnard protested in the strongest terms. He also told the
> merchant he would oppose it; but he found the Governor deaf to all remon-
> strance or argument.[42]

Sir George, she made clear, would not let a pesky employee get in the way of
his big payday. Instead, 'anxious to avoid all further conversation or respectful

opposition from Mr. Barnard, he gave the orders for the landing and selling of the slaves, and all necessary arrangements, himself, without bringing them through the Secretary's office, as is customary'. In less than five months at the Cape, she went on, the Lofty Twaddler had made a habit of sidestepping Barnard whenever it suited him. While 'every fair, broad, and proper request invariably goes through the Secretary of the Colony to the Governor,' she wrote, 'every matter of an unsound or equivocal nature proceeds by the other road'.[43]

It's hard to say whether Lady Anne wrote the letters with the intention of causing trouble for Sir George or whether she simply wanted to vent her frustrations. Historian Kirsten McKenzie notes that while 'Yonge was by any measure a bad governor ... his treatment of Andrew Barnard may also have been a contributing factor in Lady Anne's correspondence'.[44] Either way, once her determined pals had read them, Sir George's fate was sealed.

In September 1800, Dundas told the king of England that Sir George would have to be recalled.

His conduct ... has in such a variety of particulars been so wild and extravagant as to render it impossible to continue him in that government without exposing this country to the imputation of being indifferent to the concerns of that most important settlement.

At the same time, Wellesley was writing to Dundas.

My accounts from the Cape all concur in representing that government to be in a state of great confusion. The imbecility and ignorance of Sir George Yonge entirely disqualify him for his situation ... The importance of the Cape in its relation to India increases every hour ... Yonge is employed in founding theatres and masquerade rooms. He dances with more grace and perseverance than Lord Keeper Hatton; and the fame of his brawls has not only reached the k*****s, and animated every kraal from the Cape to the desert of Sahara, but extended to the Indus and the Ganges.[45]

Sir George's 'lofty tumble'

The only reason Sir George managed to last as long as he did was the sluggish pace of transcontinental communications 200 years ago. (Not that the modern

South African Post Office is much better.) Almost an entire year passed between Lady Anne sending her damning epistles and Sir George learning his fate.

Finally, in April 1801, the *Nutwell* arrived in Table Bay with 'despatches addressed to Sir George Yonge', which stated that he was 'at once to transfer the administration to Major-General [Francis] Dundas [the nephew of Lady Anne's pen pal], and to return to England by the first opportunity'.[46]

The news was 'a subject of universal gratulation to every inhabitant of the colony'.[47] But Sir George, Lady Anne noted, did not take it nearly as well:

> The Lofty Twaddler has had the lofty tumble I foresaw ... [he] was petrified at the event. He is so conceited of his own abilities that nothing was farther from his expectation than being blamed for anything.

In fact, writes Curtis, Sir George even tried to pretend he had chosen to go of his own volition. 'Sir George's dispatches having reached him before the General received his, a proclamation was issued from the Government House, stating "that His Majesty has been graciously pleased to allow him to return home", by this artifice attempting to conceal the nature of his resignation of the government.'

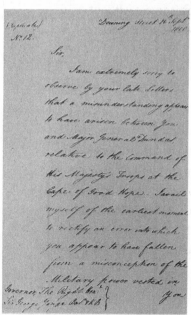

Letter from Lord Dundas to Yonge, explaining in no uncertain terms that he did not command the troops at the Cape

Once Major General Dundas received these dispatches, he wasted no time in getting rid of Yonge. '[I]n the course of an hour or so the captain's guard which had hitherto waited on Sir George's person was removed.'[48]

For the sake of appearances, Sir George begged to stay on as governor a few days longer. But Dundas was having none of it. To make matters worse, writes Theal, 'Sir George Yonge applied to the admiral on the station [Curtis] for a man-of-war [naval ship] to convey him to England, as was usual with governors of colonies returning home, but had the mortification of meeting with a refusal.'[49] Six weeks later he was finally able to hitch a ride on a private ship bound for St Helena, 'to the great satisfaction of nearly everyone in the colony'.[50]

After four months' wait on St Helena, he eventually managed to get back to his green and pleasant homeland by Christmas. There, he began 'to bombard government and the King with claims for compensation and reward for his services, but his demands for reimbursement of the expenses of his homeward journey from the Cape were rejected'.[51]

A commission appointed in October 1801 into Yonge's tenure reported 'at length' on 16 March 1802. As historian Nigel Penn observes:

> Several of the charges brought against the former governor were considered well-founded and it has been suggested that perhaps it was only Yonge's friendship with George III that saved him from prosecution for corruption. The king however, was not blind to his faults: he had not been surprised at Yonge's recall ... but he certainly had been when he heard of his appointment.[52]

If only today's monarchy had such a gift for sarcasm.

In 1802, Yonge tried to regain the parliamentary seat he'd occupied before his African sojourn. As part of the process, every voter was required to take a 'bribery oath', which 'required the voter to state that no money, gift, nor reward had come his way'. This oath was, as Frank O'Gorman writes, 'usually nothing more than a tactical device to challenge particular voters and classes of voters against whom some irregularity might be demonstrated'. It was, however, 'extremely dangerous for one side to protest and to petition against electoral practices of which both sides were equally guilty'. In fact, writes O'Gorman, 'there are instances of both sides in a contest agreeing not to tender the bribery oath'.[53] But even eighteenth-century English voters seem to have had their limits. Yonge's dream of returning to Parliament went, quite literally, up in smoke when (as the *Oxford Dictionary of National Biography* records) 'he was spat on and his wig was set on fire when he tried to administer the bribery oath'.[54]

The Lofty Twaddler finally tumbled from his mortal perch in 1812. He was buried in the north aisle of the chancel of Colyton Church in the Yonge vault. His burial was not recorded in the register, but in 1844 the floor of the vault collapsed during a vestry meeting and several members fell into the vault. On the floor were four brass coffin plates, one of which bore Sir George's name. It was later mounted on the wall of the church.

Forever Yonge

Apart from a few diehard thespians who memorialise his role in establishing the Cape's first European-style theatre, Yonge's name has (thankfully) been expunged from the South African landscape. Not so in Canada, where Toronto's main drag – the fifty-six-kilometre-long Yonge Street – still bears his name.

Ontario's first colonial administrator, John Graves Simcoe, apparently named the street after his buddy in recognition of the Lofty Twaddler's interest in ancient Roman roads. Yonge had written 'an excellent memoir on the subject of Roman roads and camps, in connection with some discoveries that had been made in Nottinghamshire, and hence the peculiar fitness of naming Yonge Street after him, it being precisely such a road, and adapted to similar uses, as those he had been engaged in examining'.[55]

Even more bizarre is the fact that Yonge-Dundas Square – the beating heart of downtown Toronto – has set in stone the fraught relationship between the inept governor and the man who effectively fired him. A search of Canadian newspaper archives suggests that modern Ontarians are blissfully unaware of Yonge's chequered past.

It is tempting to think of Yonge's brief and calamitous tenure as an aberration, but sadly the Cape would soon see his ilk again.

CHAPTER 3

LORD CHARLES SOMERSET

Taking Advantage of Birth
1814–1825

'A most unwholesome state of affairs came into existence.' – G.E. Cory

Lord Charles Somerset, the Silver Fox Hunter

'Our trusty and well-beloved Charles Henry Somerset'

In 1814, Lord Charles Somerset arrived to take up his position as governor of the Cape Colony. The position came with an annual salary of £10 000 (R15.2 million today), and he arrived with a private chaplain, a secretary, a butler, a cook, a footman, two servants 'out of livery', a boy, three lady's maids, a 'woman cook', a laundry maid, a 'girl of colour' and a secretary's servant.[1]

While such perks would have kept most men happy, they were not enough for Lord Charles. Not by half. On arriving in the Fairest Cape, he set about grabbing what he could get for the sake of what could be got. One of his first acts as the ruler of one of Britain's newest colonies was to allocate himself sackloads of cash while liberally spending public money. Still not content, he would go on to gift himself four official residences at a time when growth in the Colony's economy was stagnant and its currency, the rixdollar, was in free fall.

Indeed, Lord Charles Somerset took up that tainted torch of corruption handed down from Willem Adriaan van der Stel and our Lofty Twaddler with a sense of complete entitlement. And to it he added his own distinctive style in theft, corruption, autocracy, bribery, nepotism, unlawful detention, banishment and press censorship. As one historian put it, Lord Charles Somerset is 'one of the villains of South African history'.[2] And that's before we get into his penchant for extramarital affairs ...

As the second son of the Duke of Beaufort, Charles made his way up the ranks of the British Army unimpeded, as was the norm for privileged families in those days. His old man paid nearly £2 500 (over R5.5 million today) for young Charles to be promoted to lieutenant, and then used family connections to gain his son further promotion without paying a thing. On 25 December 1787, Lord Charles Somerset was made captain of the 77th Regiment of Foot. However, when the regiment was sent to India, where there was a real chance of facing action, his hagiographical biography simply states that 'he did not accompany it'.[3]

Lord Charles's military career would end with a soldierly disaster when his horse was shot from under him. Sadly for Charles and his rather fragile ego, the incident did not occur in the throes of battle. Instead, it happened at a festival, when a celebratory shot fired by a soldier in the lower ranks hit his horse in the head. The horse collapsed in a heap, as did Charles's military career – he broke his leg in the incident, rendering him unfit for service. With an army career now out of the question, he eloped and had several children, after which he came back to make amends with his furious and long-suffering father, who was unhappy with his errant son's choice of bride.

Charles would need his family connections from now on, because neither he nor his new wife had any money. And so, with the help of his blue-blooded Plantagenet family (who had once ruled England), a career as a member of Parliament was created for him. As a young politician, Lord Charles supported two 'suppressive bills': 'one declared writing, preaching and speaking against the King's authority to be treasonable; the other made all political meetings, unless advertised, illegal'.[4] This would be a set of laws that he would hold dear for the rest of his life.

In 1791 he was appointed as 'Gentleman of the Bed Chamber' to the Prince of Wales, and in 1797 he became a member of 'His Majesty's Privy Council'. But, as a second son, Charles's position was always precarious. When his sine-cure (a paid position that required no work) as joint paymaster of the forces was abolished, taking with it his annual pocket money of £2 000 (about R6 million today), the prime minister himself intervened to compensate him with the gov-ernorship of the Cape. The acting king, the prince regent, would finalise this appointment with the proclamation:

> Our Trusty and Well-beloved Charles Henry Somerset, to be our governor and Commander-in-chief of the said settlement of the Cape of Good Hope in South Africa with its Territories and Dependencies.[5]

The Cape Colony at the time

In 1820, the Cape Colony had an estimated 43 000 people designated 'Europeans' or 'Christians' living within its borders. The majority of these people were Cape Dutch, though the census taken then did not differentiate between British and Dutch. There were also said to be about 25 000 indigenous Khoikhoin and around 33 000 slaves whom the Dutch had transported to the Cape from their colonies in the East. About 2 000 people were termed 'free blacks'. These people were either freed slaves or descendants of political prisoners exiled to the Cape by the Dutch.

Lord Charles's first act on arriving in Cape Town in 1814 was to allocate himself a £6 750 supplement (R10.3 million today) to the £10 000 the PM had already wangled for him. Just why he felt he was entitled to this amount is unclear. But, with few financial and legal regulations in place at the Cape, he took the money without so much as a second thought. He would fast become a law unto himself, a task made simpler by the fact that the Cape's Roman-Dutch legal system was in urgent need of reform. It was, in reality, an administrative dung heap and the perfect patch for Lord Charles to sow his corrupting seed.

As G.E. Cory, another father of South African history, put it, being both the chief justice and the sole head of the Court of Appeal, Lord Charles

> could, if he were of a despotic disposition, interpret [the laws] in such a manner as to render them very oppressive. This Charles Somerset undoubtedly did. A most unwholesome state of affairs came into existence. Public Money was spent on objects of doubtful public utility, and men of questionable ability and probity were entrusted with important offices for little reason other than that they were the personal friends of Lord Charles Somerset. We find the Governor himself combining the high and dignified duties of the King's Representative with the business of the horse-dealer ... we find officials obtaining grants of land under false pretences, and, lastly, we find honest and able men rewarded for their outspokenness and refusal to deviate from the path of duty and rectitude by persecution and, in some cases, ruin.[6]

Somerset was effectively in complete control of the judiciary and the fiscal – the equivalent of director of public prosecutions. There was no need to capture the state because it was simply handed to him. Soon enough, writes historian Jeff Peires, 'the Cape Court of Justice forsook its supposed judicial neutrality to uphold the political authority of Lord Charles Somerset'.[7]

Sir Richard Plasket, who was a secretary to the Cape government towards the end of Somerset's governorship, described in a letter to the Colonial Office the state of collapse and bankruptcy he discovered on his arrival:

> Almost every single Department under this Government is in a state of total incompetence to carry on its business.
>
> In the Court of Appeal, I have already stated to you the Governor decides in civil cases, without any assessor.
>
> Our Audit office is a perfect farce, and does more harm than good, as it gives a semblance of sanction to what is really never fairly investigated into.
>
> The office of Captain of the Port is as bad. The Chief is Mr Blair, Collection of Customs, who makes a sinecure of it.

In the Sequestrator's office, the arrears are so great and the business in such confusion, that the whole community are up in arms against it.

A number of other offices, not of any consequence excepting as swallowing up a great portion of the revenue, are held by Military officers belonging to Lord Charles' staff and other sinecurists.

And to wind up the whole of this melancholy concern, the Burgher Senate, which is one of the most important branches of Colonial Administration, is in such a state of absolute nonentity that it has become the laughing stock of the place, and the Government money entrusted to it is squandered away without authority or control.

As to the Burgher Senate, I have proposed to Lord Charles and the Commissioners to place at the head of it, for two to three years, Captain Stockenström that Landdrost of Graaff Reinet, who is universally allowed to be the most intelligent Dutchman and the best man of business in the Colony. He is one of the very few men here who could bring that chaos into anything like order, but I fear I shall not succeed in my plan.

I fear however I shall tire you with my constant complaints … We are perfect bankrupts, and it is needless to conceal it, as we have not enough money to pay our own salaries.

I have no doubt that the Commissioners of Enquiry will touch upon all these points, and to them would I willingly leave, were I not afraid that we shall be all ruined before their Report can be received and acted upon.[8]

As several commentators have pointed out, Somerset was in one way rather unlucky to live in a time of administrative liberalisation and reform. Some twenty or so years prior to his arrival at the Cape, his actions may well have been 'the done thing' for a ruler in a faraway colony most people knew next to nothing about (provided he didn't make quite as many enemies as Sir George Yonge). But the winds of change were blowing through Britain's colonies. Alas, Lord Charles simply took them for an inconvenient and temporary cold winter draft in his Newlands mansion and did his best to ignore them.

Colonial bureaucrats in Britain were at the time playing a delicate game of trying to remove out-of-touch and corrupt governors like Somerset while at the same time not falling into a party-political game of Tories (conservatives) vs Whigs (liberals). But in this 'softly, softly, catchee monkey' approach, they did allow a most lamentable state of affairs to develop at the Cape. Only after eight years of reports of Somerset's shady shenanigans did the British government see fit, in 1822, to appoint the Commission of Eastern Inquiry. This commission was given the widest possible brief to investigate all aspects of Cape administration and to make specific recommendations 'for the purpose of prospective regulation and practical improvement'.[9]

Had Somerset been left to his ways, he would have got on just fine with the vast majority of Dutch-speaking burgers who fell under his rule. Unlike the Lofty Twaddler, he had few problems with the slave-owning burghers of the Cape. And just to make certain that he would get no pushback from this quarter, there were allegations that 'Lord Charles had bribed some Afrikaners with offers of free land', which, Jeff Peires suggests, 'only goes to show that the governor spoke a language which they understood'.[10]

But it was his own people, the new English, Scottish and Irish immigrants – people generally referred to as the 1820 Settlers – who would begin the stir. In Chapter 1, we saw how the free burghers' fight against Willem Adriaan van der Stel was not political but based purely on financial survival. But by 1820 a great deal had changed: Britain's new metropolitan middle class was well educated and politically aspirational. One of the great bugbears they had with the ruling upper class was corruption. And that was something Lord Charles excelled at.

Lord Charles had, from the very start of his rule, helped himself to the public purse. The colonial secretary at the Cape, Colonel Bird (he of the famed bath at Kirstenbosch), had initially pointed out to Somerset that he was not due the public funds he was handing himself and suggested that he should pay back the money. Lord Charles seems to have thought this matter was for the birds and refused to do any such thing, despite the colonel's threats to write to the Colonial Office about the matter.

Bird did not send the letter for two years, perhaps because Somerset was his new boss and he had no desire to fall out with the man who controlled the Colony. But a belief in financial accountability was on the rise in Britain. And when the Colonial Audit Office was formed in 1816, it demanded that Colonel Bird hand over the Colony's finances. Bird now had to admit to the officials that his boss was 'overdrawn' by a considerable amount. Finally, on arriving in London for a sabbatical in 1820, Lord Charles was confronted by the Colonial Office about the public money he had taken.

Far from admitting guilt, he wrote to Colonel Bird to say that he was going to refuse the auditor access to his accounts – accounts which he freely admitted he did indeed have. Lord Charles seems to have felt that, really, he was entitled to this money. He even wrote to the Colonial Office asking if he couldn't just keep it. Absolutely not, was their response. In a letter which could well have been penned by JZ after the Constitutional Court ordered him to pay back (some of) the Nkandla money, Somerset noted:

> The Auditors have come to the subject of my salary. I think I have managed badly. I went to Lord Bathurst and the decision is, I am to pay [back] half.[11]

And when he finally did pay back half the money he had stolen, Lord Charles took advantage of a weakening rixdollar and walked away with a profit of £7 087 (R13.2 million today).

The truth is, Colonel Bird, who would later be dismissed by Somerset due to a concocted claim that as a Roman Catholic he had not taken the correct oath of office, had always objected to Somerset's practices. One of the primary complaints he had lodged with his boss was the illegal and exorbitantly wasteful expenditure he had used on his palatial home in leafy Newlands (sound familiar?). The final amount spent on the house has been calculated at £28 226 (around R53.4 million today).

Lord Charles Somerset's Newlands House

Madame Rose de Saulces de Freycinet – the first woman to record a circumnavigation of the world – had the chance to visit Lord Charles in his Newlands mansion and recorded it in her diary:

> The Governor resides in a splendid mansion, delightfully situated. It is sheltered by a high mountain from those terrible gales that have to be endured by the town dwellers. He's like a Viceroy in this land. He has considerable revenues and even the court of a Prince ... He talked to me all evening with a particularity and affability that may derive from his adoration of our sex. It is even said he likes it a little too much ... We were received by the Governor in splendid style. The meal was superb. It was the first time I've experienced such a degree of ceremony.[12]

Horsing around

Lord Charles was above all a man of leisurely pursuits. He was the direct descendant of the man who invented the sport of fox-hunting. As Sir Humphrey F. De Trafford wrote in that must-have bible of the English upper class, *The Foxhounds of Great Britain and Ireland*, Lord Charles came from 'the greatest hunting family the world has seen, the ideal centre of England's grandeur in all that had to do with horse and hound, and just the best remnant with it of all that fealty existing in feudal times between the Lords of territory and their retainers'.[13]

Fox-hunting on the Cape Flats.
Lord Charles Somerset is believed to be the figure on the left

As we have seen, Lord Charles had little interest in legal reform in the Colony, whose laws reflected very much those that his family had benefited from for centuries. Instead, as Peires says, 'Lord Charles's main positive contributions towards Cape history during his first period of governorship (1814–19) were limited to a new constitution for the South African Turf Club and a thorough reform of the local hunting regulations.'[14]

His interest in horses, however, was not purely a sporting one. He soon became the main horse breeder in the Colony and took to using horses as a means of bribery. One of the many people to lodge charges against Lord Charles was the inspector of lands, a Mr D'Escury.

In March 1823, D'Escury dispatched a letter to the Colonial Office with a charge of corruption in a matter of land tenure. The head of the Colonial Office, Earl Bathurst, duly forwarded the charges to the Commission of Eastern Inquiry. One of the charges was that Lord Charles

> [c]orruptly made a grant of land to Mr Redelinghuys at the Hantam Berg in consideration for a sum of money amounting to 10,000 rixdollars [about R1.6 million today] paid by Mr Redelinghuys under the colour and pretence of a sale of a horse [by the name of Sorcerer].[15]

Seemingly, Lord Charles, who had the power to grant anybody free land, would gladly give you a farm – so long as you bought a horse from him at a grossly inflated price. D'Escury also notified officials that Lord Charles sold a horse by the name of Kutussoff for £750. Kutussoff died before being delivered to its new owner. The amount had, however, already been paid by the time of the horse's death, and Somerset refused to pay the money back.

Lord Charles then discovered that D'Escury had been writing letters to officials, and the two became open enemies. Somerset's previous promise to give him a higher-paying job was withdrawn. The commission of inquiry, which had begun its work in the Cape, was made aware of the complaints and was caught in a position of having to take sides in the matter. Did they accept D'Escury's substantiated evidence and find Somerset guilty of soliciting bribes, or did they fudge it and slap Somerset on the wrist while at the same time suggesting D'Escury's claim needed to be investigated further? As have many commissions in South Africa then and forever after, it did the latter. But in doing so, the commission did register that the governor's behaviour was sufficiently concerning to offer this sanction:

I cannot but regret that your desire to improve the breed of horse at the Cape ever led you to embark in their importation and sale on your own account ... there is an unfortunate coincidence that the parties concerned in the treaty for the horse were in both instances at the same time applying for land grants, and it is to be lamented that under such circumstances you did not impose upon yourself a circumspection which would have set male-volence at defiance.[16]

D'Escury, being the inspector of lands, was also at the centre of the Groote Post farm controversy. Groote Post was a government-run farm meant to improve farming practices in the Cape – an early version of the Vrede Dairy Project. But improve farming it certainly did not do. Lord Charles nevertheless diverted government funds in order to sustain it, while at the same time dissolving the governing board and taking direct charge of the 25 000-acre farm himself. Despite the fact that it could never turn a profit, Lord Charles continued to keep the farm, using it as a hunting spot and for entertaining guests.

D'Escury, who was simply doing his job, cited it as a losing concern that was woefully managed and a drain on public funds. He recommended that it be split up and given to farmers who could run it at a profit. No financial audit was ever done on the farm, and Lord Charles got away with selling his own privately owned horses to Groote Post. Like Van der Stel before him, he had pulled off the perfect corrupt act: a transaction where he was both (private) seller and (government) buyer. Only after Somerset left the Colony was D'Escury's recommendation put into place and the farm split up and auctioned off, à la Vergelegen.

One Mr Burnett (a gentleman we will meet again later) seems to have acquired copies of official documents verifying all of D'Escury's stories. He ended up making a considerable nuisance of himself in England over them. The Colonial Office then accused D'Escury of having leaked the documents to Burnett, and he was subsequently dismissed from the Colonial Service. D'Escury denied outright that he was the source of the leak, but was never able to clear his name. He died while sailing back to Britain to submit his testimony.

'Go to the Orange River and live on springbuck'

As Cory put it, for Lord Charles 'honesty was not ultimately the best policy'.[17] He would go on to find all manner of ways to drain public money into either his purse or that of his family. As Plasket stated in his letter bemoaning the state of the Colony, military officers on Lord Charles's staff (and some of his friends) were 'swallowing up a great portion' of public money while doing absolutely no work. This seems to have been a reference to the fact that Lord Charles, like Yonge before him, had corruptly increased military expenditure for the Cape Corps. As Bird would testify to the commission of inquiry,

> I believe great irregularity to have prevailed in the payment of the expenses of that useless and extraordinary burden to the Colony, the Cape Corps, which ought to be paid on the footing of a British Corps, but in the payment of which many items have been falsified, and many circumstances which would not have been overlooked by the strict Audit of the War Office.[18]

Lord Charles seems to have concocted a story to get more funds to the corps with zero justification. Totally disregarding solid information from Colonel Scott on the Cape's eastern frontier that there was no threat of war with the Xhosa chiefs, Somerset wrote to the Colonial Office stating that there was a decided and imminent threat of war. He stated that the Colony must augment the Cape Corps with immediate effect. (Increasing military expenditure when there is no threat. Now just where has one heard that before?) Taking Lord Charles at his word, the Colonial Office in Britain unquestioningly provided him with an extra £4000 per year. As Cory tells it, Colonel Bird did the right thing by pointing out that this was 'a premeditated and gross deception. He suspected that the whole thing was a ruse to obtain promotion and a command for Lord Charles' son, Captain Henry Somerset.'[19]

Young Henry's career, like those of several delinquent sons in this book, was certainly on the rise thanks to dear daddy, despite the fact that history has judged him to have been a 'notorious incompetent' and a bald-faced liar. In 1818, when Henry was posted to the Cape, his father 'in an act of nepotistic patronage, appointed him commissioners of stamps, which topped up his salary by a princely £600 a year [R1.1 million today]'.[20] Later, when applying for free land in the small settlement at Grahamstown, Henry wilfully misrepresented the land's location, claiming that it was four kilometres outside of town. In fact, it was slap-bang in the centre of town, some 500 metres from the spot where the Cathedral of St Michael and St George was to be built. In 1822, Lord Charles found it appropriate to hand his son a further 356 acres adjoining this land.

Captain Henry Somerset

Somerset had promoted his son to the rank of captain in the Cape Corps, which also had within its ranks the atypical Boer landdrost Andries Stockenström. Descended from Swedish stock, Stockenström was made of very different stuff to most of his fellow frontiersmen – Afrikaners and Englishmen alike. He was a staunch believer in the impartial and universal principle of justice, and would later declare, 'I have the cause of truth to serve; I am to call "murder", "murder" and "plunder", "plunder", whatever be the colour of the perpetrator's skin.'[21]

When Stockenström fell under the command of hapless, dull and incompetent Captain Henry Somerset, he would tell Colonel Bird, 'I know that I am no match for the Governor with his Downing Street and his Horse Guards at his back, but if Lord Charles Somerset expects me to submit to his son's domination I would rather dash both Civil and Military Commissions in his face, and go to the Orange River and live on springbuck, which, as a bachelor, I can do.'[22]

When Lord Charles caught wind of Stockenström's complaint to Bird, he confronted him in Cape Town. In characteristic self-entitled rage, he is said to have shouted, 'I understand you have been complaining to the Colonial Secretary of my son's proceedings. I know he will do his duty and I will not allow him to be interfered with. Let me tell you, Sir, that no one has ever embroiled himself with any of my family without regretting it.'[23]

But Stockenström would not go out to the Orange River and live off springbuck. After refusing to act upon certain 'hints' that he should resign to allow Captain Henry Somerset to take complete command of the Cape Corps, he demanded that a military inquiry take place.

Unfortunately, every single officer of the Cape Corps refused to give evidence against the Somersets, and as such Stockenström was effectively blacklisted. As Stockenström would write,

[W]ith an infatuated parent who could not believe it possible for his son to be in the wrong, who possessed despotic sway in the Colony and all powerful influence in Headquarters, Civil and Military, it was but natural that the young aspirant Captain should become the focus of a set of hangers on and flatterers.[24]

Espionage, informers and slave disguises

Stockenström did, however, find a friend by the name of Mr Bishop Burnett, a man who would prove a nasty and recurrent thorn in the side of the Somersets. And Burnett certainly had reason to be so.

Burnett had come to the Cape with the 1820 Settlers, bringing with him some innovative ideas about farming. He initially took on some debt, but soon owned one of the most productive farms in the Eastern Cape. On discovering that the Cape Corps needed barley for its horses, Burnett set about growing it and selling it to the force now commanded by Captain Henry Somerset. With a large amount owed to him by Somerset, Burnett had taken on further debt, believing that he would be paid soon. He was greatly mistaken. Lord Charles's son straight up refused to pay for the barley, and Burnett found himself having to appeal to the court in Cape Town. The judge in the case was none other than Henry's father, Lord Charles, who unsurprisingly sided with his son on the matter, leaving Burnett in a state of financial ruin.

In an ensuing set of court cases of staggering complexity and incompetence that had to do with his bankruptcy, Burnett found himself at a legal impasse that could only be sorted out by the governor himself. As such, Burnett sent Lord Charles a petition stating that the people presiding over his case were 'persons morally disqualified to fulfil the sacred functions entrusted to them'.[25] Instead of dealing with the case fairly, Lord Charles colluded with the fiscal to bring a case of libel against Burnett. Burnett was arrested and found guilty of having defamed the officials of the court. He was sentenced under Roman-Dutch law to banishment from the Cape Colony for 'five successive years, and [it was ruled] that he be confined in some secure place until opportunity offered for his being sent away'.[26]

The fiscal, however, seems to have been a timid man, and initially decided not to imprison Burnett. Instead, he allowed him three months to prepare for his departure from the Colony. Luckily for Somerset, he had in his crooked arsenal a man who claimed to be in the building trade who went by the name of Mr William Jones. Jones was, according to some historians, a man more commonly known in Britain as 'Oliver the Spy', and is noted in British history to be 'the most notorious covert operative of them all'.[27] Having been exposed in Britain as an agent provocateur who worked covertly for certain members of the British government, 'Oliver the Spy' had fled Britain fearing for his life.

The official line was that he had been introduced to Lord Charles as a simple builder by no less than the British undersecretary of state – not usually someone who'd be in the business of referring builders to governors. As Kirsten McKenzie points out, the proof that this man was 'Oliver the Spy' is circumstantial. But it was nevertheless believed by people in Cape Town that 'William Jones' was Oliver, and that he had come to the Cape Colony supposedly to work on the renovations (at the public's expense, naturally) of Lord Charles's Newlands mansion. According to the poet and newspaper editor Thomas Pringle, with 'Oliver the Spy' there abounded 'a frightful system of espionage ... informers and false witnesses'.[28]

This 'simple builder', Burnett believed, had kept an 'unofficial' eye on him, and soon a raid by some of the fiscal's men took place on Burnett's house. They had come in search of more documents libelling Lord Charles. As it turned out, they found nothing of the sort. After the raid, Burnett began to fear that instead of banishment, Lord Charles would send him to the penal colony in New South Wales. Burnett hid at a friend's house, but his hiding place was soon discovered by a party of constables who arrived to arrest him. Having no warrant to search the house, Burnett's friend demanded that they return with the correct paperwork before he would let them in. Here we will allow Cory to tell the ensuing tale:

> They [the constables] were able to do nothing more than inquire and, being put off with 'adroit answers,' guarded the house during Sunday. On Sunday afternoon a well-dressed lady and gentleman, guided, as was the custom, by a female Malay slave carrying a 'lanthorn,' were permitted by the police to pass to the house and very shortly afterwards they were permitted to pass from the house. It would be scarcely just to blame the police for not perceiving that the Malay slave who went to the house was Mrs Bishop Burnett in disguise and the Malay slave who went from the house was Mr. Bishop Burnett who quickly put on the same disguise. He thus escaped and with the help of some friends found a safer hiding-place in Cape Town where he remained about a month.[29]

Lord Charles did his utmost to find Burnett and forbade any ship in Cape Town to allow him aboard, threatening all the captains who docked there with heavy fines if it was discovered that Burnett had made off in their vessel. Finally, a month later, Burnett sneaked onto the brig *Alacrity*. He succeeded in getting to Britain by the end of March 1825. There he would busy himself with exposing Somerset and his corrupt practices to a broader British public.

A library, liberty and Thomas Pringle

Perhaps one of the most incongruous aspects of Lord Charles's governorship was his desire to improve certain cultural and educational aspects of the Cape. But allow a person an education, and the next minute they will be demanding that you run the place properly. Much like the problems that Mugabe and Zuma were to have with those whom Zuma famously called 'clever blacks', so Somerset was caught up by the newly educated English-speaking middle class.

A German colonist by the name of Joachim von Dessin had, in 1761, bequeathed a few thousand books, two 'skulls of savages', a collection of 'native craft' and a fund for the development of a library. With this, Somerset duly established a library in part of the Slave Lodge at the bottom of the Company's Garden. Lord Charles appointed a young man by the name of Thomas Pringle as its sub-librarian. Pringle had arrived in the Cape Colony with the 1820 Settlers. He'd had a go at farming but, like many of the middle-class settlers, Pringle was drawn to the more metropolitan and cultured climes of Cape Town.

To be sure, the literary world in the Cape was pretty limited. As one wag put it, it was sad that Von Dessin could not have donated to the Colony 'a collection of readers' to go with his collection of books.[30] But despite the dearth of readership in Cape Town, Pringle was set on pursuing a literary career and he arrived in Cape Town with an introduction to the governor from Sir Walter Scott, no less. Lord Charles was suitably impressed and offered him a salary of £75 a year (a mere 134 times less than the governor's own salary) as the sub-librarian to his new venture.

Due to the insignificant nature of his salary, Pringle also applied to supervise and edit the *Government Gazette*, started by Sir George Yonge. Pringle had edited the famous *Blackwood's Magazine* and then the *Edinburgh Review* – a role that would prejudice Lord Charles against him. The *Edinburgh Review* was a Whig publication, and the governor was a sworn Tory. Having been refused the position at the government's publication due to his liberal associations, Pringle began to take on private students and persuaded a Scottish friend, John Fairbairn, to join

Thomas Pringle, activist poet

him in Cape Town in order to start an English school.

Fairbairn and Pringle had met one another through literary circles in Edinburgh, but they shared a great deal more than literary tastes. Both had an unswerving dedication to the freedom of the press and would also place themselves at the forefront of the anti-slavery movement. On receiving Pringle's invitation to join him in Cape Town, Fairbairn wrote back saying he would do so, noting that 'your hint about Magazines and Newspapers pleases me exceedingly. What should hinder us from becoming the Franklins of the Kaap? … I have a number of literary schemes in my head … Yet surely popular lectures on Chemistry, Geology, Botany, and other departments of science, might be rendered both acceptable and useful to your new country men.'[31]

What Fairbairn had not gleaned from Pringle's letters was that one very large impediment stood between them and their dream of an ideal academy: Lord Charles Somerset. Somerset and his Cape government had in place a policy that forbade the establishment of an independent press, as well as laws against the expression or discussion of grievances at public meetings (remember, he had helped bring in similar laws in Britain). These laws, together with the flagrant corruption and 'irregularities' in the Somerset administration, had driven some of the 1820 Settlers to write a memorial to the Colonial Office – much like Adam Tas. It was this memorial that in part had led to Britain's Parliament appointing the commission of inquiry that arrived in the Cape in 1823.

Whatever initial good impression Somerset had of Pringle soon evaporated. Although he agreed to Pringle and Fairbairn setting up their school, Somerset would later say that it taught the 'most disgusting principles of Republicanism',[32] and he did his best to drain it of students. So, when this liberal-minded group of men applied to Lord Charles for permission to set up a periodical and a newspaper, they were told by the colonial secretary, Colonel Bird, that 'His Excellency had not seen your application in a favourable light.'[33] As Pringle tells it in his memoir,

Long before Mr Fairbairn had joined me, however, I had acquired a more intimate acquaintance with the character of the colonial administration and formed a truer estimate of the views, I soon saw that their professed anxiety to encourage education and the diffusion of knowledge was a piece of political hypocrisy, assumed to cloak the real character of the government from the prying eyes of his Majesty's Commission of Inquiry.[34]

When the commission of inquiry arrived at the Cape, Somerset went all out to ingratiate himself with the two commissioners. He accommodated them lavishly in Government House while he took to his luxuriously refurbished (at taxpayers' expense) house in Newlands. From there, he sent incessant invitations to the commissioners asking them to join him on hunts, to attend race meetings and to sample the luxuries of 'his' farm at Groote Post. These, by all accounts, the commissioners Bigge and Colebrooke steadfastly declined.

All the while, Somerset had been beavering away trying to stop the Colonial Office from granting Pringle permission to start a free press. And with the commissioners nosing around in official correspondence, Somerset took to writing privately to officials at the Colonial Office to oppose Pringle's attempts. 'I foresee so much evil,' he wrote, 'and a great public inconvenience might arise from the adoption of the measure.'[35]

Pringle and Fairbairn may well have given up their attempts for a free press had it not been for the arrival of a Mr George Greig. Greig was in the printing trade and had arrived in Cape Town with skills and some equipment. Despite the shade Lord Charles had thrown on Pringle and Fairbairn, with Greig's arrival the two did get permission from the Colonial Office in Britain to start a literary publication. The permission did, however, contain the caveat that the publication have 'the strict exclusion from the work of all topics of political or personal controversy' and that it may contain nothing that was 'detrimental to the peace and safety of the colony'.[36] And so, under these conditions, Pringle and Fairbairn's *The South African Magazine* was born. According to Pringle,

At the same time, Mr Greig, a printer who recently arrived from England, and established the printing press in Cape Town, commenced the publication of the weekly newspaper entitled the *South African Commercial Advertiser*. Every such attempt had hitherto been at once arbitrarily quashed by the colonial authorities; but the presence of the Commissioners of Inquiry, and the decision

of Earl Bathurst in our case deterred the government from then directly inter-
fering with Mr Greig's publication, although they went as far as they decently
could to discountenance and discourage it ... After issuing his first two numbers he found himself in want of editorial aid and solicited us to undertake
literary management of the paper. As the control of an efficient press, with a
view to the diffusion of useful knowledge throughout the colony, was the great
object of our ambition, we agreed.[37]

Pringle goes on to write that they acceded to the demand from the Colonial
Office not to engage in party politics. They also abstained from covering issues
like slavery and the treatment of the native population. This was no doubt difficult, as these were issues close to both Pringle's and Fairbairn's hearts. They did,
however,

[i]ntroduce the practice of reporting law cases and on this point the Governor
and some of these advisors happened to be particularly sensitive; insomuch
that although they had nothing to allege against the paper as respects the
impartiality and discretion with which such reports had been hitherto given,
they could not tolerate the continuance of such a privilege. The immediate
cause of their interference was this. It was a prosecution for libel then before
the Supreme Court, at the insistence of the Governor. In the course of the
trial the defendant (one Edwards, a reckless and desperate adventurer), had
brought forward certain scandalous and libellous charges against the character of the Lord Charles Somerset both in his public and private capacity.[38]

Edwards, who was masquerading as a lawyer in the Colony, was more than just
'a reckless and desperate adventurer'. He was a convict who had escaped from
the penal colony of Australia in 1821. He was also, by all accounts, a consummate
showman who knew how to play to an audience. His entrance into the Cape
courts was timed perfectly for the Cape's first (almost) free media.

What these trials and Pringle's newspaper revealed was

that under the Cape judicial system the government had unlimited powers of
search, detention and banishment; that the accused had no right to summon
their own witnesses or cross-examine the witnesses of the prosecution; that
the fiscal, or prosecutor, was also one of the judges and that there was no trial

by jury; and that none of the Cape's top judicial officers was fully conversant with the English language.[39]

Perhaps the most interesting of the cases, other than that of Bishop Burnett discussed above, was that of Lancelot Cooke, who wished to take on the services of a 'prize slave'. As you may recall, prize slaves were the slightly more fortunate variety of slave who had been on board foreign ships that had been captured by the British navy and 'freed'. They were freed only in the sense that they were 'apprenticed to an owner' in something like the manner of an indentured servant. That is, they had to work for a certain number of years before they could become truly free. If, however, the 'owner' of one of these 'prize slaves' died and the slave was capable of finding employment and taking care of themselves, they were free to do so. And this is precisely what happened to a Cape Town 'prize slave' by the name of Jean Ellé. After his master died, Ellé found gainful employment as a cook with a man named – with astonishing appropriateness – Lancelot Cooke.

However, the head of customs at the harbour, Mr Blair, was intent on spoiling their broth. Blair was in charge of the distribution of 'prize slaves', many of whom he assigned to himself or his friends. Jean Ellé was no exception. Blair promptly took him out of the services of Lancelot Cooke and placed him instead under Mr Wilberforce Bird's mastery. Ironically, Bird was related to William Wilberforce, Britain's greatest anti-slavery activist.

Lancelot Cooke did not take this matter lying down, and he persuaded the masquerading lawyer and escaped convict Edwards to take his case pro bono. Just quite why Edwards at this stage was so eager to take on the powers that be is unclear. Certainly, Edwards understood that abolitionism and the mistreatment of slaves in the Colony was a hot topic, and one that Somerset was on the wrong side of.

Edwards, it seems, felt very strongly on the issue of slavery and would write to Somerset saying,

> I have lived long enough to know that my life is only valuable in as much as it serves my fellow Creatures and if I should ever be martyred in the perseverance to destroy effectually the slavery my loved country has abolished.[40]

Together, Edwards and Cooke collected evidence from various others in the Colony, drew up a memorial stating the grievances many had with Mr Blair's conduct and sent it to the governor for it to be transmitted to England. But Lord Charles played the same legal trick he would later use with Bishop Burnett. He handed the memorial over to the fiscal, Daniel Denyssen, who charged Cooke and Edwards with 'libelling a public servant' – a charge that would result in banishment.

As McKenzie relays, 'Cooke was charged with having written and signed the memorial, Edwards with having drawn it up and forwarding it to the governor, and the clerk Jan Bernard Hoffman with having copied it.'[41] Edwards would go on to mock the prosecution, asking why, given these terms, he had not attempted to prosecute others involved in the production of the memorial, such as 'the papermaker or the goose, whence the pen which it was written was plucked'.[42]

During the trial, Edwards went on the attack, calling the governor in as a witness and pointing out the various instances of Denyssen's dereliction of duty. The court then sentenced Edwards to one month in prison for contempt. Daniel Denyssen, who essentially held the same position as Zuma's Shaun Abrahams two centuries later, soon became known in the Colony as 'Dog Dan'. According to a diarist of the time, a placard had been placed in the centre of Cape Town denouncing the 'rascally Fiscal', stating:

> Each Dog we know must have his day
> but when the farce is ended
> Dog Dan must be suspended.[43]

Edwards put his month in prison to good use, and when he was freed he produced in court an astonishing amount of legal precedents to substantiate his claims against the governor, citing everyone from the legal philosopher Hugo Grotius to the famous Tory judge Sir William Blackstone. Edwards would also reference a case in Cape colonial history in which a memorial had been written by whistle-blowers *without* fear of prosecution for libel. This was, as you may have already guessed, the case of Adam Tas and the free burghers against Governor Willem Adriaan van der Stel.

Every step of the way, Pringle, Fairbairn and Greig recorded Edwards's legal crusade and his exposure of corruption in their newspaper, the *South African Commercial Advertiser*. Thanks to Edwards's deft legal arguments and the grounds-well of popular support for him that was developing in the Colony, Edwards surprisingly won the case brought against him by Somerset after an appeal to the full court. The trial ultimately exposed the great corruptions and injustices that were entrenched under Somerset's rule in the Cape, not least the corrupt dealings with regard to prize slaves.

After assessing Edwards and Cooke's memorial, the head of the Colonial Office sent Lord Charles a letter. The letter pointed out that Somerset's case of libel against the two was deeply flawed. Libel, it argued, occurred when a statement was made in public; that is, when it was either said in a public meeting or printed in a newspaper or pamphlet. The Edwards memorial had been sent to Lord Charles privately. It was not a public document and therefore was not libellous. But now, they went on to explain, Somerset had made the memorial public and he had effectively become the publisher of the statements in the memorial. Lord Charles himself was thus guilty of libel, and not Edwards and Cooke.

Edwards is recorded to have said:

> I glory in having done my duty. I am proud to be the humble hand to open the eyes of a beneficent Monarch. I owe it to his Majesty not to leave him ignorant of the abuse of his officers. I will have the glory to be a broom in the hands of Royalty which shall cleanse this Aegean Stable and bury every pander in his own filth![44]

But neither Lord Charles nor Edwards was finished. On sending the governor two heated letters which our ever-sensitive governor deemed offensive, Edwards was rearrested and thrown into jail once again. Again, Somerset seemed to wilfully misinterpret the notion of 'publication' and charged Edwards with libelling 'His excellency the Governor'.

Edwards again went on the attack, calling a list of witnesses, including 'a manumitted female slave', 'a concubine living with Lord Charles Somerset' and Dr Barry, Somerset's rather unusual personal doctor. Edwards, seemingly insultingly, referred to Dr Barry as a 'Woman Doctor'.[45] The fiscal, Dog Dan, was perhaps right in believing that Edwards had called these witnesses in order to ridicule them and the governor in front of newspapermen, who were eager to publish a salacious story.

'Buggering Dr Barry'

With all of this theatre transpiring – and the choicest bits being published and sent around the Colony – Lord Charles intervened, demanding that Dog Dan censor the paper. Finally, Somerset ordered that the paper be closed entirely and that the press be destroyed. Initially, the fiscal merely sealed the printing press. But he failed to confiscate the type, and Greig succeeded in printing some further handbills. As these circulated Cape Town, the governor ordered that Greig be banished from the Colony.

The *South African Commercial Advertiser*: countering fake news with facts

With the press now out of commission, Greig banished and Edwards in jail, one of the most controversial and unexplained events in Cape history occurred. On the 1 June 1824, a poster was placed on the corner of Hout and Adderley streets stating:

A person living at Newlands makes it known or takes this opportunity of making it known to the Public authorities of this Colony that on the 5th instant he detected Lord Charles buggering Dr Barry.[46]

The mysterious Dr Barry

Dr James Barry spent his formative years in Edinburgh, where he studied medicine. He first served as a doctor in Cape Town and then in several other parts of the British Empire. He rose to the position of inspector general in charge of military hospitals. When in Cape Town, he is reported to have saved the life of Somerset's gravely ill daughter, Georgina. After this, Barry became a close friend of the family, frequenting the house in Newlands and becoming Somerset's personal physician.

While in Cape Town, he also performed one of the first Caesarean sections ever documented where both the mother and child survived. The child was christened

Dr James Barry

James Barry Munnik in Dr Barry's honour. The name was passed down the family and was given to James Barry Munnik Hertzog, Boer general and prime minister of South Africa (whom we'll meet in our chapter on the Broederbond.)

Dr Barry is said to have been an unusual person, diminutive and prone to violent outbursts. He also had a high voice and wore special platform shoes to bolster his stature. Florence Nightingale, who worked with him in the Crimean War, said that he was 'the most hardened creature I ever met'. But he was also well known for going out of his way to treat slaves and the poor and for his hospital and medical reforms.

Interestingly, Edwards used Dr Barry's decency against Lord Charles in court. Edwards noted that Somerset made a law one day and permitted his friends to break it the next. Somerset had made a law that all doctors had to charge a fixed fee of one rixdollar for a visit. But Edwards pointed out that when Barry charged *less* than the law dictated, Somerset allowed him to get away with it.

According to recent research, after Barry died it was discovered that biologically he was in fact a woman. Dr James Barry was born Margaret Bulkley and grew up as a girl in Cork, Ireland. Barry's recent biographers, Michael du Preez and Jeremy Dronfield, claim that Barry may well have had an affair with Somerset. Barry would describe Somerset as 'my more than father – my almost only friend'.[47]

Just who placed the notice on the street corner no one will ever know. Two theories existed at the time, neither of which was backed up by any evidence. One was that Edwards, while in jail, got somebody to do the deed. The other was that Lord Charles himself had arranged it all in an attempt to gain sympathy.

Lord Charles made a great show of trying to discover the perpetrator, raiding people's houses and seizing their papers, all to no avail. No substantial evidence ever came to light as to the identity of the man or woman who put up the notice. The fact that Dr Barry was biologically a woman and was, by all accounts, dedicated to Lord Charles might suggest that somebody at the Newlands residence had seen them at it. Whatever the truth, the Colony was thrown into total chaos by the scandal. Pringle gave up on any hope of a newspaper and returned to Britain with his young, adopted Tswana son. Edwards was sent to the Australian penal colony, where his true identity as an escaped convict was discovered.

And what of Lord Charles?

In mid-1825, Britain's House of Commons 'granted' Lord Charles 'a leave of absence' from the Colony. It seems the British Parliament wanted Charles to come and explain his actions, as complaints about his administration were arriving on an all-too-regular basis. But Lord Charles decided to take his merry time about leaving the Cape and only arrived in Britain almost a year later (where have we heard this before?). Before he had arrived, Bishop Burnett – who was still banished – published in London a searing and indicting pamphlet with copious evidence of Lord Charles's corrupt activities at the Cape.

There had been a leak in the colonial administration, and Burnett quoted verbatim from secret government documents. Just who leaked the information has never been established, but Lord Charles's governorship was now effectively over. The British government tried its best to stall and delay a further inquiry into the well-connected Somerset's corruption, but the British public now knew just how the Colony was being run. In the parliamentary hearing on these matters, a Mr Lombe demanded that Lord Charles be impeached. On the night of the impeachment debate, however, Lombe failed to appear, and the 'noble' Lord Charles was offered an unqualified acquittal.

As McKenzie points out, Somerset was supported by the Tories not because he wasn't corrupt, but because he was a Tory. In a moment particularly reminiscent of the African National Congress (ANC) nearly two centuries later, Lord Bathurst wrote to Somerset saying, '[A]s you will be attacked upon party principles ... you are entitled to party support'.[48] But Somerset, unlike Zuma later on, saw the writing on the wall and resigned as governor, retiring to Brighton, where he died peacefully in 1831. He did so safe in the knowledge that he would be left alone and not continually dragged into court – a privilege other corrupt dignitaries would not be afforded.

PART TWO
DIAMONDS AND GOLD

From the 1870s onwards, the discovery of diamonds
and gold attracted a new kind of skelm to South Africa.

CECIL JOHN RHODES (I)

The Young Swindler
1875–1894

'My character was so battered at the Diamond Fields that I like to preserve a few remnants.' – **Cecil John Rhodes**

Young Cecil John Rhodes with a gun – a sign of things to come

'Send for Mr Rhodes!'

Colonel Crossman, the head of the royal commission in Kimberley, had faced an incendiary opening morning to his inquiry. But with the appearance of Mr Heuteau, a thirty-five-year-old engineer from Mauritius, things had calmed down. Heuteau was giving testimony concerning the failure of his dredging equipment at the De Beers mine. Colonel Crossman stared at Heuteau and demanded, 'Who is the man who bribed you?'

Crossman's Kimberley Commission of 1876 had been set up to look into a miners' revolt at the diggings, which became known as the Black Flag Rebellion. On arriving in Kimberley, Crossman found that his commission would have to take on a rather wider brief than was initially conceived. All kinds of shenanigans and malfeasance had been carrying on in the largely unregulated scramble for riches in Griqualand West.

Under examination, Heuteau, the Mauritian engineer who manned the water pumps at the De Beers mine, had admitted that the failure of his dredging equipment was due to sabotage. What was more, Heuteau confessed that it was he who had sabotaged it. Why, the commission asked, would he have done this to his own equipment? Well, the engineer answered, the reason was really quite simple – a man had given him £300 (R665 000 today) to do so. Colonel Crossman was confused. Just who would have done that? Heuteau now found himself in a slightly awkward moral dilemma and explained to Crossman that he had given his word to the man who had bribed him that he wouldn't divulge his identity.

But the colonel insisted, threatening the Mauritian with legal action. Heuteau took some time to answer; the situation was an uncomfortable one. Then he came up with a rather brilliant solution. Instead of getting himself into hot water with the commission, Heuteau reasoned that he had only promised the man who had bribed him that he would not speak his name. Writing it down? Well, that was another matter. In his thinking, writing the name down was not part of the agreement. By doing this, Heuteau technically kept his word, but not his promise. 'I am prepared to write the name,' the Mauritian is said to have offered the commission. A small piece of paper was then handed to him and, in a second, the deed was done. The hall was silent as the piece of paper was handed over to Crossman. On turning it over, the colonel immediately announced in a ringing tone: 'Send for Mr Rhodes!'

Cecil John Rhodes had little to do with the Black Flag Rebellion and could easily have expected not to have to come before the commission. He was then a man of only twenty-two who had, a year before, returned to the Cape Colony from an unfinished degree at Oxford. What he did have something to do with, though, was the graft and shady shenanigans that were part and parcel of the ragtag swarm of men and women who had gathered at Kimberley on the discovery of diamonds in 1867. And it was this that the commission began to focus on as one of the causes of the revolt. Crossman had spent the first morning of the commission listening to and shouting over the various claims and counterclaims of the miners. But in the heat of a January afternoon in Kimberley, the court had settled down after its aggressive beginnings and Crossman had now clearly got to the bottom of what had happened to the dredging equipment.

Although the mines at Kimberley were hugely productive at first, they had run into some hurdles along the way – the latest of which was flooding. In February 1874, significant rains flooded the mines. This effectively brought mining to an end. But young Cecil Rhodes, ever the opportunist, saw the flooding as a chance to make money. He approached the board that controlled the mine and asked for exclusive rights to pump it. The De Beers board turned him down, but he and his friend Charles Rudd were later successful in securing the rights to pump the Dutoitspan mine, some six kilometres away down a dusty wagon track. Rhodes had made a promise with little hope or idea as to how he would fulfil it. He had no equipment to back the agreement up. And so, with a questionable contract in his pocket, he left Kimberley to find a machine to pump the mine.

After hearing that a farmer named Devenish some kilometres away had recently bought pumping equipment for his farm, Rhodes headed out there with an ox wagon and a driver to see if he could buy it. With dogged persistence and £1 000, Rhodes managed to secure the pump. By all accounts, he camped on Devenish's land until the farmer could bear him no longer. Devenish sold him the equipment in an effort to be rid of him.

On starting the pumping at the Dutoitspan, Rhodes and Rudd managed to secure the contract to pump the larger De Beers mine. But this was a classic case of overreach. Rhodes and his pumps simply did not have the capacity to perform the task. By May 1875, Rhodes had botched it. Much of the De Beers mine still lay under water, and its mining board informed him that he had failed to honour his contract with them. The board decided to take over the pumping of the mine themselves.

Rhodes did, however, agree with them that he would take over the dredging again once the equipment he had ordered from Britain arrived in the next few months. For some slightly confusing reason (some suggest it was Rhodes's charm), the board agreed to enter into another contract with a man who had already failed them. But this contract would only be effective once Rhodes had his new pumping equipment.

The board then appointed Mr Heuteau, who performed the task of pumping the mine rather well – doing it far more effectively than Rhodes. In fact, Heuteau kept the mine dry at the time of the heaviest rainfalls of 1875. What was more, his operating costs were far lower than the pending contract price Rhodes and the mine had agreed to. The board began to openly question why they should revert to Rhodes when Heuteau was performing the task more effectively and at far lower cost. Rhodes had, after all, already failed miserably at the job.

Up until Christmas, Heuteau had his pumps working almost perfectly. However, on Boxing Day of 1875 there was trouble. In a spectacular disaster, Heuteau's pumping operation failed catastrophically and water flooded into the De Beers mine, forcing operations to grind to a halt. On inspecting Heuteau's equipment, it was discovered that 'the plunger, gland and collar of the pumping engine [had been] removed, sabotaging and flooding the claims'.[1]

Days after the discovery of the sabotage, Heuteau sat before Colonel Crossman in the royal commission, explaining just what had happened. Under examination, Heuteau was nervous. It appeared as if he simply couldn't explain what had transpired. When Crossman had grown impatient, Heuteau had confessed he had sabotaged the dredging equipment himself. But to most people, including the colonel, this did not make sense. Why would Heuteau want to destroy all the good work he had done?

What Crossman had not taken into account was the precarious position Heuteau found himself in at the De Beers mine. Although he had done a good job, he knew that Rhodes had the contract to take over from him in the coming months. What's more, Rhodes was worried that the mining board was beginning to contemplate cancelling his contract. This would have been financially devastating, as he was now sitting with expensive equipment on board a ship in the middle of the Atlantic heading to Cape Town – paid for and possibly of no use. Heuteau had not only proved better than him at keeping the mine dry, he had done it more cheaply.

After Crossman called for Rhodes to appear before him, the young Cecil could not be found. As the local paper the *Diamond News* reported:

> Character was at stake, and the Royal Commission did all in his power to prevent Rhodes remaining under the stigma longer than was unavoidable if [Heuteau's] statement was true.[2]

When Rhodes did finally appear, just before the commission adjourned for the day, he explained that he had been hard at work tending the water-pumping equipment at the Dutoitspan mine. On hearing the accusation against him, he flatly denied bribing Heuteau, stating that Heuteau's claim was 'fictitious'. With the commission wanting to end for the day, Crossman demanded that Rhodes appear before him in two days' time.

Now Rhodes got busy. The next day he met with the De Beers board and asked them to help him clear his name. The board refused point-blank. The chairman told him that Heuteau had 'some months ago' informed him that a man had tried to bribe him. In fact, there had been other rumours, some months before the sabotage took place, that a 'speculator' had approached Heuteau offering him £300 to sabotage the pumping equipment. At the time, many miners had insisted that Heuteau give them the name of the potential corrupter, but the Mauritian had refused to speak it. (The distinction between speaking and writing was clearly important to Heuteau.)

The *Diamond News* announced the day after Heuteau's admission at the commission that 'the character of a respectable citizen has been assailed'. The paper went on to say that if Heuteau's accusations proved true, Rhodes should face legal prosecution.[3]

After getting no help from the De Beers board, Rhodes went to his good (and lifelong) friend Sidney Shippard, who just so happened to be the attorney-general in Kimberley. Rhodes persuaded Shippard to charge Heuteau with perjury, and six days later a preliminary hearing took place in the resident Magistrate's Court. No one knows precisely what happened in the interim, although it would be consistent with Rhodes's character if another bribe was duly offered. In a dramatic turnaround, Heuteau stated before the court that Rhodes was not the man who had bribed him. After this hearing, Rhodes's attorney-general friend dropped the charges against Heuteau, and the Mauritian disappeared into the fog of history, never to be heard of again.

By February 1876, with Heuteau gone and Rhodes's name officially 'cleared', Rhodes was back in charge of the pumping. But the mine was still waterlogged. A vote was held at a public meeting, and the majority of the miners voted to have Rhodes's contract cancelled. Rhodes promised them that when his new pumps arrived all would be well. Bizarrely, the mine then agreed to a nine-month contract. As historian Robert Turrell revealed, Rhodes and his partners' working expenses 'were £256 each month, which left a monthly profit of £294 or an annual income of £3,528 [R7.6 million today]'.[4]

On securing all the pumping contracts in Kimberley (his first monopoly), Rhodes made the decision to go back to Oxford to finish his degree. As a result, he became an absentee water contractor, leaving much of the logistics and work to Rudd and Company and a Mr E.W. Tarry (remember these names). The decision to vacate Kimberley society to go to Oxford was not simply academic. As Rhodes wrote in a letter, it was also due to the fact that his 'character was so battered at the Diamond Fields that I like to preserve a few remnants'.[5]

Diamond monopolies are a man's best friend

When Rhodes returned to South Africa in 1879, he began to apply himself to two interlinked concerns: politics and, as Joseph Conrad put it, 'the tearing of the raw material of treasure from the earth'.[6] What Rhodes had managed to preserve in his absence from South Africa were his friendships, in particular with Sidney Shippard and Charles Rudd. Two other men became central to his life in Kimberley after his return. One, John X. Merriman, was said to have 'fastidious scruples' (not really Rhodes's cup of Earl Grey). The other, Dr Leander Starr Jameson, seems to have lacked any scruples at all.

Merriman and Rhodes took to riding together in the morning and engaging in long discussions on the future of South Africa. During these rides, Merriman is said to have persuaded Rhodes that 'the most intellectual occupation for a man to take in S[outh] Africa was go into Parliament'.[7] Meanwhile, Dr Jameson appears to have persuaded Rhodes on more than one occasion that war was the best policy – particularly when you wanted somebody else's gold.

But before Rhodes became obsessed with gold and war, there was his desire to amalgamate the various diamond interests in Kimberley into one company under his control. He and Rudd, working with other claim holders in the area, formed the De Beers Mining Company (named after the brothers who originally owned the farm) on April Fool's Day, 1881. One of Rhodes's first actions as the head of a growing (but still not very large) mining concern was to persuade other mine owners to crack down on the 'illicit' diamond-buying market. Black miners were often accused of smuggling diamonds out of the mines and selling them 'illegally'. (The accusations were certainly true, but given the conditions we will soon hear about, it would be surprising if they hadn't helped themselves to some of the riches they were working to extract.)

Rhodes soon realised that being a member of Parliament was not only an intellectual pursuit but could, in the grand scheming of things, be ruddy useful. And so, in 1881, he ran unopposed for the seat at Barkly West, a small town near Kimberley (more about this later). Once in Parliament, he immediately set about making sure that the draconian Diamond Trade Act (1882) was passed. According to his biographer Brian Roberts, Rhodes was very proud of the fact that he had shepherded the Act through Parliament, saying that he believed fundamentally 'in his baby the Diamond Trade Act, however unpleasant it proved to be to a proportion of the community'.[8]

Of course, the community Rhodes was talking about here was the black one. Earlier legislation had barred black mine workers from owning land claims in the mining areas, but the new Act cleared the way for segregating them entirely. Fenced compounds were created, alcohol bans were instituted (miners were given ginger beer instead) and strict curfews were set. Any black labourer found outside of what was essentially their prison after ten at night was given fifteen lashes to the bare back. As Antony Thomas puts it, Rhodes's De Beers Mining Company 'perfected' the 'native' compound:

> Over 11 000 African labourers were housed 20–25 to a room in corrugated-iron barracks, set out in a square and surrounded by a 12-foot fence, which was patrolled by company police with dogs. The whole area was roofed over by double mesh wire netting and guard towers with searchlights placed at each corner.[9]

Before being herded back into the compounds after each work shift, African miners were forced to take their clothes off and be subjected to horrific and invasive body searches which probed 'every orifice'. When a miner's contract came to an end, they were stripped naked and placed in solitary confinement in a tin hut for ten days. Their hands were chained together into fingerless leather gloves, and they were fed

Compound interest, De Beers style

castor oil. Their excrement was then inspected daily, just in case they had swallowed a diamond. Although Rhodes is said not to have instigated or invented these policies, he certainly condoned their use and saw their financial benefits.

So effective did the above policies become that Rhodes and his mates now faced another problem – overproduction. The world had limited use for diamonds, and Kimberley's newfound productivity brought with it the threat of a price plummet. At this, Rhodes set about controlling the world's production of diamonds, and, as Lord Olivier put it, 'He succeeded by irrepressible energy, cajolery, perseverance and unscrupulousness in amalgamating the principal interests in the diamond diggings and established De Beers.'[10]

He first absorbed all the smaller competitors in Kimberley. Then, with the financial help of the Rothschilds in London, Rhodes managed to buy out a large French diamond-producing company, which was his only international rival. Finally, he turned to the other big concern in Kimberley – diamond magnate Barney Barnato. Rhodes convinced Barnato to merge with him, thus forming De Beers Consolidated Mines. De Beers went on to become a cartel, controlling the world's diamond industry and capable of fixing the diamond price at will. As the South African novelist William Plomer wrote in his history of Rhodes:

It need hardly be added that the establishment of the monopoly brought distress to many private individuals who were not dominated so much by greed and ambition as by the immediate need to make a living; they could no longer even sell goods to the native workmen, for the monopoly took care of that henceforth, making, we may be sure, a cosy profit in the process.[11]

But this was not even the worst of it. The De Beers trust deed made room for the company to govern countries, annex territory in Africa, raise and maintain a standing army, and make war! Rhodes would do all four ...

De Beers did fix it

'In 2004 De Beers entered an agreement with the U.S. Department of Justice in which it pleaded guilty to price fixing and agreed to pay a $10 million fine. Four years later the company paid $295 million to settle several class-action lawsuits charging it with misleading advertising, human rights violations, conspiracy to fix and raise diamond prices, and unlawfully monopolizing the supply of diamonds.'
– *Encyclopaedia Britannica*

A ruddy liar

With the discovery of gold in the Transvaal (read all about it in the next chapter), Rhodes somehow got it into his head that another large gold reef lay to the north, in Matabeleland and Mashonaland (now Zimbabwe). Many seemed to genuinely believe that King Solomon's mines (mentioned in the Bible) would be found beneath Bulawayo, the Ndebele capital. (The Ndebele were formerly known by many as the Matabele.)

A well-intentioned missionary and colonial administrator by the name of John Moffat had got Lobengula, the paramount chief of the Ndebele, to 'admit that the Transvaal had no right to interfere in his country'. Rhodes quickly realised that this did not mean to say that the English had no option over Matabeleland. As Plomer explained, 'It need hardly be said that when Rhodes had an option over anything it was apt to be almost as good as possession.'[12]

Rhodes first used his old mate Shippard to organise a peace treaty with Lobengula. Shippard was by then 'Her Majesty's Administrator' of the Bechuanaland Protectorate (now Botswana) and was known there as *Marana-maka*, the

Father of Lies. Once the treaty was in place, Rhodes sent his pumping pal Rudd to negotiate the mining rights in Matabeleland and Mashonaland. By now, everybody, including the Boers, Portuguese, Germans and other Englishmen, was convinced that mountains of gold lay beneath Lobengula's feet.

Rudd left Kimberley incognito, claiming he was off on an ordinary shooting party. Few people seem to have questioned just why he needed for this venture a barrel organ, £10 000 in gold coins (R27.5 million today – generous pocket money) and a letter stamped by Queen Victoria. All of this was taken as gifts for Lobengula, who was deemed by Rhodes and Rudd to rule not only Matabeleland, but also the northern territory of Mashonaland (parts of which neither he nor his impis had ever set foot in.)

When Rudd arrived at Bulawayo, a protracted negotiation began, during which Rudd made several verbal promises to the chief. Most of these were simply hot air. Rudd certainly did promise Lobengula 1 000 Martini-Henry rifles and ammunition in order to 'scatter the flies' that were gathering around Matabeleland, and £100 a month. These were duly noted in the agreement. Others that were not were the promise that came from Rhodes himself of a steamboat for the Zambezi River and that no more than ten white men would be brought to dig for gold. Rudd also promised that no digging would take place near any Ndebele town. As biographer Antony Thomas says, the concession was a 'fraud built upon a fraud'.[13] Through no fault of his own, Lobengula had effectively rubbed himself and his people (not to mention the Mashona) off the face of the map.

With the ink of Lobengula's sign barely dry, Rudd took to a mule cart and was off. Passing Shippard on the road through Bechuanaland, Rudd had just enough time to share a champagne luncheon with the Father of Lies before bundling back into his cart. Shortly after this (and no doubt a little worse for wear after his midday *dopping*), he lost his way when he was overtaken by a sandstorm that lasted several days. Having run out of water and with no clue where he was, he believed that the end was nigh for him and his precious piece of paper. With thoughts of his impending death, he wrote a farewell letter to his wife and buried it and the newly signed Rudd Concession in an aardvark's burrow. Sadly for the Ndebele, a group of Tswana men found him in his confused and dehydrated state and revived him. When Rudd recovered the concession from the aardvark's hole, Lobengula's fate was sealed.

From the Rudd Concession

I, Lobengula, King of Matabeleland, Mashonaland, and other adjoining territories, in exercise of my sovereign powers, and in the presence and with the consent of my council of indunas, do hereby grant and assign unto the said grantees, their heirs, representatives, and assigns, jointly and severally, the complete and exclusive charge over all metals and minerals situated and contained in my kingdoms, principalities, and dominions, together with full power to do all things that they may deem necessary to win and procure the same, and to hold, collect, and enjoy the profits and revenues, if any, derivable from the said metals and minerals, subject to the aforesaid payment; and whereas I have been much molested of late by divers persons seeking and desiring to obtain grants and concessions of land and mining rights in my territories, I do hereby authorise the said grantees, their heirs, representatives and assigns, to take all necessary and lawful steps to exclude from my kingdom, principalities, and dominions all persons seeking land, metals, minerals, or mining rights therein, and I do hereby undertake to render them all such needful assistance as they may from time to time require for the exclusion of such persons, and to grant no concessions of land or mining rights from and after this date without their consent and concurrence; provided that, if at any time the said monthly payment of one hundred pounds shall be in arrear for a period of three months, then this grant shall cease and determine from the date of the last-made payment.

Although the concession mentioned only mineral rights, it became clear from newspaper reports that Rhodes saw the agreement as ceding the land as well. This news filtered up to Lobengula, who then called his indunas and all the Europeans in the area for a meeting. Here, a European wrote down the speech of Hlesingane, one of Lobengula's elders:

O King of the country open your ears and eyes. I have been at Kimberley Diamond Fields and one or two men cannot work them, it takes thousands to work them. Do not those thousands want water and they also want land. It is the same with gold, once it is found the white men will come to work it, and then there will be trouble. [They] say [they] do not want any land, how can you dig for gold without it, is it not in the land? And by digging into the land is not that taking it, and do those thousands not make fires? Will that not take wood?[14]

The Rudd Concession

Lobengula and his indunas were said to be furious and were eager to use the newspaper in order to publicise Rhodes and Rudd's fraud as widely as possible. They were helped in this matter by some of the whites in Bulawayo, who wrote down a letter dictated to them by Lobengula and sent it to various newspapers. The letter appeared in *The Bechuanaland News* on 14 February 1889, accompanied by a photo of the original with Lobengula's seal.

I hear it is published in the newspapers that I have granted a Concession of the Minerals in all my country to Charles Dunnell Rudd, Rochford Maguire and Francis Robert Thompson.

As there is a great misunderstanding about this, all action in respect of said Concession is hereby suspended pending an investigation to be made by me in my country.

(Signed) Lobengula

Royal Kraal, Matabeleland, January 18 1889.[15]

Of course, Rhodes did not just send ten men to dig for gold 'to Matabeleland, Mashonaland, and other adjoining territories'. Instead, in 1890, he sent a private army of a thousand men, each armed with a Martini-Henry rifle and a Webley revolver, 117 wagons, field guns, rocket launchers, 'electric mines', and Gatling and Maxim machine guns. This 'pioneer column' marched straight through Matabeleland and ended up settling in what was Mashonaland – which Rhodes and Rudd claimed was ruled by Lobengula.

Lobengula's seal

Three years later, with Rhodes's most obedient of lieutenants Dr Leander Starr Jameson at its head, this private army would start a war with Lobengula. In the most absurd piece of concocted colonial-era mendacity, Jameson picked a fight with Lobengula, claiming that the Ndebele were threatening the Mashona. In reality, Jameson had decided that the time was right to go to war and see if King Solomon's gold mines lay beneath Matabeleland. This was largely because, as historian Paul Maylam points out, the Mashona had already mined gold in Mashonaland during the pre-colonial period, and by the late 1800s no significant amount of gold was to be found there. Jameson telegraphed Rhodes asking for the go ahead. Rhodes messaged back: 'Read Luke XIV 31'.

Or suppose a king is about to go to war against another king. Won't he first sit down and consider whether he is able with ten thousand men to oppose the one coming against him with twenty thousand.

Jameson (seated left) from E.W. Fry's photograph
collection titled *Occupation of Mashonaland*

As Brian Roberts puts it, 'sanctioned by holy writ', Jameson prepared for war, signing an agreement with his pioneer soldiers that they would each receive a 6 000-acre farm, twenty gold claims and a share in the looted cattle.

On 16 October 1893, Jameson ordered his men to march south. At the same time, 700 Bechuanas marched on Bulawayo under Chief Khama III, who was a staunch ally of the British. Lobengula was taken completely by surprise, and Jameson's forces, with the help of Khama III, drove him and his impis out of Matabeleland. Rhodes then hurried up north from Cape Town to catch the last of the fighting. In Bulawayo, he gave a speech to the troops, praising their valour while at the same time suggesting that he would not allow either the British or Cape Parliament to interfere in their (his) business. Rhodes knew that there were already voices in Britain calling these men 'freebooters, marauders and murderers'. Or, as Joseph Conrad famously wrote in *Heart of Darkness* with regard to this kind of colonial practice:

It was just robbery with violence, aggravated murder on a great scale, and men going at it blind ... The conquest of the earth, which mostly means the taking it away from those who have a different complexion or slightly flatter noses than ourselves, is not a pretty thing when you look into it too much.[16]

Another writer at the time, Wilfrid Blunt, referred to the Matabele War as 'slaughter for trade'.[17] The missionary John Moffat, who had been used by Rhodes and Jameson to further their cause much to his chagrin, stated that Lobengula 'was foully sinned against by Jameson and his gang'.[18]

As Lobengula fled, he tried one last time to make peace. Coming across some of Jameson's troops, he handed them a letter of peace and all the gold in his possession. Instead of taking the letter and gold back to Jameson, the two troopers legged it into the hinterland with their booty. Lobengula is said to have died of smallpox on his retreat into Mozambique, although this has been contested and he may have killed himself in despair.

Shortly after Jameson's war, the farms, gold and cattle were divided among his men. 'Native reserves' were then created, and the remnants of the Ndebele were forced to pay a hut tax. As a direct result of Jameson's actions, Rhodes's Charter Company shares (you will read much more about them later) rose on the London Stock Exchange from 12 shillings (R1 600 today) to £8 (R23 000 today).

Hold that thought

Our late-nineteenth-century journey is now going to take a short detour to Paul Kruger's Zuid-Afrikaansche Republiek (ZAR). Known as the Transvaal by the British, Kruger's republic is an extremely important (and deliciously corrupt) piece in the jigsaw puzzle of our country's history. But once we've discussed Oom Paul and his coterie of shady concessionaires, we'll be back with plenty more about Rhodes, Rudd, Jameson and a whole host of other rogues you're yet to meet. Catch you on the other side.

PAUL KRUGER

White Minority Monopoly
1881–1900

*'I blame not so much the man who accepts the
bribe as the rascal who offers it.' – **Paul Kruger***

An undated photograph of Stephanus Johannes Paulus
'Paul' Kruger, four-time president of the South African Republic

IN THE EARLY HOURS OF 27 February 1881, a ragtag force of Boer marksmen embarked on a seemingly impossible assault of Majuba Hill, some 300 kilometres to the south-east of Pretoria. The British colonial army's position at the summit of the hill was so strong that their commanding officer, Sir George Pomeroy Colley, had not even bothered to consolidate his defence.

But Colley had not reckoned with the wiles of the Boers, some of them boys as young as thirteen, who used their superior rifle skills to pot the Brits as if they were springboks silhouetted against the skyline. When the dust settled, the Boers had lost only one man to the Brits' ninety-two. A further 134 *rooinekke* were wounded and fifty-nine captured.

In the wake of Majuba, the Brits toyed with retaliation (they even went as far as sending out reinforcements) but they eventually decided to sign a peace treaty which gave the Boers back partial control of the Zuid-Afrikaansche Republiek after four years in British hands. If the uneducated and impoverished *mielieboers* wanted their desolate patch of the Highveld so badly as to risk their (and their sons') lives for it, British logic went, they could bloody well have it. (London would rapidly change its opinion of the territory when gold was discovered there five years later.)

The Boer passion for this parched soil was epitomised by one man. Stephanus Johannes Paulus Kruger spent almost his entire life fighting for his people's right to live in what they believed was the Promised Land. When he was only nine, Kruger's family had bundled all their possessions into an *ossewa*, rounded up their livestock and abandoned the family farm in the Eastern Cape. The Krugers, who called it quits in 1835, were among the very first people to take part in the Great Trek. In the years that followed, they would be joined by at least 6 000 other whites (and their slaves) who had grown sick and tired of British rule and the decision to ban slavery in the Colony. But then again, with folks like Yonge and Somerset at the helm, can you blame them?

In the words of Sir Benjamin D'Urban, the British governor who presided over the mass exodus, the causes of the Great Trek were 'insecurity of life and property, occasioned by recent measures, inadequate compensation for the loss of slaves and despair of obtaining recompense for the various losses by K****r invasion'.[1]

Kruger had an unconventional education. What it lacked in textbooks (the only book he ever read was the Bible) it made up for in life experience. By the time he was a teenager, he had trekked well over 1000 kilometres, fought with the Tswana against an Ndebele force that numbered around 5000, learnt to speak several African languages and had even killed a lion. At the age of sixteen, Kruger was granted two farms in the Magaliesberg area. A year later, he got married and was elected a deputy field cornet, 'a singular honour at seventeen'.[2]

In 1859 he played a leading role in the formation of the Dopper Church, an ultra-conservative splinter group that rejected the liberal theology (go figure!) of the Nederduits Hervormde Kerk (Dutch Reformed Church). The Doppers, who were fundamentally opposed to *dopping*, took their inspiration from the Old Testament and saw themselves as 'a people chosen by God'. Their churches had no organs, and dancing was forbidden. Their manner of dress was unique, as Martin Meredith explains:

> Objecting to long coats, men wore short jackets and broad-brimmed hats with wide trousers pinched up at the back; women always wore hoods or bonnets with their hair behind their ears. Outside their own circles, the term 'Dopper' was synonymous with extreme conservatism and uncouth manners.[3]

In the years that followed, Kruger distinguished himself as an effective military leader, emerging victorious in the Transvaal Civil War and in several battles with African peoples. When the scandalous liberal Thomas Burgers (he did not believe in the devil!) was elected president of the ZAR in 1872, Kruger resisted the urge to join several hundred Dopper families in what would later become known as the Dorsland ('Thirstland') Trek across the Kalahari Desert and into Angola. (In hindsight, this was a wise move, as the majority of Dorsland trekkers did not survive the ordeal.) Instead, Kruger decided to stay behind and fight the system from within, eventually accepting the role of vice-president in 1877, mere months before the ZAR was annexed by Britain for the first time.

Kruger's Dopper dress and uncouth habits (he was known to reek of Magaliesberg tobacco and to spit profusely) caused many Brits to discount him as little more than a boorish dinosaur who could easily be outwitted. He was described at the time as

an elderly man, decidedly ugly, with a countenance denoting extreme obstinacy, and also great cruelty. His conduct at the public luncheon on Tuesday
was as the Belgian consul described it 'gigantically horrible'. His dirty wooden
pipe was visible for it stuck out of his breast pocket; his scanty hair was in
such a condition of greasiness that it lay in streaks across his head, the drops
of rancid cocoanut oil gathering at the ends of each streak of hair and thus
rendering necessary the use of the pocket comb during lunch.[4]

But the Brits underestimated his guile. He was, as we shall soon see, not as virtuous
as one might expect such a religiously devout man to be. As one of his contempor-
aries, gold commissioner D.M. Wilson, put it, the 'oligarchic' government he ended
up presiding over was 'a synonym for business firm of Kruger & Co. Ltd, limited
in the number of favoured members who formed the company, unlimited in the
extent of its field of operations ...'[5]

Be careful what you wish for

Which brings us back to 1881 and the aftermath of the Boer triumph over the
British at Majuba Hill. For the second time in as many months, the leaders of
the ailing republic were faced with an uphill battle. But this time they could not
shoot their way out of it. As Helga Kaye writes, 'The war of 1880–1 gave back to
the South African republic, not only its partial independence, but also its state of
bankruptcy.'[6] (This was not entirely dissimilar to the economic disaster the ANC
was saddled with after apartheid. In the early 1990s, South Africa's economy had
been recording negative growth and high rates of inflation. Corruption, as we
will discover, was also rife.)

Desperate to develop the economy and infrastructure of the republic, Paul
Kruger introduced the concessions policy, which was at the heart of many of the
ZAR's later problems. J.S. Marais explains:

The concessions were actually monopolies, and their purpose was said to
be the promotion of industrial development in the Transvaal. Influential
burghers and foreigners obtained these grants from the government without
much difficulty ... The original concessionaires were usually mere speculators
hoping to sell their rights to others.[7]

The idea was not even Kruger's. On 8 September 1881, Alois Hugo Nellmapius – a slippery and loquacious Jewish-Hungarian adventurer who was described by his future business partner Sammy Marks as 'able to talk and say what is not quite the truth'[8] – submitted a handwritten application to the Boer leaders.

'Must flour be imported from Australia?' he asked.

> Because it will not grow here, and coffee, sugar, leather for harnesses and soap and clothing and candles and blankets?... I maintain that they can be produced here. Only the enterprise is lacking ... I myself wish to help the Government and people [by building] a factory for distilling liquor from grain and other raw materials ... and for producing sugar ...

But, he continued, 'he who begins a new enterprise runs a great risk' and

> [f]or my security I now request the Government to grant me the privilege of the sole right to build such a factory or factories and to manufacture the two above-named products. The concession must be [in force] for at least 15 years. [In return] I am prepared to make to the Treasury an annual contribution of £1 000 sterling [R2.7 million today].[9]

Less than a month later, Nellmapius's application was granted. Now came the small matter of securing the capital required to build the factory. Marks seems to have cast aside his misgivings about Nellmapius to first advance the Hungarian £2 000 towards the construction of the distillery and then go into a full-blown partnership with him.

Working with Nellmapius was not easy. He was overly generous ('Mr N. would rather pay £3 for an article he can get for £2'), fond of cutting corners and wholly untrustworthy. But still Marks avowed that Nellmapius was 'not one of the worst men one can meet with ... Most men have some folly or other and Mr N's is I think that he believes he knows everything.'

Sammy Marks and his father,
Mordechai Feit Marks

One thing he did know was 'his way around the *voorkamers* of power in Pretoria', and he was only too happy to tutor Marks in the 'less than subtle art of building influence among the Boers'. In addition to the numerous material gifts he gave Kruger and his coterie (see below) and his assistance in selling one of Kruger's farms at a massive profit, Marks also gave out 'loans' to anyone who was anyone in the Boer government. As Richard Mendelsohn notes, 'the schedule of debtors in Marks's balance-sheets reads like an abstract from the Transvaal civil service list'.[10] It goes without saying that the repayment of these loans – which could run into thousands of pounds depending on the importance of the official – was never of much concern to Marks. As the man himself explained in a letter to his business partner:

> I note what you write nearly every week ... But when I inform you that this money is in nearly every case advanced to influential officials, whom we may require at any moment, I think you will agree with me that it is worth our while to forgo the interest on say £10,000 which would amount to £800 per annum to keep on good terms with them.[11]

More sinister still was Marks's keenness to assist in securing loans for the government. By acting as an intermediary between Kruger and the banks, Marks 'stood to earn a sizeable commission [and] the gratitude of the government' at no financial risk to himself.[12] Over the years, Marks acted as a middleman for some eye-watering loans. In 1892, for example, he persuaded London's Rothschilds to advance Kruger's government £2.5 million. While we don't know what commission he received on this deal, we do know that he pocketed £40 000 (R115 million today) from a much smaller transaction (£350 000) later that year.

But back to the subject of the booze monopoly and Nellmapius's distillery in the still-impoverished fledgling republic ... In June 1883, a month after being elected president, Kruger the teetotaller presided over the opening ceremony of De Eerste Fabrieken in de Zuid-Afrikaansche Republiek. Somewhat ominously, his attempt at smashing a bottle of champagne against the factory wall went so badly wrong that he cut his hand. Later, in front of a large poster that proclaimed 'A Concession Policy is the Making of the Country', some 300 dignitaries enjoyed a three-course luncheon washed down by the factory's barely drinkable gin and brandy.

In hindsight, Marks would admit that Nellmapius had convinced him that 'we could make any kind of common brandy and it would sell well. We did so

Workers and managers at the Eerste Fabrieken distillery

and the result was a failure. People stated that the stuff was not worth drinking and neither was it.'[13] For decades afterwards, any inferior spirit was known as a Nellmapius (or a Mapius for short).

While the quality of the grog would gradually improve, the factory did not turn out to be the mint Marks and Nellmapius had hoped it would be. As we shall soon see, Nellmapius quickly lost interest in the distillery. Marks, however, would not give up so easily, and he put in the hard yards required to set up a sales and distribution network and to try to persuade people to buy his products. His efforts were given a major boost by the discovery of gold, as, observes social historian Charles van Onselen, 'the number of licensed canteens on the Witwatersrand rose from 147 in 1888 to 552 in 1892'.[14] (Marks's overreliance on the 'native market' would come back to bite him when the mining bosses clamped down on drinking among their workforce.) At his side almost every step of the way was Kruger, who despite never touching the drink himself, placed great value on the fact that the distillery paid his farming constituents for their surplus grain.

In January 1895, Marks added another loss-making arrow to his politically expedient quiver with the establishment of a jam factory, which bought any fruit offered by the Boers – including stuff that was so badly damaged that it was fit only for the compost heap. Within the first year the company had amassed almost eighty tonnes of jams and marmalades of every imaginable flavour. If only they could get some money for their jam. While Marks insisted that his product was 'splendid', South African consumers preferred imported products.[15] (This marketing obstacle persisted until the Anglo-Boer War, when Boer commandos turned down Marks's offer of free jam.)

Before long, Marks's business partner was again writing from London to suggest he close the factory. Marks's response was all too familiar: 'There are several little matters in which we require the aid of the Government ... I think it will be better to keep faith with the Government and to keep the concern going for another 12 months.'[16]

From bad to worse for Nellmapius

Nellmapius soon turned his attentions to another concession he'd been granted for the manufacture of gunpowder and ammunition. Teaming up with Kruger's secretary of state, W.E. Bok, might have seemed like a good idea to Nellmapius, but without the steadying influence of Marks, things at the new factory rapidly went south.

Nellmapius in the uniform of the Portuguese consul – an odd position for a Hungarian to hold

The company was managed from London 'on very slovenly lines', and although Nellmapius – the firm's 'man in South Africa' – moaned frequently about having to pay the factory's debts out of his own pocket, his English bosses saw it differently. In 1885 he was accused of having embezzled £3 000 (R8.7 million today) and was duly arrested.

After a lengthy audit of the company's 'chaotic' books, Kruger's government did an about-turn, ordering all criminal charges against Nellmapius to be dropped and even going so far as to buy 8 343 shares from the Hungarian for £4 505 (R12.2 million today).

These are a few of the Oom's favourite things

Oom Paul was never one to look a gift ox in the mouth, or to turn down the offer of an ego massage, as these gestures from Nellmapius, Marks and other businessmen attest:

- Marks made a point of giving Kruger very carefully thought-out birthday presents. One year, he ordered the Big Beard a set of seven ivory-handled razors from Sheffield (one for every day of the week). A later birthday was marked by a Meerschaum pipe, mounted in gold and engraved with the president's name and date of birth. Marks paid equally close attention to Kruger's wife: one year he even gifted her a prize cow after hers had stopped producing milk.

- In 1883, while Kruger was in the UK trying (in vain) to persuade Queen Victoria to grant increased freedoms to his republic, Nellmapius built him the spacious single-storey house in Church Street, Pretoria, where he would live until he fled the country in 1900. The stone lion sculptures on either side of the front entrance were also gifts – from Rhodes's rival Barney Barnato.

- Most famously of all, in 1895 Marks pledged £10 000 (R30 million today) for the construction of a marble statue of Kruger. After an unknown Dutch art teacher by the name of Anton van Wouw was given the commission, it was decided that bronze would be more suited to the Transvaal climate. Towards the end of 1896, Van Wouw sailed to Rome to supervise the statue's modelling and casting. When it was suggested that Kruger's top hat would cast a shadow over his face, Van Wouw stood firm – no Afrikaans burgher would ever go hatless in the African sun. In October 1899, the very same month the Anglo-Boer War broke out, Van Wouw finally returned to South Africa to supervise the installation of his magnum opus. Kruger, however, insisted that he wait until the war was over, and the statue was duly put in storage in Lourenço Marques (Maputo). Once the Brits had unleashed their foulest tricks (scorched earth, concentration camps, etc.) to effectively win the war in 1902, Sir Alfred Milner vowed 'to wipe out the last trace of Afrikanerism' from the Transvaal. When Kruger died in exile in 1904, he could never have imagined that his likeness would end up gracing the squares of Pretoria after all. In 1913, three years after the establishment of the Union, the statue was finally dusted off and erected in the slightly out-of-the-way Prince's Park. Forty-one years later, once the apartheid government had taken over, it was moved to its 'rightful place' in the heart of Church Square, where it stands to this day. (Thanks to the attentions of the #RhodesMustFall movement and Julius Malema, it is now fenced off and inaccessible to the public and there are suggestions that it will soon be moved to a 'cultural, heritage park.')

Suspicion soon fell on Mr Bok, who had, in the words of one of the prosecuting lawyers, 'compromised himself thoroughly; the President is a tool in his hands … the government is so deeply implicated in the affair that they cannot permit the case to go before a criminal court'.

Despite the efforts of Bok and Kruger, Nellmapius did end up facing criminal charges, even though Dr W.J. Leyds, the Dutch-born state prosecutor, admitted that the factory owed Nellmapius money. As Leyds said, 'it is no argument so say if someone lent a horse he would have the right to steal a horse from the borrower'. Nellmapius was, according to Leyds's wife, so confident he would be found not guilty that 'he had driven in state in his carriage with all lights blazing to hear his sentence, although he could easily have walked to his new home'.

His 'new home' was, of course, the prison in which he was sentenced to spend eighteen months plus hard labour. And so began what Kaye describes as a 'tug of war between State and Legislature'.[17] The day after his conviction, Nellmapius wrote to Kruger to ask for a pardon. The following morning, presiding Judge Brand received a memorandum from none other than Bok asking for his opinion on the possibility of a presidential pardon.

Clearly annoyed, Brand asked why Nellmapius's petition had not been forwarded to him and reminded Bok that the matter was now before the Court of Appeal. Bok duly forwarded him the petition and requested, once again, his immediate opinion. With annoyance giving way to outright anger, Brand took it upon himself to visit Kruger (at the home Nellmapius had built him). Without even bothering to take a seat in the *voorkamer*, he explained that he could not accede to the president's request to release Nellmapius on bail as the trial was no longer before his court.

Now, in an effort to put the proverbial ball back in Brand's court, Nellmapius's lawyers took the unusual step of withdrawing their client's appeal. Instead, Brand took the opportunity to 'bring to the notice of the Honourable Executive Council that it cannot interfere in the administration of Justice in this State'. 'Judges,' he memorably reminded them, 'are there for that purpose.'

Later that same day, Bok informed Brand that the executive council had granted Nellmapius a full pardon. Brand was left with no choice but to resign his position. As *De Volksstem* noted,

Mr Nellmapius was released from gaol and conducted home by his friends, where, we understand, toasting and speechifying were indulged in … The action of the Government ... has excited in Pretoria a mixed feeling of dismay, indignation and alarm.

But there would be yet another twist in the tale. Brand telegrammed Chief Justice Kotzé (who was serving on the country circuit), asking him to return to Pretoria post-haste. After examining the details of the case, Kotzé ruled that the government had overreached its powers and promptly had Nellmapius rearrested.

The executive council was furious, and after a session which lasted well into the night, Kruger barged into prosecutor Leyds's bedroom to argue the details of the case. Here we'll let Mrs Leyds take up the story:

At 3.45am there was a knock on the door. It was the President. He was worried about the case and wished to discuss it with my husband. I, lying in bed, was worried about my furniture and upholstery, for not only words of wisdom came out of Oom Paul's mouth, but also the accompanying sputum.[18]

For almost two months, Nellmapius languished in Pretoria prison while the stand-off between government and judiciary continued. Eventually, the Appeal Court set aside Nellmapius's sentence, and he was released from prison.

It is only fitting that Mrs Leyds should have the final say: 'Kotzé has annulled the sentence against Nellmapius. Between ourselves I think this cowardly. He dared not take a further stand against Kruger and therefore put an end to the affair.'[19]

After the court case, Leyds – the astute and hostile prosecutor – would go on to wheedle his way into Kruger's inner circle.

Nellmapius, meanwhile, carved a new niche for himself as a lobbyist. As tensions between the Uitlander (foreign) mining bosses and the government rose after the discovery of gold on the Witwatersrand in 1886, his well-known rapport with Kruger meant he was in high demand. Soon, he was an almost full-time government go-between for Hermann Eckstein of the famed Corner House mining company, 'obtaining licences, putting proposals, opposing unpopular decisions and soothing out differences of all kinds' for his wealthy employers.[20] Eckstein was the same man who planted three million trees in Sachsenwald, aka Saxonwold, the later playground of the Guptas.

In this new gig, Nellmapius should have done very well for himself – if he'd only been able to resist his dangerous entrepreneurial inclinations. Instead, true to form, he speculated heavily and foolishly. While his death in 1892 at the age of only forty-six was considered a national tragedy – flags were flown at half-mast and his funeral was attended by 2 000 mourners – the winding up of his estate was a far less triumphant affair. Much like Dr Nico Diederichs, whom we will meet later, his assets did not nearly cover his liabilities.

The most explosive scandal of the lot

Almost overnight, the discovery of gold in 1886 transformed the ZAR from a worthless backwater into one of the most desirable prospecting and financial opportunities in the world. These high stakes would provide a potentially fatal test to Kruger's concessions policy (which had already proved creaky in an impoverished agrarian state). As Van Onselen writes,

> Given imperfect connections in the wiring system linking political to economic power, and the strong charges emanating from the positive and negative terminals, there was constant short circuiting and the danger of an even bigger explosion. In the South African Republic, as in most systems characterised by disparities in power and wealth, the classic short-circuiting mechanism was corruption.[21]

It goes without saying that the glitter of gold would attract a new class of speculator who put the likes of Marks and Nellmapius in the shade. And none was shadier than the German concession hunter Edouard Lippert.

In 1887, Lippert was granted a sixteen-year monopoly on the manufacture of dynamite. It was Kruger's hope that forcing wealthy mining houses to buy their dynamite from a local producer would grow the republic's economy and infrastructure at very little cost to government. As C.T. Gordon writes in *The Growth of Boer Opposition to Kruger (1890–1895)*, Lippert was

> permitted to import all raw materials and machinery free of duty; but not dynamite itself. The necessary factory was to be erected within a year, and once its output was able to meet the entire demand of the Republic, no further import of dynamite would be allowed.[22]

And so Lippert's company, the Zuid-Afrikaansche Maatschappij voor Ontplofbare Stoffen Beperkt, was duly registered in London. After attempting to interest the Anglo-German Nobel Trust (Alfred Nobel, of Nobel Prize fame, had patented dynamite in 1867), the concession was ultimately passed on to a French company, the Société Centrale de Dynamite, with Lippert becoming the French firm's head agent in South Africa.

No sooner had production commenced than complaints about the 'inferior quality and danger of the local product' began to surface.[23] In an age-old South African tradition, the commission of inquiry set up to investigate these complaints found there to be nothing wrong with Lippert's *ontplofbare stoffen*.

The complaints continued throughout 1890, however, and were, once again, rejected by a government inquiry. It soon became apparent that not a single stick of dynamite had been manufactured on South African soil and that the 'factory' was 'merely a depot in which the already manufactured article was manipulated to a moderate extent'.[24] This was completely contrary to the concession, which stated emphatically that the dynamite had to be manufactured in the ZAR so as to develop the local economy. When it was put to the Volksraad that 'dynamite was being imported from abroad and that no local materials whatsoever entered into its composition',[25] Kruger and Leyds (who was now Oom's most trusted henchman) defended the concessionaires stoutly and insisted that the dynamite was being manufactured locally.

A Cape scientist saw it differently, declaring that the 'so-called "guhr imprégné" and "cellulose imprégné", which the company described as the raw materials from which dynamite was made, were neither more nor less than dynamite itself'.[26]

The Jock within

During the time of the gold rush, Kruger made enemies among both the Afrikaner volk and the (predominantly) English-speaking Uitlander community. Arguably the most complete record of this antipathy is Percy Fitzpatrick's *The Transvaal from Within*, a one-sided repudiation of everything the ZAR stood for. Fitzpatrick, who worked for Eckstein's Corner House and served as secretary of the Reform Committee of concerned Uitlanders, had been arrested in the wake of the Jameson Raid (much more about that later) and forced to abstain from politics for three years. When it finally came out, the book was an instant success in both South Africa and the UK, selling over 250 000 copies. In 1907, Fitzpatrick would write another runaway best-seller: *Jock of the Bushveld*. He went on to become an influential politician and, in 1919, he was credited with the 'invention' of two minutes of silence in memory of those who'd lost their lives in World War I.

The Uitlander mining houses, epitomised by Percy Fitzpatrick, were outraged by the revelation that the dynamite had been imported from France. Nellmapius the lobbyist was sent to argue their case with Kruger. Paying through the nose for inferior dynamite had been bad enough, he explained, but this was an even more bitter pill to swallow. Eventually, the British government got involved, declaring that the duty-free import of French dynamite flouted the rules of the London Convention of 1884. (They probably wouldn't have pointed this out if the original concession had gone to the Nobel Trust.)

After much ducking and weaving, the government eventually agreed to conduct tests on the supposed 'raw materials' being imported by Lippert. Even after the government experts had declared the stuff to be dynamite, there were still some members of the Volksraad who refused to believe it. The report of what followed, which appeared in *Land en Volk*, the opposition newspaper edited and owned by the inimitable Eugène Marais, is worth quoting from at length:

> Rarely has such a scene taken place in a free Republic as occurred during the eleven o'clock adjournment of the Volksraad last Saturday morning ... The whole Volksraad decided to go and test the material to see if it was explosive. Between 10.30 and 11 the President got hold of Jan Meyer [a prominent anti-Kruger voice in the Volksraad] and quite audible to the Press Gallery – indeed in the street – shouted at him that it was grossly unfair to make such a test. He and everyone else knew well enough that it was explosive. The only question was, was it dynamite? Jan Meyer was weak enough to give way, and the tests thus took place only in the presence of the State Mining Engineer, the Minister of Mines, the Manager of the Dynamite Factory and the scientific experts. The stuff that Mr Lippert alleged was not dynamite exploded with terrific force, throwing great masses of rock into the air.[27]

The debate in the Volksraad following this unusual coffee break was equally volatile. One member demanded that Lippert and co. face criminal prosecution for smuggling. Others insisted that the concession be cancelled altogether. But Kruger hadn't trekked all the way to the Promised Land only to give way to a few pesky naysayers. To cancel the contract, he told the Raad, 'would destroy the credit of the State completely and bring rejoicing to our enemies'.[28]

'A worker in a science yet unborn'

Marais, who worked as a journalist for only
six years in his late teens and early twenties, was
so much more than a muckraker. He was also a
poet, lawyer, writer, scientific visionary, agnostic
and lifelong drug addict. After his wife died in
childbirth in 1895 and he became addicted to
morphine, he moved to London to study law.
Before long, he was admitted to the English bar.
When the Anglo-Boer War broke out, in an effort
to drum up Dutch support for the cause, Marais
began translating *The Transvaal from Within* into
Dutch.

Eugène Marais

In April 1902, he left the UK with British
permission, in order to restart *Land en Volk* 'with an editorial slant aimed at
convincing Boers after the war to reconcile themselves to British rule, and to be
obedient subjects', according to his biographer, Carel van der Merwe.[29]

After five years working primarily as an advocate in Pretoria and Johannesburg,
adds van der Merwe, Marais and a friend moved to the Waterberg to prospect for
tin. There he spent the best part of three years observing a troop of chacma
baboons, making him, writes Robert Ardrey, 'the first man in the history of
science to conduct a prolonged study of one of man's primate relatives in a state
of nature'.[30] With very little scientific training, and no library of books, he had the
freedom simply to observe the creatures around him.

Back in Pretoria and working as a lawyer and poet (you probably came across
Winternag in high-school Afrikaans class), he wrote two books which were
rediscovered in the 1960s by Ardrey, an American film-star-cum-naturalist.
The Soul of the Ape was, in Ardrey's words, the first work to discuss 'the dawning
of humanity in the psyche of the higher primate'. *The Soul of the White Ant*
(Marais also spent a lot of his time in the Waterberg gazing at termites), meanwhile, introduced the concept – now regarded as scientific fact – that when it
comes to social insects, the entire colony should be seen as a single organism.

In 1926, Marais's work on ants was plagiarised in almost its entirety by the
Belgian Nobel laureate Maurice Maeterlinck, who, despite stern legal opposition
from Marais, got away with the theft pretty much scot-free.

In 1936, after a few days without a morphine fix, Marais borrowed a shotgun on
the pretext of wanting to kill a snake and shot himself – first in the chest and then,
to make sure of things, in the mouth.

It is only fitting that *Land en Volk* should describe Kruger's next plan:

> We cannot credit the President's behaviour. We understand his reluctance to expose the rottenness of his concession-politics, but to suggest to the Volksraad that the State buy the factory and appoint the fraudulent company as officials is too much! We expect but little of the Volksraad; but will the people allow this?... Lippert is having coffee with the President every morning.[31]

In the end, Kruger, who had a presidential election to worry about, did temporarily cancel the concession. The dynamite concession played a major role in the 1893 election campaign, which was described by Kruger as

> the most violent electoral struggle through which the Republic ever passed. I was accused by the Opposition of being autocratic, of squandering the national money, of giving away all rights and privileges in the form of concessions and of awarding all the offices of state to the Hollanders [a direct reference to W.J. Leyds].[32]

So close was the election that Kruger was only able to defeat the Progressive candidate 'Slim Piet' Joubert (who himself owned twenty-nine farms) by 52 per cent to 48 per cent. Joubert did not take the result lying down and lodged an official complaint, which stated among other things,

> That the ballot boxes had been opened and the votes counted by landdrosts and mining commissioners ... instead of being sent straight to the Executive Council.

> That innumerable unqualified people had been allowed to vote, including lunatics, children under 16, persons resident in other constituencies, persons whose names had been removed from the voting lists and persons who had not even been to the polls.

> That qualified voters had been refused permission to cast their votes.[33]

After the election, a commission was set up by Kruger to, in the words of the pro-Kruger newspaper *The Press* (which had been founded by none other Nellmapius a decade earlier), 'rescrutinise the scrutinised scrutiny'.[34] The commission, like some other South African commissions, 'regarded speed as the essence of its task',[35] taking only three days to prepare its report on Joubert's complaints! While the report acknowledged errors in the electoral process, they were not considered grave enough to impact the result, and Kruger was declared president.

The speed with which the commission into the election had reached its conclusion caused the historian C.T. Gordon to remark memorably that 'a court of law would not have decided a dispute about the possession of a stray donkey – let alone the legality of the most crucial presidential election in the history of the Transvaal – in this cavalier fashion'.[36]

Be that as it may, the freshly reanointed President Kruger wasted no time in returning to business as (un)usual. First, Marais was charged (and subsequently acquitted – read into that what you will) with libel for suggesting that Kruger had claimed expenses for a trip to Colesberg that had already been paid for by the Cape government. And within a few months, Fitzpatrick noted, 'the [dynamite] monopoly was revived in an infinitely more obnoxious form'.[37] The new government decided to take over the monopoly for itself, but reappointed Lippert and his cronies to their previous roles. *Land en Volk* would have plenty to say on the matter:

> The Kruger Government has had the inordinate impudence ['*verregaande brutaliteit*'] to give the Dynamite Agency to Messrs. Lippert & Vorstman. Those whom the Gods wish to destroy, it seems they first make mad! This is the man whom people hoped would take warning by the last election! So, the agency goes to the French Company which the President ... admitted in the Raad had committed a great fraud upon the Transvaal. There is no more shame in these people ... Our birthright is being sold to pedlars, Jews and Hollanders. Believe no one anymore who talks of our 'independence'! – our independence![38]

Determined not to be excluded from the world's largest dynamite market for a second time, the Nobel Trust now got busy, entering into direct negotiations with the Société Centrale de Dynamite. They resolved to form a new company with a capital of £450 000.

The two companies held almost the same number of shares, but the operation would be managed by the Nobel Trust. Lippert would receive 25 000 shares and a royalty of eight shillings per case for the first three years, and six shillings thereafter. Sammy Marks – yep, him again – was granted a royalty of two shillings per case of dynamite for his role in brokering the deal. (Richard Mendelsohn's unpublished research shows that 'as a result of negotiations in Pretoria in May 1894, Marks's royalty was materially reduced. The firm got 1 shilling and six pence on the first 40 000 cases sold per annum; 1 shilling and three pence on the next 20 000; and 1 shilling on subsequent quantities.'[39] Still, pretty good going for minimal effort.)

The terms of this new deal stated that a new factory would be built (at Modderfontein) that had to be capable of producing enough dynamite to meet the needs of the mines by April 1896. Despite missing this deadline by a full two years – and being allowed to continue to import dynamite during this period – eye-watering profits were made by the firm. Over 1.1 million cases of dynamite were sold at a profit of forty shillings (around R6 000 today) per case between June 1894 and September 1899. Once Lippert and Marks had also taken their cuts, the government was left with only five shillings per case.

'Such being the position,' notes J.S. Marais in his seminal work *The Fall of Kruger's Republic*, 'it is natural to ask how it came that the monopoly survived all the attacks made upon it. These attacks came from many quarters. The monopoly had in fact few friends.'[40]

A commission set up by the British government in 1900 ascribed the survival of the monopoly to bribery. It pointed the finger at two figures in particular: Max Philipp, the German chairman of the Nobel Trust, who 'was convinced that he could further his ends by bribery' (much like European arms manufacturer Thales, who would allegedly agree to pay Zuma R500 000 a year in the Arms Deal), and Lippert, who held similar views. The commission provided concrete evidence that a number of members of the Volksraad had accepted cash payments and shares in the company.

Be careful what you wish for (again)

As many a small, underdeveloped African nation has learnt since, the discovery of vast mineral wealth within one's soil can be a curse. The ZAR's metamorphosis after 1886 was startling. What was once South Africa's far dustier and more impoverished version of Amish Country suddenly teemed with Uitlander diggers hoping to strike it lucky. Hot on their heels came investors, speculators, entrepreneurs, parvenus and prostitutes.

While the gold rush allowed Kruger to give Pretoria a stately makeover, to finance a government-sponsored road to his farm and to increase his annual salary from £3 000 to £8 000 (R24 million today), it also spawned the birth of Johannesburg – or Duiwelstad (Devil's Town), as Kruger called it. The British journalist (and Rhodes propagandist) Flora Shaw, who visited as a correspondent for *The Times* in 1892, said Johannesburg was 'hideous and detestable, luxury without order, sensual enjoyment without art, riches without refinement, display without dignity'. Olive Schreiner (who you will hear a lot more from in the next chapter) was in agreement, describing Johannesburg as 'a great, fiendish hell of a city which for glitter and gold, and wickedness, carriages and palaces and brothels and gambling halls, beat creation'.[41]

This must have been quite a lot to stomach for Kruger, who, as Martin Meredith put it, 'resembled a seventeenth century zealot rather than a nineteenth century politician'. This was, after all, a man who was so sure that the earth was flat 'that when an American traveller was introduced as being on a voyage around the world, Kruger retorted: "You don't mean round the world ... It is impossible! You mean *in* the world."'[42]

Moral and scientific dilemmas aside, Kruger's even bigger problem was one all too familiar to the leaders of tinpot African nations. The profits made by the British- and European-registered mining houses did precious little to advance the republic. He resented the lavish lifestyles of the Randlords, who, in a real-life version of the board game Monopoly, soon all owned houses on London's Park Lane.

The feeling, as we've already seen, was mutual. The Johannesburg Uitlanders resented the fact that, despite paying taxes, they were not allowed to vote; they loathed Kruger's monopolies and they despised the corruption which characterised his administration. Which is not to say that they were above using bribes and Rhodes-like delinquency to advance their own interests.

The few Uitlanders who chose Pretoria as their base – people like Marks, Nellmapius and Lippert – did so for very obvious reasons.

In an attempt to ease the antipathy of the Uitlanders, Kruger eventually agreed to establish a second Volksraad, which gave them limited political say. (In 1984, P.W. Botha's apartheid-era government would try a similar thing with his Tricameral Parliament, which purported to give coloureds and Indians a seat at the table. Both Kruger's and Botha's attempts at inclusivity excluded black Africans entirely.) It soon became obvious that the Second Volksraad lacked any real political clout, and the tensions between the burghers and the Uitlanders continued to simmer. (Word on the street was that the unofficial 'third Volksraad' of people close to Kruger, like Marks, Nellmapius and Lippert, had far more sway.)

In addition to the pesky dynamite concession, Lippert was involved in a very dodgy concession for the manufacture of cement in the ZAR. As further proof that lucre was the only political ideology he could comprehend, in 1891 he also assisted Cecil Rhodes in strengthening his grip on Matabeleland. As Martin Meredith tells it, Lippert obtained a concession from the Ndebele chief Lobengula that gave him rights 'to grant lands, establish banks and conduct trade ... thus trumping the Rudd Concession which related only to mineral rights'.

Rhodes's knee-jerk reaction to the Lippert Concession was to denounce it as a fraud. But then he came up with a much craftier idea. The result of his evil machinations, writes Meredith, was:

> [a] contract that was kept secret from Lobengula. In exchange for handing Rhodes the Lippert Concession, Rhodes agreed to give Lippert £50,000 [R146 million today] worth of shares, £5,000 in cash and the right to select an area of 75 square miles in Matabeleland with all land and mineral rights there. To complete the deal, Lippert first needed to renegotiate his concession with Lobengula to put it on a firmer legal basis, while leaving Lobengula under the impression that he remained an enemy of Rhodes and implacably opposed to his designs.[43]

The plan worked, and Rhodes soon had free rein to do his very worst on Matabeleland (more about that in the next chapter). The Lippert Concession was eventually declared null and void almost thirty years later, but by then it was far too late for the Ndebele.

And then there was Kruger's nepotism. He made one grandson master of the Supreme Court, another chief inspector for roads and a nephew assistant state secretary. But the plummest gig of all went to Kruger's son-in-law, Frikkie Eloff (Monopoly enthusiasts will recognise Eloff Street as the South African equivalent of Park Lane), who was shown to have made £20 000 out of a deal to supply water to Johannesburg 'without so much as digging a spadeful of earth'.[44]

The so-called Stands Scandal – which is strangely reminiscent of the property dealings in Kaiser Matanzima's Transkei (see Chapter 10) and of State President

Nico Diederichs's transactions (see Chapter 7) – saw government officials and their friends buying plots of prime mining land and selling them at handsome profits the following day. One chap who clearly had friends in very high places applied for thirty stands at £20 each but ended up only having to pay £15 a pop. When asked if this did not strike him as unusual, he replied, 'No, I only thought it jolly nice, that's all.'[45]

Sammy Marks became an indirect object of the Uitlanders' ire due to his involvement in the liquor industry. While the mining bosses had, in the 1880s, been only too happy with the proliferation of licensed canteens because 'the many migrant workers who spent their wages on liquor saved less of their earnings than their more abstemious colleagues, and thus tended to labour underground' for longer periods, the tide of Uitlander opinion turned in the mid-1890s, when as much as 25 per cent of the black labour force was 'disabled by drink' each day. Their motivations, of course, had everything to do with the productivity of their workforce and nothing to do with humanitarian concerns. As Charles van Onselen notes, the fact that 'it was a common thing to find "boys" lying dead on the veld from exposure and the effects of the vile liquids sold them by unscrupulous dealers' was regarded as a mere commercial inconvenience.[46]

Speaking of which ... When a total prohibition (for natives) was implemented in 1897, and fully enforced two years later, it dealt a blow to Marks's firm, which he would spend several years recovering from.

Profitability of Eerste Fabrieken, 1893–99[47]

YEAR	GALLONS SOLD	NET PROFIT OR LOSS
1893	272 616	+£47 404
1894	316 046	+£48 399
1895	386 281	+£98 274
1896	298 130	+£69 569
1897	63 191	−£46 988*
1898	153 594	+£10 490
1899	86 998	+£2 737

*R131 million today

A Jameson-induced hangover

The already fraught relationship between Boers and Uitlanders was dealt an irreparable blow in the first few days of 1896. The members of Fitzpatrick's Reform Committee, who had been carefully plotting the overthrow of Kruger's republic, were left with serious egg on their faces (not to mention the prospect of lengthy jail terms and even the death penalty) when Dr Leander Starr Jameson invaded the ZAR.

Because of Rhodes's major involvement in the plot, Jameson's (disastrous) raid is covered in the next chapter. Suffice to say that the raid drove a wedge between the English and the Afrikaners, which would make the Anglo-Boer War pretty much inevitable. To highlight just how deep the resentment ran, consider the words of Judge Kowie Marais, uttered some eighty years after the event:

> Before the Jameson Raid my father used to write to my mother in English. It was the smart thing to do for middle-class Afrikaners. After the Jameson Raid he never allowed English to be spoken in the house again.[48]

After the Jameson Raid, the crop of scandals in the ZAR was 'as the rolling snow-ball,' wrote Fitzpatrick, adding that 'it is unnecessary to refer to them all in detail'.[49] But one episode that warrants a mention for sheer comic value is the so-called Donkeys and Mealies Scandal of 1897. This saw the government heavily subsidise farmers for the purchase of donkeys (from Ireland and South America) and vast quantities of inferior maize, which would serve purportedly as ballast for the top-heavy ships that carried the donkeys. As it turned out, only 10 per cent of the donkeys the farmers profited from actually existed, the remainder braying only on paper.

The dynamite concession, which by now was costing the mining industry some £600 000 a year, was as irksome as ever, and the construction of railways was another major bone of contention. A proper telling of the shenanigans involved in the construction of the main line from Pretoria to the Mozambican border (Kruger dreamed of a route to the sea that avoided British-run territories) would double the length of this chapter. A précised tale of the much smaller line to the Selati Gold-fields should give you a clear enough idea of the kind of issues that were at play.

After initially being granted to Volksraad member Barend J. Vorster, the Selati Concession was sold to Eugène Oppenheim – a suave Frenchman in the Lippert mould. Oppenheim contracted Louis Warnant to construct the 308-kilometre railway line at the full cost of £2 million. Three days later, Warnant farmed out the contract to another firm, making £519 600 (R1.5 billion today) for Oppenheim at 'the stroke of a pen'.[50] To conceal this windfall, the Frenchman indulged in some audacious book cookery.

Slow progress and grave financial difficulties, which led to a request for further funding, precipitated a commission of inquiry, at which Oppenheim admitted spending £30 000 on payments 'to different members of the Executive Council and Volksraad and their relatives and friends as the price for granting the concession'.[51] According to Fitzpatrick, these gifts included 'American spiders [a fast and light-weight carriage; the BMW Z3 of its day], Cape carts [more of a Toyota Hilux], gold watches, shares in the Company and sums in cash.' Kruger was gifted a portrait of himself 'executed by ... South Africa's one artist', which had cost £600.[52]

Oppenheim even went so far as to name all the people he had bribed. And although Kruger was unmoved – declaring in the Volksraad, 'I blame not so much the man who accepts the bribe as the rascal who offers it'[53] – Fitzpatrick most certainly was not:

> Twenty-one members of the First Volksraad out of twenty-five! The Vice-President! The son-in-law and Private Secretary of the President! The Secretary of the Volksraad and the Minute Keeper of the Executive!
>
> The Volksraad, one would think, would be bound to take cognizance of such a statement and to cause an investigation to be held. They did take cognizance of it after the manner peculiar to them. But the last thing in the world to be expected from them was an impartial investigation: nothing so foolish was ever contemplated.[54]

After a few more twists and turns, Oppenheim and company took the audacious step of suing the ZAR government in a Brussels court. Both the trial and the construction of the line were interrupted by the Anglo-Boer War, but when the case resumed Oppenheim (the plaintiff) was found guilty of bribery and sentenced to three years in prison.

The Railway Line was eventually completed in 1912, and a decade later the first rail-based safari to the Sabie Game Reserve (which had been proclaimed a conservation area by Kruger in 1898) left Pretoria. As there were no overnight facilities for the public, the tourists slept on the train at the railway line's Sabie Bridge. The itinerary 'proved so popular that rangers later accompanied the tourists on the train and even arranged short bush excursions'.[55]

In 1927, the Sabie Game Reserve was renamed – you guessed it – the Kruger National Park. While the line was rerouted in the 1960s, the defunct Sabie Bridge remains an icon of Skukuza Rest Camp. In fact, plans are afoot to establish a luxury train-hotel which will be permanently stationed atop the Sabie Bridge. Fittingly, the new project's launch (originally slated for January 2020) has been delayed without any clear explanation from the company that won the tender.

But back to 1899, when Boer–Uitlander antipathy reached a point of no return at the Bloemfontein Conference – a last-gasp attempt to avoid war convened by the president of the Orange Free State. Desperate to claim the lucrative goldfields for Her Majesty Queen Victoria, the British high commissioner, Alfred Milner, made three demands of Kruger:

1. That Uitlanders be granted immediate enfranchisement and the right to vote.
2. That English be adopted as the official language of the Volksraad.
3. That all laws passed by the Volksraad be subject to approval by the British Parliament.

As Lord Roberts (aka Bobs) advanced on Pretoria, Kruger's
saying that someone who wanted to kill a tortoise should
first wait till it has stuck its head out of its shell would be put to the test

Given what we know about Kruger, it should be clear that Milner's demands were tantamount to a declaration of war – a war which duly came in 1899. The Brits suffered a disastrous start to the campaign, but things were turned around when massive reinforcements were sent with General Roberts at their head. And with Roberts's army 'marching to Pretoria, hoorah', as the song goes, Kruger fled the ZAR's capital on 29 May 1900, six days before it was captured, to seek refuge in Machadodorp. In September, as the Boer prospects went from bad to worse, he fled the ZAR, weeping openly as his train crossed the Mozambican border.

Oom Midas

Wherever Kruger went, gold was never far away...

- In 1898, Sammy Marks was allowed the 'extraordinary privilege ... of private use of the state mint for a day'. Using his own gold, Marks struck 215 golden tickeys as 'keepsakes for his relatives and friends, including naturally, the President and members of the Volksraad'. The whole affair, notes Richard Mendelsohn, 'says as much about his special relationship with the Kruger state as it does about the pre-modern informality of that state, with its blurred divide between public property and the private property of the ruling elite'.[56]

- On 4 June 1900, the day before Pretoria fell, gold coins and bullion worth around £2.75 million (R7.9 billion today) were removed from Pretoria and supposedly taken by train to Machadodorp. While legend has it that the Kruger millions are buried somewhere beneath the Lowveld, D.W. Krüger's (no relation) book *Die Krugermiljoene* confirms that the majority of the funds were used to support Boer commandos in the field, and that a further sixty-two cases of gold bars were shipped to Germany. Once the war had ended, the remaining £170 000 was used to further the Afrikaner cause, with the last £25 being used to buy 100 shares in Nasionale Pers – the preferred media house of the Broederbond (see Chapter 7).

- Bertha Goudvis, a journalist who met Kruger in Lourenço Marques just before he left Africa for the last time, 'noticed that the President wore earrings – small gold rings, called "sleepers" – which I had worn as a little girl'. His earrings 'lent some oddity to an otherwise grave and dignified appearance,' wrote Goudvis, who observed that he wore them in the stubborn belief they 'strengthened the eyesight'.[57]

- Perhaps the most famous connection between Kruger and his preferred mineral was made long after his death, when his ideological descendant Dr Nico Diederichs (the prime villain of Part 3) minted the very first Krugerrand on 3 July 1967.

PUNCH, OR THE LONDON CHARIVARI.—June 13, 1900.

TO PRETORIA

SWAIN Sc

SHIFTING HIS CAPITAL.

["It is not true," Mr. Kruger is reported, in the *Daily Express*, to have said, "that I have brought with me gold to the value of two millions. *Whatever monetary resources I may have with me are simply those we require for State purposes.*"]

The mystery of the missing millions has fascinated – and amused – for over a century

Although the official reason for Kruger's departure from the ZAR was to drum up support for the Boer cause overseas (even in Britain many saw the conflict as a shallow, money-grabbing endeavour), he would never return to his Vaderland. Kruger died in Switzerland (coincidentally, the favoured banking destination of his similarly funny-hatted descendant Nico Diederichs) at the age of seventy-eight. His body, however, was repatriated, and he was given a state funeral in Pretoria on 16 December 1904.

CHAPTER 6

CECIL JOHN RHODES (II)

The Colossal Corrupter
1889–1898

*'The body politic was virgin soil for the new infection
to which in 1889 Rhodes subjected it.'* – **James Rose Innes**

Cecil John Rhodes – planning conquest and fraud

The business of politics

By 1889 Rhodes had been a member of the Cape Colony's Parliament for eight years (he became an MP in the same year that the ZAR achieved independence). He had also, two years previously, founded the mother of all diamond companies, De Beers Consolidated Mines, with his pumping pal Charles Rudd.

Politically, the most important man close to him was his friend John X. Merriman, whom we met in Chapter 4. Merriman, who went on to become one of the Cape's most prominent liberal politicians, would often ride with Rhodes in the morning talking politics. In the initial stages of their friendship these two men were said to agree that the 'native question' was paramount in Cape politics.

Rhodes claimed to support Merriman's belief that the only solution to the question was a liberal one. Whether Rhodes was just mirroring the beliefs of his riding buddy or whether he had a later change of heart is not easy to tell. But whatever the case, Rhodes's political interventions with regard to the 'native question' were far from liberal. The minute he assumed political office, he showed few signs of engaging productively with the plight of black people in the Cape Colony.

Rhodes on Record about the 'Native Question'

'[Is it right that] men in a state of pure barbarism should have the franchise and vote? The natives do not want it.'

'There must be Pass Laws'

'The native is to be treated as a child and denied the franchise'

'I am not going to the native vote for support'

Perhaps unsurprisingly, Rhodes's reasons for entering politics seem to have had much more to do with advancing his own business interests.

Rhodes and railways

Interestingly, considering the image most people have of Rhodes and his dream of a railroad from the Cape to Cairo, he became prime minister of the Cape as a result of the question of railways. In 1890, Prime Minister Gordon Sprigg had taken the decision to widen the railway network in the Cape Colony at a cost of around £7 500 000 (R20 billion today). Rhodes, now a member of Parliament as well as a businessman, was opposed to the broader expansion, largely because he wished to extend the railway in a more local direction. That is to say, he wanted a railway that would serve his interests in Matabeleland and Mashonaland.

His public reasons were, however, stated somewhat differently. He was quoted in the *Cape Argus* as saying that Sprigg's 'huge Railway Bill ... would be financially ruinous to the Cape Government'. His choice of publication was no coincidence. Rhodes had, in great secrecy, bought a controlling share in the *Cape Argus* in 1881 (the same year he became an MP), largely to further his own political and financial ends. And with Sprigg politically vulnerable, Rhodes put his stealth weapon to good use. With the *Argus* leading a 'full scale onslaught against the hapless Prime Minister', the Sprigg government fell.[1]

Prime Minister Sprigg's reason for developing the railway systems was an attempt to regain the support of the Afrikaner Bond members of Parliament. This loosely affiliated political party served Dutch (largely rural) interests in the Cape at this time. It was widely seen to be led and controlled by Jan Hofmeyr – a man referred to as 'Onze Jan' ('Our Jan') by his supporters and 'the Mole' by John X. Merriman. As Merriman said, '[T]he Mole is an industrious little animal ... You never see him at work, but every now and then a little mound of earth, thrown up here or there, will testify to his activities'.[2]

The Bond and 'Onze Jan'

Not to be confused with the Broederbond, the Afrikaner Bond was a Cape political party that was formed in 1881. It claimed to represent all those '*Afrikanders*' who felt that Africa was their home. This meant both English- and Afrikaans-speakers. In reality, it represented primarily rural farmers of Dutch extraction. The Bond was avowedly anti-imperialist, its aim being to bring South Africa together in a federated state that was free from British influence. Its leader, Jan Hendrik 'the Mole' Hofmeyr, never had the desire to take over direct leadership, always preferring to burrow behind the scenes. His influence and power were nevertheless enormous, and he and his political machinations were hugely effective.

Sprigg's plan for a railway network turned into a political disaster. With his policy failing to gain traction with the Afrikaner Bond, and taking huge hits in the Rhodes-controlled media, he was forced to resign as prime minister. But there was now a problem. J.W. Sauer, the liberal Afrikaner lawyer who was the unofficial leader of the opposition, was widely disliked by the largely rural members of the Bond, including the Mole. And Hofmeyr, given his mole-like nature, was not interested in the position himself. So, Sauer, knowing he lacked popular support in Parliament, recommended Rhodes for prime minister.

Rhodes had also formed the British South Africa Company (BSAC), or Chartered Company, after receiving a royal charter from Queen Victoria in 1889. The BSAC had been created in the expectation that a huge gold reef would be found in either Mashonaland or Matabeleland (soon to become Rhodesia).

Despite what is often stated in history textbooks, Rhodes was by this stage certainly not an avowed imperialist – far from it. If Rhodes had an ideological standpoint (which is doubtful), it was that of an independent colonialist of the Cape. The Cape's interests were of far more importance to him than any imperial dream – mainly because they could be used to serve the needs and purposes of one Cecil John Rhodes. Having the British imperial government nosing around in his interests was the last thing he wanted. A largely independent and roughly unified southern Africa suited him far better.

The British South Africa Company and corruption

Chartered companies were reintroduced by British prime minister William Gladstone in the 1880s. The most famous chartered company was the Honourable East India Company (a rival of Willem Adriaan's VOC), which effectively ruled India (dishonourably) until the mid-1800s. Chartered companies were formed as associations with investors and shareholders and were granted exclusive rights by 'the royal charter' – not unlike the concessions. Royal charters were seen as a way of initiating imperialism on the cheap. Rhodes's British South Africa Company was granted its status by the British Parliament when Rhodes went to London in 1889. And as one colonial source put it, Rhodes's charter 'had a questionable aroma attached to the getting there of'.[3]

Rhodes set up the company with the help of the English press and, in particular, the most famous female journalist of the day, Flora Shaw, who is said to have come under Rhodes's 'spell'. Rhodes also bribed several politicians in order to achieve his goal. Perhaps the largest impediment of getting the charter through British Parliament was Charles Parnell's anti-imperialist Irish Party. The Irish Party had always been strongly opposed to royal charters, and with eighty-five seats in Parliament they held the balance of power between the Liberal and Conservative parties. Rhodes had paid them £5 000 the year before and promised them £5 000 more once he had received his charter. Unsurprisingly, with a £10 000 reward on offer, Parnell's nationalist, anti-imperialist Irish Party did not oppose Rhodes's application. The British South Africa Company would then go on to effectively rule Rhodesia until 1924. During this time, the company found it necessary to wage wars, appropriate land, take sole control of mineral rights and generally exploit the local population at will.

Capturing the Bond

There's no doubt that Rhodes had an inbred contempt for the democratic pro-tocol instilled in the Cape constitution of the time. But he was willing to become prime minister because it would serve his purposes. That is to say, it would help him build the railway to his new BSAC interests in the north – at the Cape govern-ment's expense and not his.

Better still, Rhodes's BSAC would get the contract to build the railway. The contract was signed between the Cape government and the BSAC in the lavish home of Mr James Sivewright (more about him later) in Somerset West. Later, Rhodes's Cape government would pay Rhodes's company £730 000 (R2.2 billion today) for the railway from Kimberley to Vryburg. (And he would get the British imperial government to help the BSAC finance the section through Bechuanaland.)

Rhodes had, since his election to Parliament in 1881, cosied up to the Afrikaner Bond. Many of his interests were aligned to theirs. Of course, corruption and bribery would never be far away, and Rhodes set about handing shares in his new British South Africa Company to his political allies in the Bond – shares that were not being offered on the open market. As Rodney Davenport puts it, 'the distribution seems to have taken place both before and after Rhodes's assump-tion of the premiership in July 1890'.[4] Rhodes, it was often noted at the time, was in the 'habit of giving priority to members of the Bond when jobs were to be filled or shares in one of his under takings to be allotted'.[5] (The Broederbond and Jacob Zuma would later play the same game.)

Another interesting detail concerning the distribution of shares in the BSAC is a letter to Rhodes from James Rose Innes dated 14 February 1890. It contains a polite but firm undertone on the question of free shares.

My dear Rhodes,

I received a circular the other day stating that 750 shares in the Chartered Company had been allotted to me.

I must thank you for bearing me in mind, but at the same time I hope you will not take it amiss if I decide not to take them ... it would be better not to become a shareholder in your company. I shall occupy a sounder political position if I hold no shares. You know my views and you know that in most matters we are likely to be found on the same side, but my support will be much discounted if I am known to be interested in the Company. On every ground I would rather keep aloof from any pecuniary connection with the Company. I hope you see my position and reasons and will not resent my refusal for your very kind offer. Yours faithfully,

J. Rose Innes Jr.[6]

Rose Innes's rebuke was not unlike Mcebisi Jonas's rejection of the R600-million 'golden handcuffs' the Guptas offered him to act in their interests as finance minister more than a century later. But Rose Innes's stance – like Jonas's – was clearly a minority position, and many Bond members pocketed the shares without question. Rhodes, without doubt, could not have become prime minister without the Bond's help. And now, with some of its members' (and many prominent Englishmen's) pockets filled with free BSAC shares, the Afrikaner Bond promised Rhodes 'fair play' and backed him unanimously in Parliament. Lo and behold, as if by mere verbal persuasion, the Bond agreed to support Rhodes's plans to build a railway to the north – while at the same time going against Sprigg's attempt to expand the railways to aid their own electorate!

The Bond did this overtly because Rhodes promised to support a pro-white, racist 'native policy', as well as offering Afrikaner farmers agricultural protection. But their newly acquired shares in the BSAC surely helped to grease those political wheels. Bond MP and Hofmeyr's son-in-law D.C. de Waal, who had been strongly opposed to building the railway, is said to have been suddenly 'won over to Rhodes plans' to build the railway to Rhodesia.[7] Interestingly, De Waal is noted to have had 2500 BSAC shares 'gifted' to him by Rhodes at a similar time to this change of heart.

As Rose Innes would write in his autobiography, 'the body politic was virgin soil for the new infection to which in 1889 Rhodes subjected it'.[8]

The lying Scotsman (and Bondsman)

Another member of the Afrikaner Bond in the Cape Parliament was, surprisingly, a Scotsman, by the name of James 'Jimmy' Sivewright. Sivewright was a larger-than-life character, witty and popular in the mould of so many self-made venal South Africans. Sivewright, who had started off his southern African sojourn by embroiling himself in several corrupt dealings in Kruger's ZAR, was a perfect match for Rhodes.

When Rhodes took power, he would go on to appoint the (slightly oxy-moronic) Scottish Afrikaner Bondsman to his cabinet. Sivewright took over the public works portfolio, which included – surprise, surprise – the railways. In a piece of pragmatic (but what turned out to be foolhardy) politics, Rhodes also appointed an 'ill-assorted' cabinet, including the liberals Rose Innes, Merriman and Sauer. With this unlikely set of political figures on board, his cabinet would fast head towards a political train smash.

It is said that Merriman had a deep mistrust of Sivewright and that he had reluctantly resumed riding with Rhodes in the morning for the sake of Cape politics. As Merriman wrote about his inclusion in Rhodes's cabinet, '[I have] a good many things to gulp down. I therefore hardly like to predict a very long life for our craft … [and] I cannot say that I feel either proud or pleased.'[9]

Rhodes's liking of Sivewright went as far as arranging him a knighthood in 1892. He was knighted, more than a little ironically considering what was to follow, for his achieve-ments in negotiating the building of the railway north of Kimberley. It is said that Rhodes in par-ticular enjoyed Sivewright's 'antagonistic attitude towards Africans'. As the *Cape Times* stated at the time, Sivewright was part of the 'slave-driving' sec-tion of Rhodes's cabinet. What was more, as histor-ian Robert Rotberg says, 'Sivewright was a crook'.[10] No civil servant in the Cape had anything like Sivewright's wealth – and he would only get richer. One purchase, which no doubt raised some eye-brows at the time, was Sivewright's acquisition of the vast estate at Lourensford for £24 000 (R67 million today) which, ironically, had once been owned by Cape governor Willem Adriaan van der Stel.

James Sivewright

'I do not like hanky-panky!'

Just how Sivewright managed to acquire his wealth soon became apparent. On 5 November 1892, a letter was published in the *Cape Times*. It claimed that a contract for the refreshments along the railway line from Cape Town to the Orange Free State had been given to one man, a Mr James Logan. Logan, a friend of Sivewright's, ran the bar and refreshments room at Matjiesfontein. The letter to the paper was signed 'An Astonished Colonist'. Precedents and a framework for government tenders had long since been established in the Cape Colony. These processes were strictly vetted. Government calls to tender were put out in the press, and tenders had to be submitted in writing. A decision was then made by the general manager. These contracts were normally granted for five years.

The news of the illegal contract broke just one day before Rhodes and Sivewright set off together on a trip to the UK, Europe and Egypt. In the days that followed, the extent of the corruption was revealed. Sivewright, the *Cape Times* uncovered, had handed his friend and fellow Scot Logan the monopoly of food and beverage sales on all trains and all stations in the Cape Colony for the next eighteen years.

One whistle-blower was Sivewright's fellow cabinet member James Rose Innes, whose tone and anger rose several degrees when he wrote to Rhodes:

My dear Rhodes,

I was astounded the other day to find it stated in the papers that Logan had been granted the monopoly of supplying refreshments at all stations upon the entire system for a term of years. Hardly believing the report, I sent down to the Railway Department and they sent me a copy of the contract. Anything more improper, in my opinion, it would be difficult to conceive. Logan is to have a monopoly for fifteen years ... The lease was never submitted to this office and is very badly drawn, but that is a trifle. The real point is that no tenders were called, though in the past tenders have always been called, even for the lease of a single refreshment room. No one knows what our passenger traffic may not be in twenty years' time, yet a contract of this magnitude is given away without any call for tenders and without the Cabinet knowing anything about it ... Please show this to Sivewright I should like him to see. This is not a cheerful letter. However, I can't help it. I like fighting, but I do not like hanky-panky! Kindest Regards, Yours very truly,

James Rose Innes[11]

Two other members of the Rhodes cabinet were not keen on hanky-panky either. Merriman and Sauer were now fed up with both Rhodes's and Sivewright's shenanigans. Sivewright, rather predictably, cabled back to South Africa claiming that he had never seen Logan's contract. Neither Rhodes nor Sivewright knew at the time that Rose Innes and Merriman had in their possession an endorsement of the Logan contract written in Sivewright's own hand. With this, leaks began to spring from everywhere, linking Sivewright to graft and corruption.

Sauer was told of a bribe Sivewright had demanded while at the Johannesburg Water and Gas Works (in Kruger's republic) before he would endorse a contract. In fact, Rose Innes had written to Rhodes back on 21 May 1891 informing him that he had seen a report on the Johannesburg Water and Gas Works implicating Sivewright in wrongdoing. Rose Innes later uncovered the person who had the gas concession in Johannesburg – a man by the name of Julius Jameson (no relation to the more famous Leander Starr), who admitted that Sivewright had demanded 20 per cent of all Jameson & Co.'s profits. According to Jameson, Sivewright also did not allow work to proceed until 'he received a Commission'. Rose Innes further revealed to Rhodes that he had discovered that Sivewright's name appeared in Jameson & Co.'s books, which reflected that he had been paid a bribe (much like Zuma in the Arms Deal).[12] Other information also emerged about Sivewright's involvement in sharing the money from another transport contract.

The writer and one-time friend of Rhodes, Olive Schreiner, also linked Rhodes, Sivewright and Logan in what Paul Walters and Jeremy Fogg call 'an unholy and corrupt trinity'.[13] Schreiner had befriended Rhodes shortly after returning from London and moving to Matjiesfontein. But in 1892 something led her to break irrevocably with her friend. Her disgust with Rhodes's developing racist political agenda was certainly one reason for this. But in two letters – one to her mother and one to her brother W.P. Schreiner (later prime minister of the Cape) – she mentions another: 'I never gave up all hope of him till one day on Matjiesfontein station when he and Sivewright and Logan were talking together,' she stated to her brother.

She offered a little more to her mother a year later:

A little time after this I gave up all political hope of Rhodes. It was an affair with Logan and Sivewright and Government ground and other public matters, and it would take too long to explain, but there came a day when Rhodes and Sivewright were on the Matjiesfontein railway station; we had a talk, and my disappointment at Rhodes' action was so great that when both he and Sivewright came forward to shake hands, I turned on my heel and went to my house.[14]

Just what she was referring to has never been uncovered, but it was enough for Schreiner to call the issue that pertained to government land 'flagrantly and shamelessly dishonourable'. And as we have seen with Kruger, Van der Stel and Yonge, and will see with the Matanzimas and Dr Diederichs, corrupt government land deals are a particular favourite in our beloved country.

By the time the Logan Scandal broke, and with the political temperature rising, Rhodes was planning to rid himself of Rose Innes and his old frenemy Merriman. But he had no intention of getting rid of Sivewright, despite the mounting evidence against him.

Although Rhodes and Sivewright initially cancelled the contract with Logan, they had a 'change of heart' and reinstated it after Logan threatened to sue. Rose Innes, Merriman and Sauer scrupulously obeyed all cabinet protocols with regard to secrecy and refused to leak anything to the press. But this was not true of Sivewright and Rhodes. Confidential cables were leaked to the papers, and Rhodes's paper, the *Cape Argus*, went on the attack, referring to Rose Innes, Merriman and Sauer as 'the three mutineers'. The Rhodes mouthpiece continued its attack on the three liberal politicians, suggesting that their claim that Sivewright was corrupt was simply motivated by personal jealousy.[15]

Rhodes even wrote to Merriman, denying the attacks in his newspaper had anything to do with him. He went on to say that he wished the two of them could continue their morning rides. In a private meeting with Rose Innes and Merriman, Rhodes appealed to them not to resign from the cabinet, saying he simply could not drop Sivewright because if he did the Scotsman would 'besmirch him in mud'.[16]

The reality was that Rhodes and Sivewright were bound together in corruption, and Rhodes was desperate to protect Sivewright. After Rhodes returned from his overseas trip, he did continue his morning rides with the now deeply unimpressed Merriman. On one of these rides, Rhodes would tell Merriman that he had asked Sivewright for an explanation regarding the Logan contract and the corruption in Kruger's ZAR. He claimed that Sivewright had given him a perfectly satisfactory explanation: the Logan contract was an 'error', while the case in the ZAR was simply a matter where his name had been mistakenly used.

Merriman's wife would express a sentiment not unfamiliar to many South

Africans today: 'How is it possible to believe Mr Sivewright's statement in the face of all this evidence?'[17]

Jan 'the Mole' Hofmeyr also defended Sivewright in a speech in Stellenbosch. Behind the scenes, the Mole and Rhodes – the arch-schemers – had been talking. They planned to redeploy the troublesome Rose Innes by making him a judge. As for Merriman, they conspired to send him off to Britain to become agent general or ambassador. In the end, there was no need for any of this as Rhodes arranged for Sprigg (the man he had replaced as prime minister) to return to the fold so that he could jettison the liberals after calling an election.

With this agreement in place, Rhodes resigned. The papers blamed Merriman for this unnecessary public inconvenience. A new election was called which Rhodes, despite his public associations with corruption, won by a two-thirds majority. And with Sprigg now on Rhodes's side, the liberals were forced into opposition. As Vere Stent, perhaps the most famous journalist of the day, suggested, Rhodes's parting with the three liberals Rose Innes, Merriman and Sauer meant that he lost 'high honesty and a nice sense of honour, brilliant biting wit and moral courage, erudition and fearless criticism ... and the door was open for sycophancy, opportunism and time-serving'.[18]

Rhodes also quietly found the time to drop his friend Sivewright from the cabinet nearly a year and a half after the Logan controversy was first made public. This did not mean that Rhodes became unsympathetic to Sivewright – they would continue to remain strong political allies. In the 1950s, historian Eric Rosenthal wrote something that in hindsight seems laughably naive, saying that Sivewright, 'in the annals of South African money-making, probably stands unique as the only civil servant who managed to enter the millionaire class'. In 1895, Sivewright was worth over £1 000 000 (R2.5 billion today). True to form, he signed a significant amount of this over to his wife in order to avoid paying tax.[19]

Many have seen Rhodes's dealings with Sivewright as the great turning point in his life, claiming that he was corrupted by both Sivewright and his parliamentary powers. However, it is far more likely that the lip service Rhodes had paid to democracy, justice, liberalism and 'the native question' was largely an act of pragmatism. These values may have got him somewhere with the politically intelligent Merriman and the literary colossus that was Schreiner, but when they proved inconvenient to his financial and political aspirations, they were simply jettisoned. Lest we forget, Rhodes showed himself to be a *skelm* the moment he arrived in Kimberley and started sabotaging pumping equipment.

Over the next few years Rhodes would continue to further his political and financial aims, adding one more string to his political bow – war. While wilfully provoking the Ndebele, he also attempted to snatch stretches of the Bechuanaland Protectorate from the Tswana in order to build his railway to the north. His railway was never really going to Cairo – that was simply imperial bluster to gain support from Britain. The anti-imperialist (and morally compromised, thanks to his bribes) Afrikaner Bond were also aiding him in his project. His aim was to connect his interests in what had fast become his own private fiefdom in Rhodesia.

Don't give that man a Jameson!

As we saw in Chapter 4, in 1893 Rhodes and his ever-faithful friend Dr Leander Starr Jameson concocted a war with the Ndebele – a war that was fought and won by a private army – the 'pioneers' of the British South Africa Company. Once the inconvenience of the Ndebele had been dealt with, Rhodes and Jameson would turn their sights on Kruger, the Transvaal and its gold. There, however, they would meet their Waterloo with the Jameson Raid.

Towards the end of 1895, Jameson, with the clandestine backing of Prime Minister Rhodes, had gathered a small army of the British South African Police from Rhodesia and some paid members of the Bechuanaland Border Police. Armed to the teeth, they entered the Transvaal on 29 December 1895.

They did so in the belief that they would be supported in Johannesburg by a group of English miners called the Reform Committee. Rhodes and Jameson had secretly sent the Reform Committee guns and uniforms in oil drums labelled as 'mining equipment', and had arranged with them that when Jameson invaded, they would rise up in revolt and help overthrow Kruger. One of the leaders of the Reform Committee just so happened to be Frank Rhodes, Cecil's older brother.

Jameson's raiders also crossed the Transvaal border with another belief: that the telegraph cables to Pretoria had been cut.

On both these counts the raiders were mistaken. Their fellow conspirators in the Reform Committee in Johannesburg had lost confidence and begun arguing among themselves. They entered into negotiations with Kruger and, thinking that Kruger was ready to make an agreement, they sent him a list of all their names. All the men on the list were duly arrested by Kruger. They were, after all, conspirators, and crafty Oom Paul had the paper to prove it ... He had got the naive fools to write it themselves.

Meanwhile, Jameson and his men were engaged in an epic fail of their own. The group of troopers who were meant to cut the telegraph lines had gotten monstrously drunk the night they went out to do the deed and, mistakenly identifying a farmer's fence for a telegraph line, they left communication open from Zeerust to Pretoria. One particularly drunken trooper is even said to have buried the farmer's fence, which he swore in his drunken state was a telegraph line, with the great satisfaction of a job well done.

An artist's impression of Jameson's men cutting the telegraph lines

With communication to Pretoria still open and his movements widely communicated, Jameson's army was met at Doornkop by Commandant Piet Cronje. There, Jameson ended up surrendering after a skirmish in which thirty of his men were killed. The whole affair had been an ignominious shambles from beginning to end. As one of the brothers of the raiders related, the raid had been 'a regular drunken frolic'.[20] It was, the editor of the *Cape Times* wrote afterwards, a piece of dramatic irony that what Jameson and his men had needed (and would prove their undoing) was a little 'Dutch courage'.

In the ensuing parliamentary investigation into the Jameson Raid, Rhodes used his trump card of the 'gift' of BSAC shares to blackmail Hofmeyr into silence. An ex-Bondsman by the name of Smartt alleged in 1898 that Hofmeyr had made a profit in BSAC shares of £30 000 (R88.2 million today). Hofmeyr would later deny this and, several years after the Jameson Raid, published a certificate from his broker showing that his profits from BSAC shares only totalled a meagre £2 456 (R6.7 million today). But there was also proof that Hofmeyr had done a much larger deal on preferential terms in 1895 on Rhodes's De Beers

THE PIED PIPER OF RHODESIA.

"All the little boys and girls   · For he led us, he said, to a joyous land   And flowers put forth a fairer hue,
Tripping and skipping, ran merrily after   And everything was strange and new.' "
The wonderful music with shouting and laughter.   Where waters gushed and fruit-trees grew,   *Robert Browning.*

Sir M-ch-l H-cks-B-ch (*apart*). " UM—HA—*I* 'M NOT GOING TO FOLLOW *THAT* MUSIC ! "

Rhodes depicted as the Pied Piper in *Punch*

shares, and it was this that helped to seal Hofmeyr's lips. Simply put, Hofmeyr had sold at least some of his soul to Rhodes. What is more, Hofmeyr's son-in-law and fellow Bondsman MP D.C. de Waal (of De Waal Park fame), who owned 2500 'gifted' Charter Company shares, tried to persuade his fellow Afrikaners in Parliament that Rhodes was not the Hertfordshire shithouse he seemed to be and that he was not responsible for the raid. There were, in fact, several of these Bondsmen who supported Rhodes, and they were collectively referred to as 'the wobblers'.

As James Rose Innes said, Rhodes saw money as a great source of power. But this financial power did have its limits. The majority of Parliament could not be bought, bribed, bamboozled and bullied. In the aftermath of the Jameson Raid, Rhodes was forced to resign as prime minister. Meanwhile, Jameson was sent with his men to Britain to be tried in the High Court in London and was sentenced to fifteen months in prison for an unprovoked attack on a friendly state.

Frank Rhodes, Cecil's beloved elder brother, was initially sentenced to death for his role in the Reform Committee activities in the Transvaal. But, after the sentence had been commuted to fifteen years in prison, Cecil organised to pay the Transvaal government a hefty amount of money to have his brother released in 1896.

One of the most telling repercussions of the Jameson Raid was the deep distrust it fomented between the Afrikaans- and English-speaking whites in the Cape Colony. This distrust would play out for over a century, possibly longer. As Jan Smuts would say after the Anglo-Boer War had finished, 'The Jameson Raid was the real declaration of war.'[21]

'Sammy's political trinity'

After the Jameson Raid, James Rose Innes – who was friendly with Percy Fitzpatrick – travelled to the Transvaal to attend the trial of the members of the Reform Committee. While there, he stayed in the opulent country estate of none other than Sammy Marks of our previous chapter. As Rose Innes would write:

I had a splendid bedroom and was very comfortable; indeed they were kindness itself. On a cabinet in my room were three photos: Sivewright in court dress in the middle, flanked on either side by Rhodes and Kruger; and under the protection of the trio I slept well!!

The following morning, Rose Innes pointed to the photos of what he referred to in his autobiography as 'Sammy's political trinity', and asked his host whether he thought Rhodes would ever be taken seriously again.

Marks's reply was one for the ages: 'My dear Sir, *how* can you keep down a man with two millions?'[22]

Interestingly, Rose Innes also noted in a private letter to Percy Fitzpatrick that the fallout of the Jameson Raid had resulted in Rhodes's global investment portfolio doubling in value, a claim that surely warrants further examination.

Bribery, newspapers and the 1898 election

Marks's prediction would prove eerily accurate. By 1898, Rhodes felt he had served his time in the political wilderness and was ready to become prime minister once again – just in time for a new Cape election. The election would turn out to be 'the most corrupt, libellous and closely contested in Cape history'.[23]

One of the first steps Rhodes would take in his attempt to re-enter the political fray was to buy out newspapers like Kimberley's daily paper, the *Diamond Fields Advertiser*. The *DFA* was of particular strategic interest: not only had it previously taken a decidedly anti-Rhodes stance, but it was also circulated near to the parliamentary seat he would run for at Barkly West.

Rhodes, being one of the largest employers in the area, still had a ground-swell of popularity in the town. But the outcome of the election rested on two groups of potential swing voters: the group of diamond miners known as the River Diggers and the black vote. Rhodes had said before that he was 'not going to the native vote for support'. But, in 1898, go to them he did.

The Cape's non-racial franchise and Rhodes's racism

When the Cape received powers to form a representative government in 1853, its first parliament was elected by men of all races. The Cape constitution was one of the first in the world to have at its centre a non-racial voters' roll. There were, however, qualifications. The voters had to be men with a minimum property ownership of £25 (R60 000 today). As the British colonial secretary wrote in one of the Cape Parliament's foundational documents,

> it is exceedingly undesirable that the franchise should be so restricted as to leave those of the Coloured classes who, in point of intelligence, are qualified for the exercise of political power, practically unrepresented ... It is the earnest desire of Her Majesty's Government that all her subjects at the Cape without distinction of class or colour, should be united by one bond of loyalty and common interest, and we believe that the exercise of political rights enjoyed by all alike will prove one of the best methods of attaining this object.[24]

By the 1890s, several parliamentary Acts initiated by Rhodes had gone some way to undermining what was known as the non-racial '£25 vote'. With the Franchise and Ballot Act (1892), Rhodes managed to raise the qualification from £25 to £75 (R175 000 today). And in the 1894 Glen Grey Act, he pushed through legislation that excluded certain kinds of black landownership from the £75 voting qualification. However, black voters remained well represented in the 1890s in certain areas in the Eastern Cape and around Kimberley.

Barkly West had one of the largest proportions of black voters in the Colony. Rhodes also knew that he would be facing stiff opposition from Olive Schreiner and her husband, Samuel Cronwright-Schreiner, who were living in Kimberley at the time. Rhodes seems to have possibly been behind getting Samuel Cronwright-Schreiner struck off the voters' roll in revenge for both Olive's book *Trooper Peter Halket of Mashonaland* and Samuel's famous speech in the Kimberley town hall, 'The Political Situation', both of which had excoriated Rhodes for his reactionary racist policies.

Unable to contest the election himself, Cronwright-Schreiner had convinced a young, single-minded lawyer by the name of Henry Burton to take up the challenge of defeating Rhodes. Burton had become well known in Kimberley for defending black citizens who had fallen foul of the racist laws in the Cape Colony in the 1890s, in particular the pass laws. Burton was widely considered to be a 'friend of the native'. However, Burton (like many liberals, including John X. Merriman) had found himself needing to align with the Mole's Bond Party in order stand up to Rhodes and his Progressive Party. Only, James Rose Innes refused to align himself with either, instead running as an independent.

Voters of all races at Barkly West polling station in 1898

Strange fruit hanging from the Bulawayo tree

The political campaign of 1898 would focus heavily on the events of 1896. Not only was this the year of the Jameson Raid fiasco, which poisoned the Afrikaner Bond against Rhodes, but, shortly after the raid, the Ndebele had risen up in Rhodesia in what would be called the First Chimurenga. Rhodes was in Rhodesia at the time, trying his utmost to escape the parliamentary inquiry into his involvement in the Jameson Raid. There, he had taken charge of a column of BSAC troopers in the north that had tried to suppress the rebellion. In 1897, Olive Schreiner published *Trooper Peter Halket of Mashonaland.* At its heart lay a criticism of Rhodes's racial and warmongering policies in Rhodesia.

From a photograph taken in Matabeleland.

The shocking photograph published in Schreiner's book

Perhaps one of the most controversial elements of the book was the inclusion of the frontispiece photograph. The image shows, in graphic detail, three Ndebele 'spies' hanging from a tree in the main street of Bulawayo while some of Rhodes's BSAC men look on. As the 1898 campaign kicked off, Burton and his friend Samuel Cronwright-Schreiner set about trying to persuade black voters to vote against Rhodes. In doing so, they distributed the image of the hanging. On the pamphlet were written the words 'How the Natives are ruled under Cecil Rhodes' Company'.

How the Natives are ruled under Cecil Rhodes' Company.

From a Photograph taken at Bulawayo.

The pamphlet distributed by Burton and Cronwright-Schreiner

Rhodes was now eager to win the native vote and changed his election slogan from 'Equal rights for all white men' to 'Equal rights for all civilised men' (back then, 'civilised' generally and roughly meant people of all races who could read and write). Rhodes was reported to have held several meetings with the black population of Barkly West, where he was said to have explained away Burton and Cronwright-Schreiner's image of the hanging. As Rhodes's paper the *Diamond Fields Advertiser* reported on 4 August 1898:

> Rhodes met about 200 natives, mostly voters, and explained the matter to them. He answered what he described as the lies which had been told about him. At the meeting he showed that the blacks had equal rights with the whites in Rhodesia, for he said, 'If I wish to do otherwise I could not, as the country is directly under your Queen.' In referring to the Glen Grey Act, Mr Rhodes said the Bond wished to drive the natives from the territory concerned, where, as he said the land was reserved for them. As to the [image of the hanging] he

knocked the bottom out of the Bond myths by explaining that the persons hanged were not hanged as natives but as murderers. 'Would you not do the same?' he asked. 'Yes' answered a chorus of natives in their mother tongue.[25]

What was perhaps most untrue among these statements was that black and white people in Rhodesia had equal rights. To say the Queen had control over Rhodesia was another barefaced lie, as the country was run entirely at the whim of Rhodes and the rules of his British South Africa Company. Also false were his claims about the 1894 Glen Grey Act. Calling it a piece of legislation created to protect black interests was disingenuous to say the least – it was, in fact, the first case of Bantustan (or homeland) legislation in South Africa. Rose Innes and Merriman opposed the legislation and even London objected to it, but it passed into law with the support of the Bond. The legislation fined any black male ten shillings if they did not work outside their district in the Eastern Cape – thus enforcing migrant labour. Rhodes's defenders have claimed that, through the Glen Grey Act, he intended to 'stimulate' men through taxation to, as he put it, 'recognize the dignity of labour'.[26] Here, one can't help but remember that above the gates of Auschwitz hung a sign saying *Arbeit Macht Frei* – Work Sets You Free.

What was more, Rhodes had openly pursued a policy of terror in Rhodesia. While leading his column of troopers, he had urged them to 'kill all you can as it serves as a lesson to them'.[27] Rhodes participated in burning settlements and encouraging the indiscriminate massacres of men, women and children. He is said to have taken great pleasure in personally counting the dead bodies after such events. Witnesses also attested that the men hanged at the tree in Bulawayo were not murderers, as Rhodes had claimed when speaking in Barkly West. As Frank Sykes wrote in his 1897 book *With Plumer in Matabeleland,*

What rebel spies were caught were summarily tried and hanged. There is a tree, known as the hanging tree, to the north of the town, which did service as gallows. Hither the doomed men were conveyed. On the ropes being fastened to their necks, they were made to climb along an overhanging branch, and thence were pushed or compelled to jump into the space after a 'last look at Bulawayo'. Their bodies were left suspended for twenty-four hours.[28]

The election campaign of 1898 was full of false claims, obfuscations and electoral bribery, but by the end of it, Rhodes (and his running mate James Hill) came up trumps. Rhodes had clearly convinced enough of the miners in the area, and a sizable black contingent of voters, that he was the man for the job. In the end, Rhodes acquired 1 405 votes to Burton's 844.

As Hofmeyr would write to Burton shortly after the election, 'defeat was not such a very great disappointment to one', and considering Rhodes's wealth and status, 'you made a gallant fight of it'.[29] One person whom Burton did persuade to vote for him was a young court translator called Sol Plaatje. Plaatje, one of the founders of the ANC, admitted as much in his diary, noting the local missionaries' displeasure with his decision (the missionaries in the area largely supported Rhodes).

But Burton had not given up the fight. After Hofmeyr promised him £200 for legal fees, he launched a petition against Rhodes and Hill, stating that they had engaged in both 'Bribery and Corrupt Practices' during the election.

The case would be heard in front of Judge de Villiers, a man whom Rhodes had briefly tried to make prime minister after the Logan Scandal. Interestingly, De Villiers is listed as an original shareholder in the British South Africa Company, holding 750 shares 'gifted' to him by Rhodes. Rhodes had also offered De Villiers the chairmanship of the local board of the BSAC. This De Villiers refused. And considering what was to follow, it is worth noting that these offers, which were directed at the likes of De Villiers (and Rose Innes), were considered at the time to be 'approaching bribery'. Now Rhodes and De Villiers would face one another as accused and judge.

Burton, it would seem, believed he had good prospects of having Rhodes and Hill removed as members of Parliament. The crux of the case lay with the legal definition of bribery and how it related to the election laws. Burton accused Rhodes of having attempted to bribe the group of voters known as the River Diggers. That is, he had offered them the mining rights of privately owned land in return for their vote. This promise of personal enrichment came, Burton submitted to the court, in the form of a notice placed – on the day of the election, *nogal* – in two local papers: the *Diamond Fields Advertiser* and *Barkly and Diggers News*. As Burton put to the court:

On 26 August, the day before the poll, the following circular was printed at the office of the *Barkly and Diggers News*, a paper supporting the respondents [Rhodes and Hill], and a copy of it appeared in that paper on the morning of the polling day.[30]

> Good News for the Diggers and Everybody Else.
>
> Messrs. Rhodes and Hill, the Progressive Candidates, have already arranged with the owners of the Vaal River Estate to throw open their entire property. First instalment of good works! Don't forget to record your votes for Rhodes and Hill. Longlands, Delport's, Niekerk's Rush, Laaken's Vlakte, and the other diggings will now boom.

What's more, Burton produced two further claims of corruption and bribery. One was that Burton's black election agent, a man by the name of Pukwane, had been offered £50 and, when he refused, £60 by Rhodes's election agent – a Mr Brown. Burton, who had paid Pukwane £11 for his services, saw this to be a bribe. Pukwane, it seems, also saw it this way as he refused the money and reported the incident to Burton. The other claim that came up in testimony was that Rhodes had paid a black Kimberley-based missionary by the name of Reverend Davidson Msikinya £286 (R688 000 today) in order to promote Rhodes among the black population of Barkly West. This same Msikinya had apparently set up the meeting between Pukwane and Rhodes's agent Brown.

Burton claimed that the promise to open up the Vaal River Estate, a privately owned area, to the River Diggers was simply a bribe. But the court was unsure. Wasn't this a legitimate election promise of a social benefit? No, Burton and his team argued, this was about promising a particular group of people personal individual enrichment. As they would point out, under the Election Act 'candidates could not do acts of private beneficence on the eve of an election'. In terms of the

Rhodes's bribery note

law, Burton's lawyers argued, an election should be won by argument alone. The fact that the newspaper actually named the beneficiaries meant that it was a private and not public benefit. That is to say, this was a case of bribery and not electioneering.

Rhodes and his lawyers led a classic Stalingrad defence, denying almost everything and refusing to submit the required documentation. Rhodes had, by his own admission, promised to help get the Vaal River Estate thrown open. He denied, however, that he had anything to do with the placement of the notice in the paper the day before the election. But this was not the whole of it. Rhodes first attempted to deny that the Vaal River property was owned by his old De Beers and water-pumping pal Charles Rudd of Rudd Concession fame. In fact, Rhodes's own name appeared on the title deeds of the Vaal River Estate, which showed that he had sold his concern to his friends Rudd and Tarry in 1885.

The documents clearly showed that Rhodes had had a financial interest in the property. But in his court testimony, he played the game of selective amnesia. After lengthy attempts to get him to admit his financial dealings, Burton's lawyer, Sir Henry Juta, asked him for the last time if he was interested in the Vaal River property.

RHODES: Not that I can remember.

JUTA: Cannot you try and remember?

RHODES: No, I don't think so. In 1885 I sold out entirely ...

JUTA: Did you have no interest with Rudd at that time?

RHODES: I had no interest with Rudd and Tarry's Business that I can remember.

JUTA: Not at this time?

RHODES: No, I had interests in other matters.

JUTA: I am talking of this matter.

RHODES: Not that I can remember.

Finally, Rhodes did admit that he had spoken to Rudd about throwing open the land to the diggers. But he was still firm on the fact that he had not authorised the printing of the announcement the day before the election. The question was then: if he had not, who had? On the day the announcement had been placed, Rhodes was electioneering in Windsorton – the very same place from which the cable containing the wording of the notice had been sent to the paper.

JUTA: Can you suggest any way in which persons at Windsorton could have sent a wire to Kimberley and have this advertisement put in the *Diamond Fields Advertiser*?

RHODES: No; but it was from nothing that I said, I feel sure. I was careful to make no promises, only say I would do my best.

JUTA: But I want to know whether you can suggest any way in which any person acting on your behalf could've wired to Barkly West to have this advertisement printed.

RHODES: No, nothing but ill-considered zeal.

JUTA: Who could have been the too zealous party?

RHODES: I have not the slightest idea.

'You eat your dinner; you do not cook it'

Rhodes's total lack of a feeling for accountability and his appetite to pass the buck is all too familiar in our current political environment. But something else was there too: a bald-faced lie. Rhodes had a controlling interest in both the *Argus* and Kimberley's *Diamond Fields Advertiser* newspapers, although he had managed to keep this a secret. Rhodes had only gained control of the *DFA* shortly before the election in 1898, a fact he was, of course, equally eager to deny. But Juta could smell a rat.

JUTA: The *D.F. Advertiser* was being run in your interests?

RHODES: No.

JUTA: Were you not aware of that?

RHODES: It supported me [in the election].

...

JUTA: And you supported it.

RHODES: No.

JUTA: Was not the *D.F. Advertiser* run by you – you know what I mean?

RHODES: If you mean it was paid – certainly not.

JUTA: And the *Barkly and Diggers News*?

RHODES: I believe it was supporting us. You will see by the columns.

JUTA: But was it paid?

RHODES: What do you mean paid?

JUTA: That during the election it was, as it were, retained?

RHODES: That was my agents' matter; you had better ask them.

The alacrity with which Rhodes chose to lie in this matter was symptomatic of a man who had got used to both lying and escaping legal consequence. Rhodes again sailed close to the winds of falsehood and evasions when he was asked what his relationship with Rev. Msikinya was – the man paid to do his election bidding in the black community at Barkly West. Rhodes's answers were once more filled with negations and 'forgetfulness'.

JUTA: You know the Rev. Mr. S. Msikinya?

RHODES: I cannot say I do.

...

JUTA: Don't you remember a certain meeting you had with a native minister proposing a vote of confidence in you?

RHODES: Yes, at Barkly West.

JUTA: You know the man?

RHODES: Yes, but not by the name of the Rev. Msikinya. I know him as a native parson.

JUTA: Didn't you know his name?

RHODES: No, I did not know [his] name. They are so difficult. I did not know him by that name.

JUTA: You knew he was acting as one of your agents?

RHODES: I did not know that the Rev. Msikinya was acting as one of my agents.

JUTA: Or that he was working on your behalf?

RHODES: No; I saw him at Barkly West. He called a meeting and I was asked to attend. I made a speech. I was not aware that he was touring on my behalf. But I gathered from his conduct that he was a favourable supporter.

JUTA: But beyond that?

RHODES: No. Beyond that I knew nothing.

JUTA: Have you no knowledge of any of your agents?

RHODES: No, I left everything to Brown, and it took me all my time to go 'round and make speeches.

JUTA: You took some interest in obtaining the native vote?

RHODES: My agents did, no doubt. I did not.

JUTA: No personal interest yourself?

RHODES: My dear Sir, you eat your dinner, you do not cook it. That is the answer. I did not know any of the details of the canvassing or the appointment of agents or supporters or committees. It simply took me all my time to go to the different places, make a speech, get to bed, and go to the next place.

Rhodes would also go on to deny any knowledge of the bribe offered to Pukwane, Burton's agent. He would claim that it was certainly not the case that he had authorised Brown to do so. Pukwane claimed that he was told to go and see Rhodes himself for the payment. But Pukwane refused to go, staying faithful to Burton.

There are many things in this case against Rhodes we will never know, because when it finally came to the question of the election campaign accounts there was another problem:

JUTA: Who kept all the accounts?
RHODES: Mr Brown.
JUTA: You had nothing to do with it?
RHODES: No.
JUTA: Nothing whatever?
RHODES: No.
JUTA: Did you see them afterwards to check them?
RHODES: No, I just saw some of them, but did not think they were complete yet.
JUTA: Did these accounts disclose the names of the agents?
RHODES: Not that I can remember.
JUTA: Gave you no information and would give us none?
RHODES: No.
JUTA: As to who the agents were?
RHODES: Not that I can remember.
JUTA: Have you got [the accounts] with you?
RHODES: No, I have not. I had no time for those sort of things.
JUTA: You've got the accounts at your house?
RHODES: I think not.
JUTA: Who's got them?
RHODES: I think Mr Hill ... I cannot remember that.[31]

No accounts of the election campaign were ever submitted to the court for the simple reason that Hill (or perhaps Rhodes himself) destroyed them. As the court stated, it was 'regrettable' that 'Mr Hill has had a copy of the accounts in his possession, but destroyed it, and has not instructed his counsel to offer any explanation as to why he took such a step while the proceedings were pending'.

What Burton and his legal team could not prove in court was that Rhodes had ordered the newspapers to print the notice that the Vaal River Estate be opened to the River Diggers. There were documented political speeches of Rhodes and Hill stating very much the same thing. But the two managed to wriggle out of this by stating that they had said they would attempt to do this but had not promised to do so. Who had got the notice printed remained a (rather easy-to-solve) mystery. What's more, with the destruction of the electoral accounts, the court rendered unsubstantiated any definitive evidence as to whether Rhodes and Hill had bribed anyone and who had paid for the printing of the notice.

When Judge De Villiers finally came to the judgment, he felt he could not find Rhodes guilty. He did, however, offer sanction, stating that Rhodes's election agents 'had come perilously close' to bribery, but had not 'entered into the forbidden territory'. (Whether Rhodes had come perilously close to entering into the same territory by personally 'gifting' BSAC shares in 1890 to people like De Villiers is, of course, another question.) De Villiers's right-hand man, Judge Solomon, also agreed that what Rhodes and his agents had done was a 'reprehensible procedure'. He argued that although it was not strictly unlawful, the election laws should be changed so that these kinds of actions 'should be a corrupt act [and] should be sufficient to unseat candidates whose agents were responsible for such a proceeding. I certainly would concur with that being done [i.e. the law being changed]'.[32]

In the same year, Rhodes's friend and long-time political ally James Sivewright *was* unseated by an election petition. This time it was proved that Sivewright and his agents, who were part of Rhodes's Progressive Party, had involved themselves in bribing members of the electorate. With this, Sivewright was duly removed from his seat at Stellenbosch. At the final count, Rhodes's Progressive Party won thirty-eight seats to the Bond's forty, while James Rose Innes was returned unopposed to his seat as an independent. Rhodes nevertheless won the popular vote, but could not buy his way to the prime ministership. That honour fell to W.P. Schreiner (Olive's brother), who had, like Burton, run as a Bond candidate.

The 1898 election results

PARTY	VOTES	%	SEATS
Independent–Afrikaner Bond Alliance	52 388	38.04	40
Progressive Party	73 097	53.08	38
Independents	12 232	8.88	1
Total	137 717	100	79

Rhodes's gift to the nation

Although Rhodes's guilt was not proved in court, he did lie about his involvement in the *Diamond Fields Advertiser*. He was also evasive with regard to his interests in the Vaal River property, and was clearly not willing to hand over his accounts of the election campaign to the court. In fact, very little of his testimony seems to have been offered in the pursuit of justice.

Rhodes's willingness to avoid accountability, his brazen contempt for the law and his total lack of interest in the truth seems to have rooted itself into South Africa's body politic.

So many of Rhodes's business and political actions appear to have been littered with lies, criminality and corruption. There can be little doubt that corruption was in Rhodes's DNA, and that this was directly proportional to his rise in both South African business and politics. He may never have had children, but the progenies of his political and business practices certainly were passed down from one South African generation to the next.

As Shakespeare might have put it, Rhodes bestrides our narrow history like a colossus, while those 'petty' men Rose Innes and Burton have found themselves peeping out at the sidelines from forgotten graves. When Rhodes died in 1902, the Cape government afforded him the grandest funeral tour of any politician in the history of South Africa. A funeral train took his coffin from Cape Town to Rhodesia, along the very railway line his corrupt practices had helped to build, stopping at every single railway station along the way to allow mourners to pay their last respects. But, thanks to the likes of James Rose Innes, the profit made from the sandwiches and beer sold at the station refreshment stalls would not go into Rhodes's political allies' pockets.

PART THREE

GRAND AND NOT-SO-GRAND APARTHEID

The rise of Afrikaner nationalism after the Anglo-Boer War
culminated in the National Party taking power in 1948.
And with this were blasted in the foul airs of not only racism
but state capture and full-blown corruption.

CHAPTER 7

THE BROEDERBOND

Bound in the Capture
1935–1978

'A mad, fatal idea.' – *J.B.M. Hertzog.*[1]

Broeder Nico Diederichs with
top hat and many corrupt tales

No pointy hats or secret handshakes?

The mention of the secret society known as the Afrikaner Broederbond may conjure up images of pointy-hat-wearing religious and racist zealots greeting one another with ludicrous handshakes and engaging in sexually dubious initiation practices. But nothing could be further from the truth. Zealots they may have been, but these secretive 8 000 or so 'Super-Afrikaners' captured a country's economy – and they didn't have a handshake and wore only sombre black suits at their meetings. But despite their austere habits, their leaders drove Mercedes-Benzes, and their one time chairman and ideological father, Nico 'Dr Gold' Diederichs, was thought to be the wealthiest politician since Cecil John Rhodes – that is, until it was discovered just what he owed to his creditors! At his death, he was initially found to have left behind a surprisingly large estate and had, according to one High Court judge, R1.8 billion (in today's terms) knocking about in a Swiss bank account.

What makes the Broederbond's story of corruption and political manipulation different to some of the others in this book is that it is a collective story; the story of how many hands made light work of capturing a 'democratic' state. Another key difference is that, having effectively captured the state, they were pretty good at covering their tracks of corruption. Many, like Diederichs, took secrets to their graves, as well as to their Swiss bank accounts.

The Broederbond's programme of social upliftment for Afrikaners has sometimes been a subject of peculiar nostalgia. Why, some have asked, did the ANC and its BEE project not follow the same methods? There are important differences that should be noted from the get-go. One is that BEE is a piece of constitutional legislation. What the Broederbond achieved by hook or by crook (and it was mainly by crook) was secretive and quite often illegal. And, as we will see later, many of Jacob Zuma's best tricks came straight out of the Broederbond's leather-lined glove compartments – right down to giving Eskom contracts to 'brothers'. But the writing was on the wall long before Broeder D.F. Malan won the 1948 election. General J.B.M. Hertzog, the original founder of the National Party, blew the whistle on their secret conspiracies as early as 1935.

J.B.M. Hertzog: not a Broeder
but from the same moeder

Hertzog, the Broederbond and a 'mad, fatal idea'

Boer War general J.B.M. Hertzog, himself a right-wing racist republican, saw the Broeders as a source of profound evil. Having seen his own party split up because of the Broederbond's interference, he decided to tear off the Broeders' mask in what has been called 'one of the most sensational speeches in South African political history'.[2] Speaking at a meeting held in his constituency of Smithfield on 7 November 1935, Hertzog made several revealing claims which might help us to understand just who the Broederbond really were.

One claim was that the Broederbond, although maintaining to be a purely cultural and non-political society, was in control of the breakaway faction of Hertzog's own National Party – a faction led by D.F. Malan. Here, Hertzog offered up papers to prove this. He then went on to state that these Broeders had a 'mad, fatal idea' that they were 'the chosen of the gods to rule over others' and that they were intent on the supreme domination of the English and other races of South Africa. Hertzog would then go on to state that the Broeders were recruiting teachers and attempting to indoctrinate schoolchildren against their English-speaking brethren. They were also advancing each other's interests in appointments and promotions in the civil service, while discriminating against all those who were not Broeders.

'A white civil war'

Despite the Broederbond's racist apartheid ideology, which they implemented through the National Party after 1948, it was actually the English-speaking liberals who were their initial target. As Max du Preez explains, '[T]he enemy in the early days was Britain and, by proxy, English-speaking South Africans as opposed to black South Africans: the *Engelse Gevaar* rather than the *Swart Gevaar*, which would come later.'[3] The contestation between the English (liberals) and the Afrikaners (conservatives) bore all of the hallmarks of what one of the heroes of this chapter, Charles Bloomberg, called a 'white civil war'.[4] Echoing military theorist Carl von Clausewitz's famous pronouncement that 'war is merely the continuation of politics by other means', the Broederbond's state capture was war performed through politics, religion, economics and culture.

This 'war' was, as Broederbond chairman Nico Diederichs once suggested, an 'economic struggle' – a concept not entirely dissimilar to the Economic Freedom Fighters' reason for being. It was the English-speakers' capitalist power that the Broederbond was most interested in toppling on their pilgrimage to the Promised

The first executive council of the Afrikaner Broederbond, 1918.
Standing (left to right): D.H.C. du Plessis, J Combrink, H. le R. Jooste.
Sitting: L.J. Erasmus (sec.) H.J. Klopper (chair)
Rev, Wm Nicol (v.chair) J.E. Reeler (treasurer)

Land. This was Diederichs's attitude. And in his maiden speech in Parliament in 1948, he would sound the Broederbond's dog whistle. 'This doctrine of liberalism,' he got up to say (liberalism being proxy for 'English'), 'that stands for equal rights for all civilized human beings ... is almost the same as the ideal of communism.'[5] Just how the English could be both the minority controllers of capital as well as communists was never explained. Diederichs and the Broeders' thinking, like all populism, was not particularly consistent.

Formed in a modest house in Johannesburg in 1918, the Broederbond operated out in the open until 1922. There is even a photograph of the founders sitting openly with one of its leading religious figures, Reverend William Nicol, nonchalantly resting his arm on a small table. (Isn't it amazing that, to this day, one of the main arterial roads in Joburg still bears his name?) Nicol is interesting for two reasons. One, he symbolises the religious NG Kerk underpinning of the Broederbond. Two, despite his name he wasn't English. Originally, all recruits to what would become perhaps the most powerful secret organisation of the twenti-eth century had to prove an Afrikaner ancestry dating back before 1820 (that is, before British colonial settlement in South Africa). This rule was later relaxed to let in Dr H.F. Verwoerd, who was born in Holland.

Just quite why the Broeders decided to go underground and adopt a clandes-tine and secretive approach to politics is not certain. All we know is that in 1922 they did so by a majority vote taken in a meeting at, of all places, Rhodes's old pal and rival Barney Barnato's Carlton Hotel. There they swore, under the cloak of secretive darkness, to bind all Afrikaners together into the *volk* – that is, into a uni-tary nation based on a supposed shared tradition, culture, language and religion.

After the electoral victory of General Hertzog's right-wing National Party in 1924, the Broederbond's dreams seemed to have come true. Hertzog's vision and racial policies were not dissimilar to theirs. But then Hertzog showed his concili-atory side by accepting that the British Balfour Declaration of 1926 had given South Africa a republican political independence, if not in name then at least in practice. The declaration had given 'autonomous communities within the British Empire, equal status, in no way subordinate the one to the other'.[6] This was simply not good enough for the Broeders. Worse still, in the early 1930s Hertzog performed a deed most foul: he reunited with the 'traitor' Jan Smuts in order to form a government. One Broederbond member, Dr D.F. Malan, strongly opposed the coalition and drew politically closer to his fellow Broeders, in particular to a group of 'Young Turks' including Dr H.F. Verwoerd, Dr Nico Diederichs and Dr Piet Meyer.

Heil Hitler

It was through these men that the Broederbond would find their ideological and corrupting voice. As journalist and historian Allister Sparks would say of apart-heid, 'it was Diederichs who laid the philosophical foundation of it, … Meyer who was its key backroom strategist, and Verwoerd who finally implemented it in its most absolute form'.[7] Although it was an ideology based on racial segregation, it would put money and the capture of the economy at the centre of its goals. The first thing that the Broederbond achieved in the 1930s was to gather money from like-minded Afrikaners. With these funds they paid for a select group of students, including Verwoerd, Diederichs and Meyer, to go to Germany to study the methods employed by the Nazis.

When Diederichs and Meyer returned home (after consorting with top Nazi officials), they founded the militant students' union the Afrikaanse Nasionale Studentebond (ANS), which was allied to the Broederbond. Diederichs would then go on to publish his influential book *Nationalism as Life Outlook and Its Relationship to Internationalism* in 1936. This work was one of the most important pioneer attempts to express the Christian National doctrine of the Broederbond. Its most striking characteristics were the adoption of certain Nazi concepts such as the 'Volksstaat'.

Like the Nazis, Diederichs argued in his book that the nation and identity was the centre of all social life: 'Of all groupings of people, the nation is the highest, the most all-embracing, the most total group. In this human world, there is nothing higher than the nation.'[8] But there was one significant difference between Nazism and Diederichs's racist vision for South Africa, and that was his insistence on the God-directed nature of the notion of nationhood and race. 'The Nation' was, he argued, ordained and instituted by the will of God and it was 'destined to fulfil a calling and contribute a portion to the realisation of the Divinely-determined purpose of universe'.[9]

With Diederichs's Nazi-like ideas laying the foundations for the Broederbond in the 1930s, it is hardly surprising that the beginning of the Second World War would cause one of the greatest political ruptures in South African history. The Broederbond precipitated not only a split in the ruling party but a divide in the country.

Losing the vote in Parliament on whether to stay neutral after Hitler invaded Poland by eighty to sixty-seven, Prime Minister Hertzog broke with Smuts, leaving Smuts to form a pro-war government. At the same time, members of the Broederbond unfurled their flags and raised their arms to salute the Nazi cause. And while 325 000 white, black and coloured volunteer servicemen were fighting the Nazis abroad, right-wing Afrikaner nationalists stayed behind and united in the pro-Nazi, Broederbond-backed movement known as the Ossewabrandwag (OB), which translates into English as Ox-Wagon Sentinel, and which would engage in acts of terrorism and sabotage during the war.

Smuts, once more prime minister of the country, soon began to realise the danger of the likes of Diederichs and the Broederbond and asked the head of military intelligence, Dr E.G. Malherbe, to investigate their activities. Malherbe set about his work with extreme efficiency, bugging Broederbond meetings and gathering a wealth of revealing intelligence – some of which was destroyed when the National Party took power in 1948.

Diederichs, the Broeders and the Ossewabrandwag

Diederichs, who was chairman of the Broederbond from 1938 to 1942, had a close association with the Ossewabrandwag. In 1941, he swore in Kommandant-Generaal Hans van Rensburg as the head of the Ossewabrandwag in a ceremony on the slopes of Majuba – the site of the famous Boer victory over the British in Kruger's time. Under Van Rensburg, the OB led a campaign of terror and sabotage in South Africa that lasted the duration of the war. In 1941, the OB's military wing, 'the Stormjaers' (Nazi-styled storm troopers), engaged in a running battle with the army in the streets of Johannesburg.

In one bomb attack in 1942, Stormjaers Julian Visser and Hendrik van Blerk blew up the post office in Benoni, killing an innocent civilian. They were sentenced to death, but when the National Party pleaded for leniency Smuts commuted the sentence to life imprisonment. (In years to come, the NP would not show the same compassion for the likes of Solomon Mahlangu or John Harris.) Visser and Van Blerk were later freed when the National Party took power. In another bombing campaign very similar to those later waged by the ANC and the African Resistance Movement (ARM), the Stormjaers blew up fifteen electricity pylons.

The Ossewabrandwag also tried to blow up a train full of South African troops destined for the fight against the Nazis in North Africa. The Stormjaers' 'General' Theron and a man known simply as 'Doors' Erasmus, however, ended up blowing themselves to smithereens under the bridge where they'd planned to

place the dynamite. Another OB tactic was to strip and beat any serviceman they found hitchhiking alone on empty country roads.

During the war, an internment camp at Koffiefontein was set up to hold militant members of the Ossewabrandwag. There, an important friendship was forged between two OB prisoners: Hoof-Generaal B.J. Vorster (a future prime minister of South Africa) and 'Lang Hendrik' van den Bergh (future head of the notorious Bureau of State Security, or BOSS). At Koffiefontein, Van den Bergh became head of the camp's counter-intelligence unit, his job being

Vorster delivering a speech
to the Ossewabrandwag

to root out spies. Vorster would later use his detention without trial and experiences in the camp to justify the imprisonment and treatment of anti-apartheid activists. As historian Christoph Marx says, although members of the OB were subjected to some 'petty harassment' in the camp, these 'cannot be equated with the "interrogations" that took place (many on Van dèn Bergh's orders) in the built-for-purpose apartheid prison that was John Vorster Square'.[10]

According to Charles Bloomberg, Smuts believed that the OB and its political puppet-masters, the Broederbond, were planning a 'Munich beerhall-type putsch' or Hitler-style coup. Malherbe's report to Smuts noted under the title 'Afrikaner Broederbond':

> The Afrikaner Broederbond has become immensely interested in the Nazi System. Dr Diederichs and a specially selected Stellenbosch student were sent over to study National Socialism. Both of them qualified as Quislings [spies] in the Nazis' Anti-Komintern training school.[11]

As he would go on to say, 'The Ossewabrandwag has waxed with the rise of Nazi power; it will wane with it. The Broederbond will outlive both, because its policy is much more patient and insidious.'[12]

An interim report compiled in 1941 and given to Smuts also revealed that Diederichs had once given a speech at Hitler's second-in-command Hermann Goering's home before the war in which he'd said that, like the Germans, the Afrikaners 'don't give way, we fall'.[13] It also revealed that Diederichs had brought over to South Africa a Nazi spy in order to 'convert and organise' young Afrikaner students along Nazi lines. Mentioning Diederichs again, the report claimed that the Broederbond had gained a 'strangle-hold' over South African education which would enable it to 'govern South Africa' in the next decade. The report drew particular attention to the Broederbond's 'subversive character' and long-term revolutionary plans for the establishment of a republic, as well as its undercover links with the Nazis.

When Malherbe delivered his final report to Smuts in 1944, he also brought forward evidence of the Broederbond's penetration into government departments in the ministries of social welfare, posts and telegraphs, food control, justice, education, agriculture, and railways and harbours, as well as the police. The report also detailed the Broederbond's 'empire' of interlinked student, cultural and economic bodies and paramilitary institutions at the time: the Reddingsdaadbond, the Federasie van Afrikaanse Kultuurvereniginge (FAK), the Afrikaans Handelsinstituut, the Afrikaanse Nasionale Studentebond and the Ossewabrandwag, among others.

Malherbe also claimed that Diederichs, as founder of the Reddingsdaadbond (a savings fund that acquired money from private members in order to help poor Afrikaners), was the head of a 'complicated financial maze' in which 'a terrific fiddling with paper assets is carried on'. The money the Reddingsdaadbond had acquired, Malherbe claimed, had been gained via 'extortion' and had been 'wrung from the poor ... There is every possibility that a thorough investigation by impartial auditors will reveal grave irregularities.'[14]

Smuts launched a campaign to try to eradicate the Broederbond from the civil service, the army and police force. He demanded that all civil servants who were members of the Broederbond resign from the secret organisation immediately. A total of 1094 civil servants complied with his request and left the Broederbond. But when Smuts lost the 1948 general election to Broeder D.F. Malan, the vast majority of them simply resumed their membership.

State Capture 1.0

With the National Party's victory in 1948, the Broederbond set to work capturing the state. The Broeders had been working tirelessly to stack the civil service and education system with young junior members. In fact, the National Party's victory against Smuts can, according to many, be put down to this covert propaganda strategy. Now, with the groundwork laid and one of their members prime minister, the Broederbond were in the perfect position to take control of all state apparatuses, to stack the courts with their judges and to hand their companies lucrative government tenders.

The scale of the capture was immense. What made it even more remarkable was that this was not an elected party setting up their stall, but a secret elite organisation with only a few thousand of what journalists Ivor Wilkins and Hans Strydom famously called 'Super-Afrikaners' in its ranks. Most of Malan's cabinet positions were filled by members of the Broederbond. And within forty-three days of taking power, Malan handed control of the defence force and railways to his Broeders. His method was simple: he did a Zuma and removed General Poole, one of the most respected and decorated Second World War officers as head of the army. Of course, the National Party claimed, as Zuma did after removing finance minister Nhlanhla Nene in 2015, that they had another job for him that was of great importance. In Poole's case, at least, the job did actually exist, and the general was spirited out of the way to Berlin on an obscure diplomatic mission.

At the head of the railways – perhaps the most important piece of public infra-structure in the country – was the young and impressive (but English-speaking) Marshal Clark, who still had another eighteen years of government service left. Clark was forced into early retirement and given an £80 000 (R60 million today) golden handshake. As Senator David Jackson (we had senators back then) pointed out, installing a Broederbonder as head of the railways ended up costing the taxpayer £95 000 (over R72 million today) once the administrative costs had been taken into account.

On retiring at the age of forty-eight, Clark stated, seemingly quite genuinely, that he was 'sad at heart that I leave'[15] and that he was looking forward to the 'other work' the government had lined up for him. On discovering that the 'other work' was a complete farce, Clark insisted on further compensation from the government. Malan duly coughed up another £80 000 pension. Clark, still seventeen years away from retirement, would then become a director of De Beers – nice work if you can get it, especially with a R120-million severance package already in your pocket!

Charles Bloomberg, one of the first journalists to investigate the Broederbond's activities, demonstrated that by 1962 every branch of the state (civil service, judiciary, police, army and parastatals) was controlled and staffed by Afrikaners. And most of the top positions were filled by Broeders. Of the forty-six top civil servants, forty-two were Afrikaners; of the country's 318 diplomats, only three were English. The Appeal Court too had been packed with sympathetic Afrikaners. Only two (old) judges were not of Afrikaner descent; and not one English surname could be found on the senior military and police lists.

As the academic Julian Hyslop argues, the country and the government did pay heavily for these policies. The new officials placed in the senior positions of the civil service, in particular, lacked the training and expertise of the people they had supplanted. This led to an all too familiar skills shortage, an issue that plagued the government over the decades to come. The new Afrikaans recruits at junior levels were also quite often from the least educated sector of the population and struggled initially with their new tasks.

To add to these problems, an almost wholesale economic capture was on the go. As Wilkins and Strydom (those laudable muckraking journalists) noted, the influence that the Broederbond had on South African business was so widespread and fundamental that it could easily be the subject of a book the length of a Voortrekker family Bible. At the centre of this was the notion of 'economic struggle' in which capitalism would be used to promote the advancement of Afrikaner business. In this pursuit, the Broederbond set up an economic committee in the 1930s fronted by the Federasie van Afrikaanse Kultuurvereniginge. The federation's committee included a list of the Broederbond's usual suspects, including Nico Diederichs and Piet Meyer.

Diederichs's dream/Nico's nightmare

In the book that Diederichs and Meyer co-authored, *Ons Republiek* (1941), Diederichs set out the Broederbond's blueprint for a Christian National nation. He argued that individual rights would be secondary to those of the *volk*. Exclusive control of the state would be held by Afrikaners and the state would take control of the press and the South African Broadcasting Corporation (SABC). He proposed that all political parties whose principles were contrary to those of the NG Kerk should be abolished. True to his Nazi beliefs, he argued that a group of European second-class citizens was to be created as a service class (presumably Jews, but he possibly also had the English in mind). Interracial marriage should be banned, he argued, as should sex between any of the 'classes', even if the individuals were both white. He also called for the nationalisation of banks, mines and key industries.

In October 1950, the Broederbond organised an Ekonomiese Volkskongres. Diederichs, in his address to the conference, stated in typically populist form that it was characteristic of the Afrikaner that *he* always 'attached more weight to the spiritual than to the material'. Diederichs went on to say that the economic strengthening of the *volk* 'was never an end in itself, but was always seen purely as a means, and indeed essential means to the fulfilment of the eternal spiritual calling of our nation'.[16] But of course Dr Gold *would* say this.

Hoes vir die volk

By this time, Diederichs was not only a member of Parliament but also the chairman of Anton Rupert's Rembrandt cigarette empire. Rupert, who would later become a *verligte* (enlightened moderate), was then a staunch member of the Broederbond. He had started his company together with the first apartheid minister of health (!), Dr A. Stals, and the ever-present Dr Diederichs. As Wilkins and Strydom were told by a member of the Broederbond, Rupert's tobacco products were always distributed at their meetings and the Bond 'were asked to smoke and cough ['*hoes*'] for the volk and vaderland'.[17]

Although Rupert always claimed that he began his company with only £10, the growth of his empire was not held back by the Broederbond and its financial institutions. By 1968, Rembrandt's combined profits amounted to R54 729 000 before tax (R4.1 billion today). As Diederichs proudly proclaimed, they 'often sold more [cigarettes] in non-Afrikaans areas than in Afrikaans areas'. Certainly, Diederichs had no problem with the 'eternal spiritual calling of the nation' being built on that most vulgar of all things, English money.

Rembrandt's first cigarette factory in Paarl made a point of employing only Afrikaner women and children. This made it seem like it was at the forefront of Afrikaner upliftment by delivering a product 'that was untouched by African hands'. (This phrase was actually used in their advertising campaigns – not surprising considering their head of PR was Piet Meyer, one-time propaganda chief for the Ossewabrandwag.) It also, historian Dan O'Meara needled, had the benefit of keeping the company's production costs to a minimum, as it was much cheaper to employ women and children.

After the 1948 election, Afrikaans business elites experienced extraordinary portfolio growth and an incomparable set of financial windfalls, not all of which could be put down to hard work. At the centre of the Broederbond's 'economic struggle' was the attempt to break the monopoly of the two English banks, Barclays and Standard Bank. They went about this by establishing a purely Afrikaans bank called Volkskas – the precursor of what has become ABSA. All the directors (which included the cigarette-producing health minister Dr A. Stals) were Broederbond members. Founded in 1935 (when it made an annual profit of R17.06), Volkskas saw unprecedented growth after the 1948 election, with its assets rising from R40 million in 1950 to R538 million in 1968.

This rapid growth came off the back of government business from public institutions. In 1979, new deposits in Volkskas amounted to R210 million. Their next biggest rival, Barclays, managed a meagre R76 million. In 1943 the building society Saambou had assets of R25 000 (and took a loss of R1 200), but by 1968 its assets had risen to R125 million (R 9.5 billion today) and it made a profit after tax of R4 138 607 (R313 million today). The life insurance company Sanlam, formed in 1918, had assets in 1949 of R34 million. By 1968 these had increased tenfold, to R334 million.[18]

Anton Rupert, Nico Diederichs and Tienie Louw of Sanlam (all of the Broederbond)
in 1948 inspect the first box of 'Afrikaans cigarettes' from Rembrandt's
machine in Paarl while a white female factory worker toils

Only in the field of mining were there problems. As 'Dr Gold' Diederichs pointed out in 1950, Afrikaners had achieved very little in mining and only 1 per cent of the industry was in their control. But what they certainly did have control over, through the National Party, was a growing list of publicly owned industries. With the nationalised railways and the parastatals Iscor, Sasol, Amcor and Eskom, the Broederbond (with Diederichs as minister of economic affairs from 1958 onwards) effectively controlled a huge section of the South African economy. Dr Malherbe, no longer the head of military intelligence, worked out that the government employed over a quarter of all white people of working age. And it was through these parastatals, and in particular Eskom, Iscor and Sasol, that the Broederbond began to make inroads into mining.

Two of Eskom's biggest power stations were deliberately built next to coal mines owned by a small company called Federale Mynbou, which was run, not surprisingly, by members of the Broederbond. Mynbou was then naturally handed

government tenders that guaranteed their survival – a trick Zuma would imper-
fectly repeat with the Gupta-controlled coal mines. Other Afrikaans-owned mining
companies were given concessions to mines in Namibia (then South West Africa)
ahead of the far more prominent De Beers and Anglo American mining firms.

Soon the Broederbond-dominated parastatals became laws unto themselves,
refusing to account publicly for their actions. These corporations, according to
Brian Bunting, became 'bafflingly secretive about their policies and activities'
while handling public money. What was more, they refused to offer any information about salaries on the grounds that 'no information about their staff could
be supplied to outsiders'. It was later revealed that their managers received pay
packets 'of up to 45% more than those of similar levels in the public service'.[19]

In the 1960s, in an all-too-familiar situation, members of the public began
to question whether 'swimming pools, massage salons, air-conditioned underground wine-cellars and sun rooms were necessary amenities for executives
employed by public corporations'.[20] And then there was the case of publicly
owned entities like Klipfontein Organic Products (KOP), which despite its name
was a chemical manufacturer that produced mustard gas and DDT (a pesticide
that was later found to have detrimental environmental effects). KOP was sold
'lock, stock and barrel' to Federale Volksbeleggings, a private enterprise controlled by the Broederbond, at below market value.

Who needs a free press?

By now the resemblance between the Broederbond and the ANC state under
Zuma should be plain to see, but there are a couple more examples that should
raise at least a little laugh. The Broederbond had always been tied very closely to
the Afrikaans press. D.F. Malan was the founding editor of *Die Burger*, while
Verwoerd held the same title at the populist *Die Transvaler*. By the 1950s the
Broederbond had also taken control of the Sunday newspaper *Dagbreek*, with
the chairmanship of its controlling company falling on the shoulders of Prime
Minister H.F. Verwoerd. What later came to light was that Dagbreek Pers received
government contracts worth £1.5 million (R680 million today) between 1960
and 1962. That is while Verwoerd was both prime minister of the country and
chairman of the company! What was more, advertisements were placed by the
government in nationalist newspapers completely out of proportion to their rela-
tive circulation – the similarity to the Guptas' *New Age* is truly uncanny.

The SABC would also come under sustained attack and finally capture. In 1949, Malan's government had made a strategic mistake by appointing Gideon Roos as general director of the national broadcaster. Roos, who was the son of the famed rugby player Paul Roos, seemed to be made of the right stuff: a proud Afrikaner with a well-established broadcasting background. But Roos made the fatal error that all political appointees make when they assume they have received the job because of their experience and credentials – he tried to do the job properly. He even told the *Sunday Times* that 'the SABC provides a service to the public, and is therefore a servant of the public, not a servant of the Government'.[21] Perhaps he didn't get the memo?

As such, Roos set about doing his job in the most impartial manner possible. The Nationalists were unsurprisingly perplexed. Did Roos not know his place? Somehow Roos managed to cling on to his position for ten years. However, when H.F. Verwoerd took the reins of the country there was no pussyfooting around. Verwoerd handed over the chairmanship (and the newly created 'executive chairmanship') of the SABC to his best friend and chairman of the Broederbond, Dr Piet Meyer. As such, Roos's position at the SABC became meaningless and Meyer finally discharged him in 1961. The position of general director simply fell away and Meyer (chief Broeder, Nazi sympathiser, possible ex-spy and PR officer for Rembrandt) now ruled supreme, taking an iron-fist approach to all broadcasting matters.

Divisions between church and state

By the early 1960s the Broederbond had control over huge swathes of South African political and cultural life. But there was one extra string to their ideological bow: the NG Kerk. In one way, the NGK acted for the National Party as the Congress of South African Trade Unions (COSATU) would act for the ANC. That is, they made sure their members voted the 'right' way.

The Broederbond was birthed in the radical Christian Nationalism of the NGK, and to begin with there was seemingly no ideological difference between the two. Dr Diederichs, opening the executive meeting of the Broederbond in 1945, read from the Bible, proclaiming that the executive committee of the Broederbond was 'an instrument appointed by the Almighty to sit in council and to show Afrikaners the way'.

The Broederbond was in many ways fused with the NG Kerk, with the likes of Rev. William Nicol being both its chairman (1924–25) and the moderator of the NG Kerk in the Transvaal. Nicol had also written an influential book called *The Righteousness of Racial Apartheid.*

In 1949, the NG Kerk's Synodal Commission report on race relations righteously defended apartheid legislation. Up until 1960 most of the NGK went along with this stance – apart for one man, Stellenbosch University professor of doctrine and ethics Ben Keet.

Die koeël is nie deur die kerk nie

Professor Ben Keet courageously declared that the Synod of 1949 had misunderstood the scriptures on the point of race. He argued that the 'mixed marriage' which the Holy Scriptures thought dangerous was between believers and non-believers, not between races. He also put it out there that the idea of racial 'impurity' was not sinful and, if it was, then the Afrikaners had been birthed in sin. The Chinese (whom the Bible did not mention once), on the contrary, were probably the most faithful of God's people.

Keet argued that the simple truth was that there were no pure races. As he said, Jesus Christ himself was not of pure Jewish origin. In Keet's view, diversity of race, nationality, language and culture was a gift of nature through which people should glorify God. This variety was the very hallmark of God's creation.

Professor Keet was what might be called a 'rank outsider', and his 'eccentric' views on racial and cultural diversity were simply ignored by the majority of the NG Kerk and its followers. But by 1960, and especially after the Sharpeville massacre, in which sixty-nine peaceful protestors were killed by the police, some of the church had started to feel uncomfortable with the heavy-handed tactics of the Broederbond-controlled National Party.

What was more, religious leaders within the NGK began to question the influence that the Broeders had over the church. The vast majority of the Broeders were not theologians and yet they had begun to control church doctrine – a control that was far more political than it was religious. As the NGK became more and more entwined in the Broederbond's system of state capture, so it began to lose its doctrinal independence, progressively becoming a political puppet.

In December of that year, many NG theologians attended a World Council of Churches conference in the Johannesburg suburb of Cottesloe. Some of them, it seems, were partly swayed by the theologically liberal concluding statement of the conference, which condemned apartheid. In response, the Broeders and their networks within the NGK stepped in to quell any dissent within the ranks of the church. As Hennie Serfontein (another journalist who took on the Broeders) pointed out, the engagement between the more liberal churches and the NG Kerk would result in most of these Dutch Reformed reformers getting 'cold feet' and returning to the conservative fold. This was after Broederbond chairman Dr Piet Meyer read them the riot act, warning them that the Broederbond would not tolerate their liberal sympathies.

But the more heavy-handed the Broederbond became with the church, the more one churchman began to doubt. And in true religious style, a twenty-two-year-old veteran of the Broederbond by the name of Reverend Beyers Naudé would have his 'road to Damascus' moment. It was a moment that would shake the Broederbond to the core and reveal the Broeders' true nature to the rest of South Africa.

Who will rid us of this troublesome Naudé?

Naudé's personal troubles began after the Cottesloe Consultation, when he started to ask himself one simple question: could a devout Christian also be a Broeder? Naudé decided to unburden himself (along with a treasure trove of secret Broederbond documents) to the theologian Professor Albert Geyser, who had already fallen foul of the Broederbond-controlled leadership of the NGK. He had been expelled from the church in May 1962 for putting forward the 'preposterous' idea that God's love knew no racial boundaries.

Prof. Geyser took photographs of the Broederbond documents Naudé had given him and leaked them to Sunday Times journalist Charles Bloomberg. Bloomberg recruited Hennie Serfontein to help him, and the Broederbond were given a bloody nose in the English press. These revelations exposed how members of the Broederbond had captured the state. The Broederbond's fightback would ultimately show just who and what sectors of the state they secretly controlled.

In May 1963, an article in the Sunday Times disclosed the Broederbond's campaign against the more verligte elements within the NGK. As Geyser would say, the minute he saw the documents he realised they were the proof that could be used to show that the Broederbond was using the church for its own set of political goals. With these and other revelations being splashed across the English press, the Broederbond snapped into action. Bloomberg, Serfontein,

Geyser and Naudé were subjected to a campaign of intimidation, receiving a barrage of death threats. Serfontein had his car tampered with. Bloomberg fled the country fearing for his life. Geyser had, of course, already been excommunicated, and Naudé would be both debarred from the church and later banned by the apartheid government. He was forced to live for many years under house arrest. Serfontein explained in his book on the Broederbond that he personally lived in a strange from of Afrikaner banishment, condemned as a traitor to his own people.

The Broederbond initially stated with no regard to Naude's leaking of papers that there had been a robbery and that the *Sunday Times* had acquired the papers through theft. One should also not forget that the Broederbond claimed at the time to be a harmless apolitical cultural organisation. But when the police arrived, darkening the doors of Naudé, Geyser and Serfontein, they were not all members of the robbery squad; some of them were from the feared Special Branch. As Geyser stated:

> Officers from the security police visited me on November 11. I answered their questions and in turn asked them if they were members of the Broederbond, which they denied. I asked them how a member of the Security Police fitted in with an investigation of a complaint of theft and burglary. They gave an evasive reply.[22]

The Security Branch's involvement in the case raised several red flags and the police commissioner and Broeder, Lieutenant General J.M. Keevy, offered a slightly confusing statement.

Verwoerd's old newspaper, the Broederbond-controlled *Die Transvaler*, quoted General Keevy as saying that Colonel 'Lang Hendrik' van den Bergh (a man who will make regular pernicious appearances in this book) acted in the capacity of an 'ordinary' policeman, and not as the head of the notorious Special Branch, when he questioned the likes of Geyser. This was perhaps akin to having Heinrich Himmler of the SS arriving at your front door to question you on the theft of your neighbour's bicycle. As these and other revelations unfolded, Japie Basson, a United Party member of Parliament, stated that the 'Special Branch police are becoming the Gestapo of South Africa'.

Another telling, and at the time truly astonishing, incident was to bring the Broederbond out of the shadows and right into the homes of millions of South

Africans. Piet Meyer, the chairman of the Broederbond and the head of the SABC, suddenly suspended radio services to take to the airwaves himself. He laid into Naudé, asking why he had never said anything against the Broederbond throughout his twenty-two-year membership of the organisation. Meyer then explained that:

> [m]embers of the Bond are Christians who do not regard themselves as better than others but who, on the grounds of ability and their undertaking to live in harmony with others, are prepared to sacrifice more, and work harder for the future of South Africa as a whole with its great variety of ethnic groups.[23]

He then went on to say (sounding very much like his close friend the then minister of finance Dr Diederichs) that members of the Broederbond worked 'without expecting honour or compensation and without striving for honoured positions or self-interest'. This from the man who reigned supreme at the SABC and had a penchant for fine art.

Meyer and the money

Piet Meyer became famous for his extravagances at the SABC. He is said to have spent R250 000 (R10.5 million today) on a party to open the new TV complex at the SABC. He also filled his offices with art and antiques and got the SABC restaurant decked out like a five-star hotel. As Wilkins and Strydom pointed out, all SABC spending was a closely kept secret under Meyer. The National Party simply refused to offer the public any information on the broadcaster's expenditure.

And then there was the time when the SABC bought Meyer's house in Emmarentia from him for R80 000 (R3.4 million today), 52 per cent more than its municipal evaluation. Despite having sold it to his employers, Meyer continued to live in the house until he retired.

Piet Meyer with his hero's moustache

The sudden takeover of the country's national broadcaster for a political message by the chairman of a secret cultural organisation was best summed up by the editor of the *Rand Daily Mail*, Lawrence Gandar, in his editorial on 22 November 1963:

> Has it struck you as odd that the SABC should interrupt its regular pro-
> grammes on both services to broadcast a summary of Rev Beyers Naudé's
> statement about the Broederbond documents followed by the furious reply
> of the Broederbond's executive committee?
>
> Do you think it remarkable that the chief of the security police should be
> investigating in person an allegation by the Broederbond of theft in connec-
> tion with these documents?
>
> Here is a clandestine political organisation, with no offices and no address,
> a completely faceless body except for piecemeal exposures in the press, sum-
> moning the assistance of the Police Force at the highest level because some of
> its circulars have been photographed and published. Here is the secret society
> apparently able to command time – at the shortest notice – on the National
> broadcasting network.
>
> Are we to assume that the security of the Broederbond is equated with
> the safety of the state?[24]

As the temperature rose over the seeming ease with which the Broederbond could use public organs such as the police and the SABC, Prime Minister Verwoerd desperately tried to skirt the issue in Parliament. Sir De Villiers Graaff, head of the official opposition, demanded a public inquiry. He argued that there should be an agreement on the commissioners and the terms of reference; that evidence should be given under oath; and that the inquiry should be public.

Verwoerd strangely agreed to De Villiers Graaff's request for an inquiry – so long as it also included investigations into the Freemasons, an obscure organi-sation called the Sons of England and the Anglo American Corporation. The two then went head-to-head in Parliament:

> SIR DE VILLIERS GRAAFF: I think it is necessary as regards the Broeder-
> bond and I think there is a prima facie case against the organisation.
> I do not think there is a prima facie case against the Freemasons or
> the Sons of England and I do not have enough knowledge to make a
> decision on the Anglo American Corporation. (*Laughter*)

DR VERWOERD: You don't dare propose such an investigation.

SIR DE VILLIERS GRAAFF: As regards the Freemasons, there are 38 books in the library and the Prime Minister can even buy a calendar of the meetings of their various lodges from the bookseller. I have sought in vain for such material on the Broederbond.[25]

Three months after this exchange, Verwoerd announced that he was now prepared to allow an inquiry into the Broederbond and that it would also include the Freemasons and the Sons of England (why he decided to drop Anglo American is not known). It should be pointed out that neither the Freemasons nor the Sons of England had been a recent source of public outcry, nor did they have any obvious connection to the government. In fact, an investigation into Anglo American's connection to and influence with the *Argus* and the South African Associated Newspapers may have been a closer like for like.

H.F. Verwoerd preaching to the converted

It is almost certain that Verwoerd decided on this course of action after a long consultation with his fellow Broeders. They, as much as he, decided on the terms and scope of the inquiry. And it was these terms and conditions that ultimately made the commission one of the greatest farces in South African history.

The secret commission investigates the secret society

Verwoerd demanded that the inquiry into secret organisations be held in secret and announced that it would be a one-man commission.

As De Villiers Graaff pointed out, there was a law prohibiting commissions being held in secret. Needing only a simple majority to change the law on this matter, the National Party quickly pushed through legislation to permit secret commissions of inquiry. As De Villiers Graaff also pointed out, the terms of reference for the commission were so ludicrously wide and diffuse as to include all kinds of acts which no organisation had been accused of. What was more, the terms of reference were framed to investigate whether the Broederbond (or any other secret organisation) was attempting to influence the government. This was the wrong way of framing it because the real issue was whether the Broederbond was the state itself. It was not a matter of whether the Broederbond was trying to capture the state, but whether the state had already been captured.

The farce continued with Appeal Court judge D.H. Botha being placed in charge of the commission. Botha, although not a proven member of the Broederbond, had been fast-tracked by the apartheid government into his position as a judge. He had been a civil servant and legal advisor to Minister Eben Dönges when he was minister of the interior. Dönges was certainly a Broeder and was responsible for some of apartheid's worst racial legislation. Judge Botha was, at the very least, a trusted pair of apartheid hands.

That said, it should be noted that some historians say that Botha did do his best in an almost impossible position. The absurdity of the whole process was ably expressed by Stanley Uys of the *Sunday Times*, who pointed out that Verwoerd had appointed a commission and a judge to look into a secret organisation of which Verwoerd himself was a high-ranking member. As Uys wrote: 'The Prime Minister should have recused himself from the whole situation. He should not have appointed the judge, defined the terms of reference, or stated the conditions under which the commission should operate.'[26] It all does sound a little familiar ...

Not surprisingly, the commission found very little. As most journalists closely associated with the Broederbond story noted, Judge Botha simply accepted the Broederbond's submissions without questioning them. What Botha did seem eager to express was the gratitude he felt towards the two men who assisted him in gathering the evidence. Mr J.P.J. Coetzer and Mr C.M. van Niekerk had, Botha said, 'displayed exceptional initiative in containing evidence relating to the commission's terms of reference. Without their assistance, it would not have been possible to complete the inquiry in the manner in which, and the time within which, it was carried out.'[27]

It almost goes without saying that Judge Botha's able helpers Coetzer and Van Niekerk (the secretary and the under-secretary of justice) were high-ranking members of the Broederbond.

And so ended another perfect piece of South African political disgrace. Little came from the commission other than it later being used to exonerate any malfeasance on the part of the Broederbond. Whenever issues arose with the

Broederbond, apartheid politicians would simply point out that an 'independent' commission had uncovered no wrongdoing. And Judge Botha would later claim that all accusations against the Broederbond were 'totally untrue'.[28]

The enemy within

The rocky road that the Broederbond encountered in the latter years of apartheid was not a result of political pressure from the liberal and left-wing elements in the country. These they almost entirely subverted via imprisonments, banning orders and wholesale state capture. The only thing that would harm them was that other plague within South African politics: factionalism. Infighting between the *verkramptes* and *verligtes* would undermine the Broederbond's almost indomitable position.

Another inbuilt inconsistency for Broederbond members was the one Anton Rupert and others began to face. The more successful their businesses became, the more they were thrown into a global economic world that was not wholly sold on Afrikaner nationalism and the brutal regime it condoned. Federale Mynbou too began to realise that they were better off teaming up with privately owned Anglo American (of all things!) than relying on the Broederbond to get tenders from the government. And, of course, chipping steadily away at it all was garden-variety financial corruption, which seems slowly but surely to have whittled away many an ideologue's belief in their cause.

The case of Broeder Diederichs

Dr Nico Diederichs, 'Dr Gold', was many things in his life: a Broederbonder, a Nazi-trained quisling or spy, a political theorist, a director of Rembrandt, a cabinet minister for sixteen years and, finally, state president from 1974 until 1978 (a mainly ceremonial position, but with powers of its own). Despite Diederichs's claims that the Afrikaner 'attached more weight to the spiritual than to the material' and that capitalism was simply a 'means' to political power and 'not an end', his life, maybe more than that of any other Broeder, was baptised in corruption.

Martin Welz, the journalist who perhaps knows most about Diederichs, told us that Diederichs had been kept out of J.G. Strydom's government in the 1950s because Strydom didn't like corruption. By the end of his life, Diederichs had seemingly amassed a private (accounted-for) fortune of over R25 million rand in today's terms.

After his death in 1978, he was linked to many dodgy and corrupt deals. One of his most well-known acts was buying a piece of land for R2 000 (R117 000 today) and selling it two years later for R125 000 (R6 million today) to a township-development property company called Glen Anil. As state president, he seems to have known that a seemingly worthless piece of land would soon be part of a development project. Some of the money he received in this deal was alleged to have been bribes paid to him by Glen Anil.

Diederichs also lucked out with the purchase of a farm near Hoedspruit. Soon after buying the farm in 1972, the land was conveniently required for a new air force base. Part of the farm was expropriated from him for what was reckoned at the time to be an extraordinarily large and undisclosed amount of money.

He was also implicated in a scandal involving the government-owned steel producer Iscor. According to Martin Welz, Diederichs, while minister of economic affairs and responsible for Iscor, had politically intervened in order to have Dr J.G. van der Merwe elected as vice-chairman of Iscor. Diederichs, it later turned out, was a partner in Van der Merwe's business that supplied sand to the foundries at Iscor. Van der Merwe was forced to resign when the scandal broke over his undeclared interest in the sand business, but he only admitted to Diederichs's involvement after the old Broederbonder's death.

In another event, which smacks of the infamous Arms Deal, a German construction company withdrew from a tender to build a dam project in Port Elizabeth in the 1950s, after Dr Diederichs demanded from them a personal 'commission' of R200 000 (about R20 million today) for his 'services' as agent between the company and the State Tender Board.

And then there was the matter of his infamous Swiss bank account. Rumours around Diederichs and his Swiss connections began at a Herstigte Nasionale Party (HNP) meeting in the mid-1970s. The HNP were like today's EFF to the ruling party, a splinter group of National Party Broederbonders that took with them a radical faction but also some insider knowledge of their estranged parent. According to the journalists Mervyn Rees and Chris Day, members of the HNP openly discussed that Diederichs had a Swiss bank account which had millions of taxpayer rands in it. The HNP's Jaap Marais, who had served as a National Party member of Parliament from 1958 to 1969, claimed such accounts were set up as a fail-safe plan for government officials in case of a hostile overthrow or revolution. He also went on to say that the account had been set up in Diederichs's name.

A similar story was told to Rees in 1980 by an Afrikaans Supreme Court judge named Joe Ludorf – the same judge who sentenced John Harris to death for the Johannesburg Station bombing. Harris was the only white political activist to be hanged during apartheid, so Ludorf was certainly no bleeding-heart liberal. But despite having certain Afrikaner apartheid allegiances, he was known for his independence (and for enjoying the odd drink). Ludorf told Rees that a trusted and very reliable source had informed him that a Swiss bank account with the account number 187-613-L1E was linked to Diederichs and held an amount of R28 million (R746 million today).

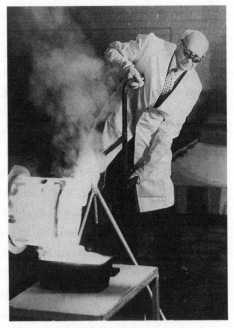

'Dr Gold' dishing out the source of his corruption

Diederichs had apparently set up the account with the help of a mysterious Mrs Patricia Owen. Owen, according to the *Sunday Express*, was a London-based woman with strong ties to 'influential people in South Africa'.[29] Police later went as far as flying to Europe to question Mrs Owen, but they could make no link to her and a Swiss bank account. Ludorf would go on to claim that Diederichs, when he was minister of finance, had agreed to move the sales of South African gold from London to Zurich on condition that he personally received ten US cents for every ounce of gold sold.

When Rees went to his editor Allister Sparks at the *Rand Daily Mail* with the story, Sparks asked him if the judge had been four sheets to the wind while relating this. Rees confessed that a few malt whiskies had been drunk but that the judge 'wasn't in his cups. He was very serious. Very concerned.'[30] Sparks would later go to Switzerland in 1980 and deposit fifty Swiss francs and later thirty Swiss francs into account 187-613-L1E, writing down the account holder's name as Dr Nico Diederichs. He discovered, unsurprisingly, that the account did indeed exist – at the Zurich head office of the Union Bank of Switzerland, no less.

Through his newspaper, Sparks managed to kick up such a stink about the matter that the government was forced to set up an inquiry. Advocate-General P.J. van der Walt was given the task of heading the investigation in 1981. Perhaps unsurprisingly, an Advocate P.J. van der Walt living in Pretoria in 1977 appears on the famous list of Broederbonders published by Wilkins and Strydom. When Van der Walt announced his findings, he stated that although the Swiss bank account 187-613-L1E did exist, it belonged to Mr David Mort, a Cape Town–based businessman. The fact that it was a South African who was linked to the account should have sounded alarm bells, but Van der Walt instead stated that it was a 'flight of imagination' and 'completely untrue' that Diederichs had salted away millions of dollars into this account.

As it turned out, David Mort was a little more than just a 'Cape Town–based businessman'. Mort was a friend of Diederichs 'and a former business associate of his family'.[31] He was also in business with Diederichs's delinquent son, Nico Junior. Mort, it was reported at the time, was involved in property 'in the new coloured township of Mitchell's Plain and also the agent for the sale of property in the now demolished District Six'.[32] What was also uncovered was that the Mrs Patricia Owen, who was linked to Diederichs and the Swiss account, was Mort's cousin.

Mort claimed at the inquiry that he had initially been unaware of the account's existence (in his own name!) and that an inheritance had been placed in it from his grandmother. It was also discovered by Van der Walt that Mort had not declared the account to the Reserve Bank and had as such contravened exchange-control regulations. Van der Walt, rather predictably, decided not to prosecute Mort. Another red flag was that Van der Walt could find no record in account 187-613-L1E of Sparks's deposits of fifty and thirty Swiss francs, so a redacted version of the account's statements had clearly been given to him. Sparks would publish proof of the actual deposit slips on the front page of *Rand Daily Mail*. (This same account was linked to the murders of Robert and Jeanne-Cora Smit, which you will read about in Chapter 9.)

Years later, Sparks would suggest to Dullah Omar, the minister of justice under Nelson Mandela, that the ANC government should find out just who account 187-613-L1E belonged to and what money was there. Sparks seems to have believed that there could be something in the region of $3 billion of South African government money in this and perhaps other accounts. Minister Omar by all accounts liked the idea and asked Sparks for the details. Sparks sent him a letter on 7 October 1997 with all that he knew about the account. When he followed up some time later, Omar told him that Mandela did not want to pursue the matter because he did not wish to aggravate race relations any further. And that is where the story of Diederichs's slush fund seems to have ended.

Blood is thicker than water

But, for all this, when the great reckoning of Diederichs's South African estate was totalled up, he turned out to be insolvent. It seems Helen Zille was wrong in one regard when she wrote in the *Rand Daily Mail* at the time of his death that 'his economic brilliance brought him recognition from all over the world'.[33] His personal finances were far from brilliant.

As Martin Welz revealed, the man who had once been on the board of the Rembrandt Group and the beneficiary of many a dodgy deal had one enormous economic *kameeldoring* in his side – his son, Nico Junior. And shame, the poor oke ... As one of Klein Nico's drinking buddies from the Clifton Hotel put it, Diederichs Jr. struggled at the best of times to form complete sentences. Over the years, the 'good doctor' seems to have loaned his son R850 000 (about R45 million today), of which Klein Nico managed to pay back precisely zilch. In comparison, Zuma seems to have had much better luck with his sons.

Even after this insane loan from daddy, Klein Nico did not have two brass farthings to show for himself. This despite being on more company boards than he had brain cells and having business interests in hotels, diamond companies and property developments in Spain, Bantry Bay, Mossel Bay and in 'coloured townships'. Try as he may, not one of Nico's endeavours seemed to make money. Instead, they all racked up huge loses and massive debts.

But as long as politically important daddy lived, money was abundantly poured into Nico Junior's businesses. Sadly, when all the creditors came for their pound of flesh after Diederichs's death, they discovered that even Dr Gold could not cover it all. The estate was left with nothing, and many of his and his son's debts were left unpaid. Mrs Diederichs went on record offering the losers in all this corruption and wastefulness a tearful apology, saying that her husband had 'served his country without giving precedence to his own interest'.

It seems that many of our more recent politicians have followed this creditable (and debitable) pursuit.

CHAPTER 8

THE
INFORMATION
SCANDAL

Financing Fake News
1974–1978

*Patriotism is the last refuge of the scoundrel. – **Samuel Johnson***

Connie Mulder, B.J. Vorster and Eschel Rhoodie preparing to cook the books

IMAGINE, IF YOU WILL, THE 1970s. A world before Twitter bots, where PR companies like Bell Pottinger were not even a glint in the Guptas' eyes. Before Vladimir Putin and Facebook, before newspapers were bought by politicians or big business. A place where the media lived in a pre-Zumarian golden age, before ANN7, *The New Age* and Independent Newspapers under Iqbal Survé. A time where you could trust a newspaper to deliver the truth to your doorstep.

Wait a moment! If this book has taught you one thing, it should be that the media has always been bought, undermined and controlled by politicians or the wealthy. And in the 1970s the media – in South Africa and internationally – would come under the threat of a new and particularly nefarious spell: the dark arts of apartheid's Department of Information.

Before 1976 and the Soweto uprising, the National Party had been pretty effective at dealing with its political dissidents. Leading figures in the ANC and Pan Africanist Congress (PAC) had been imprisoned, exiled or banned; Steve Biko had been banned and was later killed; and even liberals like Eddie Daniels and Randolph Vigne were either rotting in apartheid jails or living in exile in the UK. There were still, however, two major thorns in Pretoria's arse. One was that apartheid and its brutal and degrading actions had developed a distinctly bad reputation overseas. And another was that unsightly leaky wound called the English-language press, which continued to seep out stories of apartheid's atrocities onto the seat of South Africa's supposedly clean white pants.

Just how to deal with these two problems was the issue of the day. Long before the Guptas went to Bell Pottinger, two men named Connie Mulder and Eschel Rhoodie entered the fray. Connie Mulder, the minister of information, was *the* political heavyweight of his time. Leader of the Transvaal section of the National Party, Mulder was widely touted as the next prime minister of the country. Rhoodie, meanwhile, was a power-hungry ideologue who was hell-bent on 'improving' apartheid's reputation internally and externally at any cost – and boy, would it cost. It was these two men who, as the *Rand Daily Mail*'s Allister Sparks put it, took control of 'one of the most ambitious propaganda projects ever devised by any government'.[1] And one of the most morally and financially corrupt.

In fact, if it had not been for one person code-named 'Myrtle', three journalists, a judge and the second thoughts of a man called Retief van Rooyen, who knows just what road South Africa may have followed? As Van Rooyen told the journalist Mervyn Rees, while working with Mulder and Rhoodie, 'I had put my head through the door of political dictatorship and what I saw there horrified the hell out of me.'

Some years later, Rhoodie openly admitted that he, Mulder and General 'Lang Hendrik' van den Bergh of the Bureau of State Security (BOSS) had agreed that once they took over from B.J. Vorster, they would move the country towards a 'benevolent' or '*verligte*' dictatorship.

Just how effective these men had been in their propaganda war is shown by the result of the 1977 snap election.

The call for the election took everybody by surprise, coming eighteen months before it was legally required. Realising the strength of his position, Prime Minister Vorster took the gap, supported by his three closest allies: Mulder, Rhoodie and Van den Bergh. With these men all pulling in the same direction, the National Party rode to its greatest electoral victory ever, winning 134 seats out of 165, giving the Nats an insurmountable hold over Parliament with 81 per cent of the seats in the house. One of the most eyebrow-raising elements of the victory was just how many English-speakers had thrown in their lot with the NP. As the journalists Mervyn Rees and Chris Day (who were instrumental in uncovering what became known as the Information Scandal) would say, 'the newly launched *Citizen* newspaper played a significant role in this phenomenon'.[2]

The paper curtain

But we are getting ahead of ourselves. The story really begins with a meeting held in Prime Minister Vorster's office in February 1974. Present were Mulder, Rhoodie, Vorster and the now all-too-familiar figure of Dr Gold, the minister of finance. Mulder had been moving up the ranks of the National Party, holding all the while to the coat-tails of the Broederbond faction – the same faction that had supported Verwoerd's and B.J. Vorster's rise to power. And with him he had brought a man who was widely considered to be one of the true masters of the malediction of propaganda, the wiry and charming Dr Eschel Rhoodie.

Eschel Rhoodie, the fake news führer

Eschel Rhoodie, the papier-mâché Mephistopheles

Rhoodie is a true outlier in the history of apartheid. He was born in the small town of Caledon in 1933, but we know little to nothing of his upbringing. It is a marker of the time that every person who wrote about him noted his complexion and hinted strongly that pure Aryan Afrikaner he was not. 'Dark', 'swarthy', 'Mediterranean' and 'Arabic-looking' are some of the ways people described him. The mysterious woman code-named 'Myrtle' revealed that his nickname at school had been 'k*****' and that Prime Minister Vorster referred to him and his Department of Information as the 'k***** taxi'.

Rhoodie was unique within the National Party. For one thing, he was not a member of the Broederbond. For another, his solutions for the future of white-supremacist South Africa were a strange mix of cosmopolitanism, fascist ideology and Machiavellian backroom deals. Ruthless, charming and highly intelligent, he was a modern Mephistopheles; a hollow man capable of actions others would baulk at, not to mention acts of staggering and alarming imagination. Although those in the apartheid establishment may have questioned his racial origins, they clearly recognised his abilities. General Van den Bergh referred to him as 'one of the most intelligent men I have ever met'.[3]

In 1969 a young Rhoodie had published an influential book titled *The Paper Curtain* through Voortrekkerpers. In it he argued a point that should not be unfamiliar to the oversensitive conspiracy theorists out there. Rhoodie claimed that South Africa was surrounded not by a USSR-created 'Iron Curtain', but by a curtain of paper – a drapery created by an international media conspiracy that purposefully depicted South Africa in a bad light. There was, he claimed, a clear journalistic bias against the apartheid regime. And with this came certain buzz phrases, such as 'double standards' and 'journalistic racisms'.

What Rhoodie meant by this was that other African countries with similarly deplorable human rights records were not as harshly judged in the media as South Africa. Bizarrely, it did not seem to register with Rhoodie (and many other whites) that saying that other countries were just as bad was in fact an admission that apartheid was pretty damned abhorrent. Nevertheless, the powerful Mulder was deeply impressed by *The Paper Curtain* and befriended Rhoodie, promoting him up the ranks of his Department of Information. By 1974, Rhoodie was the bureaucratic head of Mulder's department and the two were able to sit down with Vorster and Diederichs to discuss a broad and sweeping counter-propaganda offensive. It was an attempt to win the hearts and minds of the West and to persuade South African English-speakers that the National Party was actually quite lekker.

Mulder and Rhoodie's proposal to Diederichs and Vorster was pitch perfect. No doubt the two old Nazi sympathisers were saddened to hear Rhoodie inform them that South Africa had the worst reputation in the world after Nazi Germany. But according to Rhoodie, who had a gift for exaggeration, Diederichs and Vorster simply marvelled at the ideas he put forward. In fact, they lamented that they had not been placed before them ten years before.

Then, Diederichs asked the multimillion-dollar question: how much would this cost? Rhoodie recalled that Diederichs was standing at the window at the time and that he told the old Broederbonder that he had better sit down. 'I want R25 million a year [R1.5 billion today] over a five-year period.' Diederichs simply responded that his Treasury was 'prepared to provide the money'.[4] Dr Gold then set about masterminding the financing of the project, making sure that the money would go through then minister of defence P.W. Botha's secret Defence Special Account, which could not be scrutinised by Parliament. The money could then circulate through the Swiss bank accounts so loved by Diederichs before being made available to a network of frontmen and front companies locally and across the globe.

Rhoodie, at the age of forty, was now the sole arbitrator over a secret government fund worth R7.5 billion in today's terms. (Obviously, the urge to enrich himself was great, but more about this later.) And with this money now freely available, Rhoodie set about finding out just how internationally unpopular South Africa really was. For this project he employed the New York–based PR company Richard Manville Inc. at the cost of R280 000 (R15.1 million today) to run an international survey to establish Western public opinion.

They discovered that South Africa's reputation ranked second-worst in the world, worse than both China and the USSR. The survey also proved that Rhoodie's argument in *The Paper Curtain* was wrong. One African country did have a worse reputation than apartheid South Africa's – Idi Amin's Uganda. Amin, it was rumoured, had eaten some of his enemies, and he claimed to have chopped his political opponents' heads off and had them stored in his fridge.

Advertising apartheid

Now that he knew just how low South Africa had sunk in terms of global public opinion, Rhoodie would go on to create fake pressure groups, like the UK-based

'The Club of Ten'. Despite the name, there were not ten people in the club, but two: a badly duped and attention-seeking ex-judge from the UK named Gerald Sparrow, and Charalampos Nichas, a Greek potato farmer who had emigrated to South Africa with eighty cents in his pocket. Using money that came from a secret Swiss bank account, Sparrow placed pro-South African adverts in papers such as the *Guardian*, the *Observer* and the *New York Times*. Almost all the major papers in the UK, after establishing the amount of money Sparrow was willing to pay them, clambered over each other to offer the best coverage available. Only London's newspaper 'powerhouse' the *Church Times*, with its tiny circulation of Anglican observers, refused apartheid's clandestine money and told Sparrow to take a hike.

Rhoodie would later claim to have had one Conservative and two Labour members of the UK Parliament in his pay. He also boasted to have affected election results in the US. Two anti-apartheid senators, John Tunney of California and Dick Clark of Iowa, who had outspoken views on the war in Angola, were targeted by South African frontmen with Rhoodie's money. Much to the surprise of most political pundits, they both lost their re-election bids to Republican senators – Tunney in 1976 and Clark in 1978.

In 1976, Rhoodie employed the New York–based Bell Pottinger of its day, a PR firm called Sydney S. Baron Co., for a yearly fee of $365 000 (R29 million today). By 1979 that amount had escalated to $650 000 (R40 million today) a year. (Sydney Baron was also being paid a yearly fee in 1976 by Kaiser Matanzima's newly 'independent' Transkei which was, in real terms, another payment from the South African government.)

With this dirty money bulging from their pockets, Sydney S. Baron Co. employed the services of Andrew Hatcher, a man who had been the first black assistant press secretary in John F. Kennedy's White House. Hatcher sent stories to various publications extolling the wonders of South Africa. He even went so far as to appear on a debate on NBC's *Today* show on 23 June 1976 – one week after hundreds of schoolchildren had been gunned down in Soweto – to praise South Africa's position on social change. In another interview he stated that 'the blacks of South Africa are not capable of running the country at this time'.[5] In the same television debate, his stunned opponent, a white anti-apartheid activist by the name of George Houser, replied, '[T]o see a black man defending South Africa for money is not unlike seeing a Jew hired by the Nazis.'[6]

Paper money

But this was all small fry compared to the project Rhoodie had in mind. What he *really* planned to do was to buy and control large sections of the Western press itself. He also wanted to control the local English-language media with its broadly liberal pro-democracy elements. With this in mind he would gather around him a literal gallery of right-wing rogues, including an American called John McGoff and a man who might be familiar to rugby enthusiasts, the late Louis Luyt.

Citizen Luyt

Louis Luyt was born into a poor Afrikaans family in Britstown in the Karoo. He played provincial rugby for the Orange Free State and became a self-made millionaire via the fertiliser industry. Despite having no discernible neckline, he was neck-deep in the Information Scandal from beginning to end. But as Max du Preez pointed out, Luyt was the one person to come out of the scandal almost entirely unscathed.

Luyt once told a journalist that he'd met Rhoodie during the Angolan war, when Luyt claimed to have been acting as a go-between for the apartheid regime and other African leaders. Described as a 'megalomaniac' with a painfully sensitive ego (respray him in orange and a resemblance to Donald Trump might suddenly

Louis Luyt singing from his own hymn sheet

appear), Luyt was susceptible to extreme mood swings and general paranoia. He regularly had the phones of both his friends and enemies tapped.

Most people know him now as the man who was president of the South African Rugby Football Union (SARFU) at the time of the 1995 World Cup. He can be seen in many of the trophy-lifting photos behind Nelson Mandela and François Pienaar. In what should have been one of the great moments of his life, he stood up at the final dinner of the World Cup and gave a speech which displayed a completely unrepentant attitude towards apartheid. He was booed and jeered off the stage. Pienaar told a journalist that he was 'ashamed' of Luyt's behaviour.

Luyt had always been involved in dodgy rugby dealings, illegally paying amateur players money. Nelson Mandela finally ordered a commission of inquiry into Luyt's SARFU in 1997 after minister of sport Steve Tshwete declared that the 'administration of rugby is defective, dictatorial and, perhaps, even corrupt'.[7] In return, Luyt accused Mandela of lying and bragged that he would 'hammer' him in court. In the ensuing legal battle (which bizarrely saw a sitting president forced to give testimony), the apartheid-era judge William de Villiers found against Mandela. De Villiers was lambasted in the press for stating that Madiba's 'overall demeanour is, to my mind, subject to material criticism'.[8] When the Constitutional Court overturned De Villiers's judgment, stating that Mandela had applied his mind correctly, Luyt's career in rugby was effectively over.

He then went into politics, teaming up with Rocky Malebane-Metsing (whose coup attempt in Bophuthatswana in 1987 features in Chapter 11) to form the Federal Alliance. Luyt became a member of Parliament in 1999. Strangely, Thabo Mbeki's ANC appointed him onto the Judicial Services Commission ahead of the Democratic Party's stalwart Douglas Gibson. Tony Leon, head of the DP, questioned whether Luyt was a 'fit and proper person' to be given that responsibility. A year later, Luyt's Federal Alliance merged with Leon's DP and they rebranded as the Democratic Alliance!

Rhoodie's idea was to buy out the South African Associated Newspapers (SAAN), which was, in 1976, in serious financial difficulties. SAAN, which owned the *Rand Daily Mail*, the *Sunday Times* and the *Sunday Express*, was the bastion of the liberal English-speaking press. And with Allister Sparks and Rex Gibson as editors, SAAN boasted two of the most vocal dissenting public voices in the country at the time.

To buy out SAAN without it looking like a government takeover, Rhoodie needed a wealthy businessman to act as his front. For this he selected Luyt. About R9 million (R380 million today) was sent from a Swiss account to a front company called Thor Communications. Thor, which was essentially just an office with a telephone, had as it directors Andre Pieterse, a film producer, and Retief van Rooyen, a lawyer whose only claim to notoriety by this time was that he'd represented the police in the farcical inquest into the murder of Steve Biko. From Thor's account the money was sent on to Luyt's Volkskas account.

Never one for reserve, Luyt soon began shooting his mouth off about his bid to take over one of the cornerstones of the English-language press. This drove the journalists at SAAN into a frenzy, and when asked by reporters what his intentions were, Luyt crowed that he planned to make the English more objective in their reporting.[9]

The game was up and now everybody knew that a very hostile takeover was being planned by Luyt and the strange dark forces that surrounded him. Despite another R3 million being spirited into Luyt's account via Switzerland, the owners of SAAN managed to stave off Luyt's takeover bid with money secretly raised by the Syfrets Trust (with the help of Harry Oppenheimer). And Sparks and Gibson were allowed to continue their work.

Editorial interference at the *Rand Daily Mail*

Allister Sparks pointed out that the Syfrets Trust, which represented the majority of SAAN's shareholders, had themselves intervened editorially in the *Rand Daily Mail* in the 1960s. Clive Corder, chairman of Syfrets, had ordered that the editor of the paper, Lawrence Gandar, be fired. This was after Gandar criticised the leader of the opposition, Sir De Villiers Graaff, for his inability to effectively oppose apartheid. Corder was incensed by Gandar's 'extreme' liberal position (Corder just so happened to have been Sir De Villiers Graaff's best man ...). He claimed in his memoirs that he got rid of Gandar because his editorials were 'not in the national interest'.[10]

With Luyt's botched attempt at a hostile takeover now sunk, Rhoodie decided instead to set up an English-language rival to the *Rand Daily Mail*. Although Rhoodie prided himself on thinking up names for this project (The Club of Ten, Thor Communications, and the like), he and Luyt came up with a simple translation of the well-known Broederbond-controlled rag *Die Burger*. The paper would be called *The Citizen* and Louis Luyt would be its owner. With R13 million (R558 million today) now sitting in Luyt's Volkskas account, it was agreed that Luyt would take the money and place it in an interest-bearing financial 'pool'. He would then dish it out to the pro-government newspaper when required.

On 2 April 1976, Luyt accordingly signed an agreement printed on a Department of Information letterhead and stamped 'Top Secret'. The agreement stated that Luyt would be the owner and chairman of *The Citizen*, but that he and its employees would be bound by a very particular set of guidelines. These were:

The name of the paper may not be changed;

the paper shall undertake to publish nothing that will endanger the political, social, economic position of the white population of the Republic of South Africa;

the paper shall not tolerate communism or further its aims;

the paper shall not undertake or publish anything that will endanger the constitutional[ly] chosen Government of the Republic of South Africa;

the paper supports the broad objectives of the present government in respect of separate political development of the black and the white population of the RSA, as well as anti-communism policy and security laws of the RSA.

All chief sub-editors, assistant and deputy editors, all editors, political columnists, correspondents and leader writers are a) obliged to keep the editorial character and to sign and enforce it and b) will be obliged to apply in letter and spirit this charter and any other editorial guidelines in this contract agreement, in the subbing and publication of the *Citizen*.[11]

With the agreement in place, *The Citizen* hit the ground running with the trendiest advertising campaign imaginable – the sponsorship of the South African 1976 Grand Prix held at Kyalami. (Formula 1 was to them what cricket sponsorship was to the Guptas – remember Sahara Park Newlands, Sahara Stadium Kingsmead and Sahara Oval St George's, all named after their computer company?) The naming rights of the 1976 Grand Prix would cost Rhoodie's department R220 000 (R9.3 million today), and *The Citizen*'s advertising at the Grand Prix continued until at least 1978 (at what cost per year is not known).

But there was a significant problem. The senior citizen at the paper, Luyt, proved to be of the non-law-abiding variety. By early 1977 the paper was running into serious financial problems. In April 1977, Luyt finally came, cap in hand, to Rhoodie. In a room in the Johannesburg Holiday Inn, he confessed that problems were arising because he'd invested the money not into a financial pool but rather into his own ailing fertiliser company. He was now finding it 'hard to release' finances in order to carry out the day-to-day running of the paper.

Rhoodie was flabbergasted. How could Luyt have put the money into his own company? Things became heated and Luyt is said to have become particularly abusive towards the spin doctor, sarcastically calling him 'James Bond'. In a moment straight out of *The Apprentice*, he shouted at Rhoodie: 'I hire people like you, I don't work for them.' And – seemingly forgetting the huge stash of government funds he'd placed in his own company – he shouted, 'I am doing these things for nothing for you.'[12] Later, he told the various members of the department, to whom he owed R13 million, to 'bugger off'.

Rhoodie could not just walk away from the project. Luyt not only owned a paper he could not afford but he also owed the government R13 million plus interest. And then there was Mulder, who knew that this total pig's ear of a situation could ruin his plans of becoming the next prime minister. Somehow (and it is not quite clear how), Luyt managed to raise a further 'loan' amounting to nearly R3 million from an overseas Swiss source. Although the money bore all the hallmarks of the Department of Information, Luyt would later claim that the 'loan' was in fact raised off his own bat and that it was therefore not owed to the government. Rhoodie also organised Luyt an overdraft facility of R7 million (R296 million today) at Volkskas. Our old 'friend' General Van den Bergh, it was later discovered, was the man in charge of paying government money into this facility.

Rhoodie would, however, slowly learn the maxim 'Better never than Luyt'. Luyt's friendship with Rhoodie was now badly damaged and would never recover. This was problematic because Luyt was, by then, wedded to Rhoodie's local and international scheming. Luyt was the chairman of the Committee for Fairness in Sport (CFFS), another of Rhoodie's PR schemes. Rhoodie alleged in his book, *The Real Information Scandal*, that Luyt and the golfer Gary Player were tasked with helping to improve South Africa's racist sporting image. As we know, Rhoodie had previously handed Luyt the responsibility of placing pro-apartheid adverts in Britain, New Zealand, Australia and America. Luyt was also, according to slightly dodgy UK judge Gerald Sparrow, affiliated to The Club of Ten, which did a similar job of placing political adverts in the international press. We don't know if anyone was paid for the 'services' Rhoodie claimed the two had provided. But one thing that is known is that Sparrow never did anything for free.

In Luyt's own testimony to Judge Mostert's commission of inquiry into exchange-control violations, he did stick to the basic facts stated above. He was at the same time not entirely truthful. He did admit under questioning that he had already put the money into his own company after the SAAN affair. This was before any agreement had been made with Rhoodie and Mulder as to how the money was to be used. Interestingly, Luyt made the deeply disingenuous claim that 'the higher the circulation [of *The Citizen*], the higher the costs. We got a very good printing contract, but in spite of that it became more expensive.'[13]

This was not the whole truth. The number of copies sold under Luyt's watch was always a bone of contention. In fact, Luyt was engaged in an act of deceit that would send the price of the venture skyrocketing. Luyt regularly stated that *The Citizen*'s daily circulation was 90 000 – much larger than any Afrikaans newspaper and approaching that of the highest-selling daily, the *Rand Daily Mail*. This was simply not believed by other editors. After journalists began nosing around *The Citizen*'s printing depot, they discovered the truth: 30 000 copies of the daily print run were being loaded onto a truck. When the truck was tailed, journalists discovered that it was being driven ninety kilometres out of the city to a farm called Kromdraai, or Crooked Corner. The farm certainly was just that: it turned out to be a wastepaper depot owned by none other than Louis Luyt. His readership figures were a complete lie. A third of the cost of the printing was simply being dumped on his own farm. No wonder he couldn't make a profit.

After selling the paper to the Broederbond-controlled Perskor, *The Citizen* actually did go on to become one of the most successful newspapers in South

Tony Grogan has a field day with the events at Luyt's Crooked Corner

African history. (Clearly, not all English-speakers were keen on the liberal offerings of the *Rand Daily Mail*, which went out of business in the mid-1980s.) By 1980, Luyt seems to have had paid back about R9 million of the R13 million 'loan' he had received from the government. But he was, rather like Van der Stel, Somerset and, later, Zuma and others, given a special dispensation not to pay back all the money. This was because he claimed that nearly R3 million of the cash that went into *The Citizen* was his 'own money'. By this stage, however, quite what was his money and what was the government's was difficult to differentiate. And he certainly never paid back any interest.

And then there was the matter of Luyt's aeroplane. For reasons that remain obscure, Rhoodie and the Department of Information paid R1.5 million for a half share in the plane through the mysterious front company Thor Communications (with funds from a Swiss bank account, of course). When Luyt finally sold the plane, he paid only two-thirds of that amount back to Thor. Just what all of these transactions were about is difficult to say. But Luyt's plane was part of the larger story. In 1976 it carried a large group of holiday-goers to the Seychelles, including Rhoodie. The holiday was, of course, all paid for by the taxpayer.

Although the press at the time claimed Rhoodie's trip to the Indian Ocean islands was a lavish holiday, there were some serious reasons for going to the Seychelles. One was to get Luyt's private jet registered there so that members of the Department of Information could move around the world more easily. Planes registered in South Africa were finding landing rights a growing problem. What was more, according to the editor Rex Gibson, Rhoodie had 'carried with him not only a suitcase of beach clothes but a bagful of bribe money to secure South African interests'.[14]

South Africa, the Seychelles and the 'Mad Hoare'

By 1976, with the civil war in Rhodesia escalating and the Portuguese having recently left their colonies of Angola and Mozambique, South Africa was fast becoming internationally isolated. Thanks no doubt to Rhoodie's bags of cash, it found a friend in Sir James Mancham, the president of the newly independent Seychelles.

However, Mancham was ousted in a left-wing coup led by France-Albert René in 1977. This created problems for South Africa, which was fast running out of sanctions-busting buddies. In 1981, P.W. Botha's government decided to launch a clandestine coup of their own in the Seychelles. To do this they employed the services of the famous English mercenary 'Mad Mike' Hoare, who lived in Natal. On 25 November 1981, Hoare took forty-five mercenaries disguised as members of a drinking club called the Ancient Order of Froth Blowers to the Seychelles on a commercial flight. Customised bags had been made, complete with beer-drinking stickers and false bottoms housing AK-47s.

While going through customs, a mercenary panicked when he saw one of the bags being inspected. With that he assembled his AK-47 and opened fire. A six-hour gun battle ensued at the airport and Hoare and his men decided to retreat to the runway when an armoured car joined the fray. Leaving behind five men and a female accomplice, Hoare boarded and hijacked an Air India jet, forcing the pilots at gunpoint to fly back to Durban.

Having no landing rights in Durban, the plane's arrival (with forty armed mercenaries on board, *nogal*) created an international incident. Prime Minister Botha denied that South Africa had had anything to do with the coup attempt and had Hoare and his men arrested. They were tried and sentenced to various lengths of imprisonment. Most of them were released early. Hoare was sentenced to ten years and served nearly three of them, after which he received a presidential pardon. Four of the six people left behind in the Seychelles were tried and sentenced to death. All six were, however, eventually returned to South Africa after Botha's government paid President René a ransom of $3 million (R148 million today).

But Luyt, his aeroplane and *The Citizen* were simply the tip of the iceberg. Rhoodie had much grander ambitions. He wanted to control the Western media itself. Perhaps one of the largest stones in the apartheid veldskoen was the *Washington Post*, which had rated Vorster the world's eighth-worst human being of the year 1975. Rhoodie's solution was simple: buy the paper's competitor the *Washington Star* and install *Citizen*-like editorial control. For this task Rhoodie befriended an American right-wing newspaper owner by the name of John McGoff. The Department of Information sent McGoff $10 million to buy the paper. But, alas, the American was outbid by a North Korean religious cult leader.

Like the Matanzimas of the Transkei, Rhoodie then discovered that if you try the same trick twice you might just end up with the same result. According to Rhoodie, McGoff then told him that he had bought the *Sacramento Union* newspaper in California with the interest that had accrued from the $10-million 'loan'. This was a lie. Like Luyt, McGoff had used up all the money by buying the *Sacramento Union* and investing the rest in his own companies. McGoff, however, did prove a little more reliable in another venture. With money from the Department of Information he managed to buy out a controlling share of United Press International Television News (UP-ITN), the second-biggest producer and distributor of news films in the world. McGoff then placed a close associate of his, a man by the name of Clarence Rhodes (no relation to Cecil), in the position of CEO in London.

With this network in place, Rhoodie managed to get news programmes covering the 'independence' of both the Transkei and Bophuthatswana distributed all over the world. There were also films made and distributed concerning the strategic importance of the South African Defence Force. Rhoodie claimed, though, that his most epic achievement while effectively pulling the levers at UP-ITN was getting Clarence Rhodes to do an interview with Prime Minister Vorster.

According to Rhoodie (who is perhaps not the most trustworthy of sources), he wrote both the questions for Rhodes and the answers for Vorster. The interview, which was distributed in over ninety countries, featured Vorster discussing South African troops in Angola for the first time. Vorster claimed that they were there for purely defensive purposes. He would go on to say that if the Russian-backed MPLA won the civil war in Angola, it would be the direct result of the fact that 'the free world has shirked its duty (if I can call it that way and I make no apologies for using that word) it has shirked its duty to give the FNLA and UNITA a chance to fight the superior weapons by supplying them with weapons.'[15] This was precisely the kind of message Rhoodie had wanted to spread, and it was a narrative that many in the West took up.

While the UP-ITN executives in London were said not to have been impressed by the interview, company representatives in both America and the UK strongly denied that they were in any way being clandestinely financed by South African government money. They would end up with egg on their faces when Judge Mostert revealed the stark reality of the origins of McGoff's funds. After these revelations, ITN bought McGoff's share in UP-ITN. McGoff would later face an investigation by the US Department of Justice, which charged him with accepting millions of dollars from the South African government without being registered as a 'foreign agent'. The case was later dismissed when the statute of limitations ran out.[16]

Fools and other people's money

Although Rhoodie was very pleased with the news films UP-ITN made, he would suffer one of his more epic fails with another film-based venture. Rhoodie, it seems, had an Orwellian dream for films black audiences in South Africa could watch. He also had plans about where black people could view them. The films he planned to make would be propaganda-heavy and shown in government-built facilities in the townships. Black people should, Rhoodie believed, be steered away from American cosmopolitan ideas and redirected to 'superheroes' set against 'ethnic backgrounds'.[17] Remember, this was at a time when television was only just being introduced into the country. Few whites, let alone any black people, had a 'tube'.

In order to build these township cinemas, Rhoodie formed a front company called the Film Trust Plaza with two of his favourite frontmen, Van Zyl Alberts and Andre Pieterse (who was already a director of Thor Communications). Rhoodie gave both these men interest-free loans of R825 000 (R35 million today) in order to begin building the cinemas. But Pieterse instead put his money into a film that he wanted to produce starring Irish actor Richard Harris (a famous drinker and the man who would later play Albus Dumbledore in the first two *Harry Potter* movies).

Golden Rendezvous was shot in South Africa and not only went $1.5 million (R111 million today) over budget but also proved to be a complete financial and critical flop. The *Guardian* in Britain, perhaps making up for having run propaganda adverts for apartheid, called it 'nothing but dross'.[18] Pieterse would go on to blame Harris's drinking problems for the budget troubles. Amusingly, Harris did not deny that he had drunk throughout the film, but in mitigation he stated that 'everybody on that film was drinking, we were all so fucking miserable'.[19] Pieterse tried to have Harris arrested when he was next back in South Africa, but, probably realising the international fallout that would come with arresting a famous international actor, the police backed off. Harris told the press that Pieterse still owed him $50 000.

Flopping on both sides of apartheid

In 2011, Pieterse wrote and produced a film on the life of Winnie Mandela starring American actress and singer Jennifer Hudson in the title role. Ed Gibbs of the *Guardian* gave the film two stars, saying that it was a historically inaccurate 'sugar-coated, decidedly episodic and selective affair: one that plays out much like a primetime telemovie'.[20] Winnie Madikizela-Mandela was quoted as being deeply unhappy with the production. What other people thought of the film is hard to tell, seeing as so few went to see it: it made a paltry $80 634 at the box office.

The other man to receive money to build cinemas, Van Zyl Alberts, also seems to have put at least some of the money Rhoodie gave him into a film, this one called *Tigers Don't Cry*. It also had a famous actor, Anthony Quinn, in the starring role. It too was shot in South Africa but was considered too awful for release. According to the journalists Rees and Day, Van Zyl Alberts could not pay Quinn and Quinn finally accepted as payment a flat in Clifton in a block called Valhalla overlooking the beach. Nine of these heavenly Valhalla flats had, it turned out, been bought with government funds by Rhoodie's front company Thor Communications.

This is where the sorry film saga ended, with millions of government rands down the drain, complete duds for films, and not a single sod of soil turned in the building of the township cinemas. But perhaps that was just as well.

Hands in the koekie jar

And now we should discuss what Rhoodie got out of it all. And where better to start than the Valhalla flats? According to Retief van Rooyen, a director of Thor Communications, there was something decidedly fishy about Thor's purchase of nine flats in Clifton. They were supposedly bought as investments which would bring a monthly income into the Department of Information's propaganda schemes. Van Rooyen soon realised that Rhoodie had taken one for himself and another for his brother, so those two flats generated no income – not to mention the one that went to the actor Anthony Quinn.

But that was simply the crest of the wave. For a humble civil servant, Rhoodie had a jaw-dropping collection of expensive cars, houses and properties liberally scattered around South Africa and overseas. He owned a house in Bantry Bay, which he renovated at the cost R40 000 (R1.7 million today), and which he paid for in cash. He also had properties in Nature's Valley and Plettenberg Bay. And of course there had to be a farm too. Strangely, or perhaps not strangely at all, the farm was near Hoedspruit in the Eastern Transvaal – the very area where Nico 'Dr Gold' Diederichs had bought his farm and made a cool profit.

What's more, Rhoodie regularly flew himself and his family around the world to flats and houses dotted around the globe. After an exhaustive search, Mervyn Rees discovered that Rhoodie had bought a house for R228 000 (about R10 million today) on Millionaires' Row in Miami Beach. What other houses he owned around the world is not clear, but there were many rumours. And all of these were, of course, purchased at the taxpayer's expense.

White lies

Up until October 1978, only Rhoodie, Mulder, the person code-named 'Myrtle', Lang Hendrik van den Bergh, Prime Minister Vorster, five journalists and one judge knew the extent of the Department of Information's shenanigans. The unravelling of Mulder and Rhoodie's convoluted financial and propaganda networks turned on one very simple moment. Much like US president Richard Nixon – whose fate was decided when he lied about his knowledge of the Watergate break-in – Mulder too would make one simple and completely avoidable mistake.

The journalists Rees, Day and Kitt Katzin (with the support of their editors Sparks and Gibson) had been gathering evidence for years on Rhoodie and Mulder, but they all had a problem. Although people like Retief van Rooyen and the mysterious 'Myrtle' had given them very exact details, they had no useable paperwork, nor was any person willing to go on the record. But then Connie Mulder stood up in Parliament on 10 May 1978 to make one simple and fatal statement.

As minister of the Department of Information, Mulder was being questioned by that ever-present gadfly Japie Basson, then in the ranks of the Progressive Federal Party. Basson had for some time been suspicious of *The Citizen* newspaper, its pro-National Party line and its seemingly magical ability to get access to government information. As Joshua Haasbroek points out, Basson had absolutely no proof whatsoever that the paper was funded by the government. He was simply acting on a hunch when he stood up during Mulder's budget speech and began harassing the minister. But when Mulder ignored the question, Basson seems to have realised that he was on to something and he rose again.

> BASSON: The answer that the Minister provided – he can correct me – was that the Department of Information is not the owners of the newspaper. That we know. But that was not the question ... I once again ask a simple question directed at Mulder and require a direct answer.
>
> MULDER: I will answer directly by saying that the Department of Information does not provide funds for *The Citizen*. Is it clear and does the Honourable member accept it?
>
> BASSON: And the government?
>
> MULDER: The government does not give funds to *The Citizen*.[21]

Whether Basson knew this was not true, we are not sure. But at least five news-papermen knew that what Mulder had just said was a lie.

A great deal had happened in the South African Parliament since 1910. Abhorrent race legislation had been passed, the National Party had used its tiny majority to change the Constitution, there had been a fair amount of pre-varication and the usual parliamentary bullshit too, and there had even been a murder – Prime Minister Verwoerd was stabbed to death in Parliament in 1966 by Dimitri Tsafendas. But a bald-faced lie? That was something new. For the common conservative NG Kerk-goer, this would be a bridge too far. Racism was fine, but to lie in Parliament was akin to blaspheming in church. It was simply not done. Still, the journalists had to find a way to prove that Mulder had lied and work out how to get the stories out without being sued or worse – being banned or imprisoned were both distinct possibilities in 1970s apartheid.

The journalists were helped by the fact that the old guard of the NP were ailing and dying. As the ANC knows all too well, there is nothing quite like a succession battle to test the timbers of an already slightly leaky and corrupted ship.

What had already transpired by this point was that the auditor-general, Gerald Barrie (whom Mulder had redeployed to allow for Rhoodie to take command of the Department of Information), had reported irregular spending in his old department. The *Sunday Express* had also reported on Rhoodie's government-funded jaunt to the Seychelles. That had seemed like the end of the road to Day, Rees and Katzin – until Mulder lied in Parliament.

Rhoodie, believing fully in his own powers to manipulate not only the press but also his political superiors, supposed he could be master of the situation and came out punching. He explained in a media interview after Mulder's lie that he was authorised to do whatever the hell he chose. He then also accused Auditor-General Barrie of leaking information. This forced Vorster to admit that Rhoodie had access to secret funds and that he had given prime-ministerial authorisation to Rhoodie. Vorster then accused the auditor-general of essentially meddling in affairs he knew nothing about.

There are no rules to succession
As both Thabo Mbeki and Jacob Zuma would discover, even the captain of the ship needs everybody on board to be working for them in order to arrive

at the desired destination. Vorster then appointed the newly retired head of BOSS, Lang Hendrik van den Bergh, and the auditor of BOSS, a man called Reynders, to 'investigate' the Department of Information's use of funds. Of course, Van den Bergh had been at the centre of the project right from the start. This was a move Zuma could only have dreamt of – and, to be fair, he probably did dream of it when he had Public Protector Thuli Madonsela breathing down his neck.

Vorster and Mulder thought that with an 'investigation' in the safe hands of Van den Bergh, the Information Scandal could be kept under wraps until they had both arrived at safer shores: Vorster in comfortable retirement and Mulder the new prime minister.

The situation went into overdrive when State President Diederichs, who had masterminded the money flows back in 1974, died suddenly. Diederichs was afforded an extravagant, televised state funeral, with his coffin paraded through the streets of Bloemfontein on top of a gun carriage, while army and navy units paraded alongside and crowds cheered from the pavements. But at the funeral, at which Anton Rupert gave the eulogy, it was noticed that Vorster's health was failing.

Mulder now knew he would have to act quickly to show the country and his party that his Department of Information had a clean bill of health. On 20 September Vorster announced his resignation. And on 23 September, an article appeared in the Broederbond-controlled newspaper *Die Transvaler* stating that Van den Bergh and Reynder's investigation into Mulder's department had uncovered no irregularities in spending. In doing so, it had put Mulder at the front of the queue to take over as prime minister.

But there was one person who smelt a rat. Retief van Rooyen, who was one of *the* frontmen of Rhoodie's operation, knew that Reynders had found irregularities. Van Rooyen had grown deeply disillusioned with Mulder and Rhoodie. He seemingly believed, with a fair amount of justification, that if these two gained control of the country it would lead not only to further wholesale looting, but there was also a possibility that Mulder would end up as South Africa's first real dictator (at least according to those who knew him and Rhoodie).

Van Rooyen, on reading the piece in *Die Transvaler*, went to Pik Botha, then minister of foreign affairs and himself an aspiring prime minister, with details of the misappropriation of funds. Pik in turn went to P.W. Botha, defence minister and another aspiring PM. They both confronted Vorster and the cabinet with the news of Rhoodie and Mulder's shenanigans. Many of the National Party elite were now deeply shocked that Mulder had lied in Parliament. In the ensuing election battle for head of the National Party, P.W., with the help of both Pik and the Orange Free State caucus, narrowly won the election, defeating an unapologetic Mulder. P.W. then came out fighting, claiming in his first speech that he would ensure a clean, corruption-free administration.

Botha was, however, still keen on a cover-up. After all, it was through his Special Defence Account that the corruption had occurred. But try as they might, neither P.W. nor the ailing Vorster could bury the corpse unseen. They had the press at their heels, of course, but they probably hadn't bargained for a largely unknown judge by the name of Anton Mostert, who stumbled almost unwittingly into a veritable graveyard of corrupted dealings. Mostert had been appointed by Treasury to investigate exchange-control violations. While many judges in this position would have gone about their business without causing too much of a fuss, Mostert would prove to be different.

Although he had been schooled in the Afrikaner Nationalist traditions, he, much like James Rose Innes before him (see Chapter 6), did not tolerate financial hanky-panky. Mostert had interviewed both Retief van Rooyen and Louis Luyt under oath and knew a great deal about Rhoodie's Department of Information. The journalists Rees and Day, on hearing about this obscure judge and his even obscurer commission, had gone off to interview Mostert in Pietermaritzburg. Although Mostert was frank with them, telling them he would spill no beans, they were made aware that this straight-talking judge knew that the story they were itching to tell was true.

Journalist Kitt Katzin, working for the *Sunday Express*, had also been in contact with Mostert, and the *Express* now felt confident that it could fire the opening journalistic shot. On 29 October 1978, it published the first article about what would soon become known as the Information Scandal under the banner headline 'The Citizen Secret Revealed'. The *Rand Daily Mail* followed this up the next day, with a huge front-page headline: 'Missing Millions'. The article stated that R13 million had been sent to Luyt to start up *The Citizen*. Luyt came out fighting the same day in an interview in *The Star*. Lying through his teeth, Luyt stated that he had not received a single cent from government to launch *The Citizen*. He perhaps believed that Judge Mostert would never publicly reveal his secrets and/or that the National Party would do their best to supress Mostert's finding. If he did believe these things, then he was at least 50 per cent correct.

'Thank you, Judge Mostert!'

Mostert was by then coming under severe political pressure from Prime Minister Botha to keep a lid on it. But Mostert was no pushover. On 2 November he was summoned to the Union Buildings for a meeting with the Groot Krokodil. About an hour later he is said to have come storming out, his jaw clenched, his face 'ashen'. With a bevy of journalists stampeding behind him, he turned to them and growled, 'I will speak to you at my offices at Abattoir House at 2 p.m. today. I will have nothing to say until then.'[22]

What took place at Abattoir House that day was a slaughter of sorts. In one of the most astonishing moves in South African history, with an SABC TV crew recording the event in a room full of eager journalists, Mostert dished out all the evidence he had gathered to date. In the next few hours, P.W. desperately tried to muzzle the press, but Mostert argued that he saw no legal impediment to the press publishing what he'd said. Under the headline 'It's All True', the *Rand Daily Mail* went to town revealing the whole sordid tale. Hardly surprisingly, not one word of the story and not one second of the footage of Judge Mostert was broadcast on the SABC, which was controlled by arch-Broederbonder Piet Meyer.

Bumper stickers reading 'Thank you, Judge Mostert!' soon appeared on cars. And as streams of congratulatory and adulatory messages came in, Mostert, now with the bit between his teeth, announced that his commission would continue in public. Mostert's favourite expression was Samuel Johnson's 'Patriotism is the last refuge of the scoundrel', and he was determined to prove that it applied to South Africans too. P.W. Botha summarily axed Mostert's commission and announced a new inquiry under Judge Erasmus. As Allister Sparks recently wrote, the reason for setting up the Erasmus Commission was 'to use the more compliant judge to prevent any further publication of the scandal under the *sub judice* rule'.[23]

Mostert stepped down from the bench in protest and resumed his career at the bar. In the next few days, Rhoodie fled the country, Mulder resigned from government and stepped down as head of the NP in the Transvaal, and General Van den Bergh slipped back into retirement on his chicken farm. Rhoodie was eventually tracked down in France and extradited to South Africa for trial. He was found guilty of fraud and sentenced to six years in prison. The sentence was, however, overturned in the Appeal Court and he was set free. He went to live in Atlanta in the USA and died there at the age of sixty of a heart attack

The *Rand Daily Mail* delivering what Piet Meyer's SABC censored

while playing tennis. Mulder was also charged, in his case with contempt, when he refused to give evidence at the Erasmus Commission. But he was, rather predictably, acquitted. No other politician ever faced prosecution, despite P.W.'s promise of a clean-up.

The only other people to end up in court over the whole affair were editor Allister Sparks and journalist Hamish Fraser of the *Rand Daily Mail*. They were charged with publishing an article during the commission of inquiry that was deemed to be in contempt of court. As Rees and Day remembered it,

On 17 January 1979, Sparks, Fraser and SAAN were found guilty – SAAN was fined R50, Sparks R50 or 25 days [in jail] and Fraser was cautioned and discharged. Sparks told the court that the summons was served 'with dramatic and exaggerated haste' within 48 hours of the publication of the contested report. This contrasted, he said, markedly with the 'tardiness the State has shown in bringing any kind of action against the principal figures involved in the Information Scandal'.[24]

The mysterious Ms. Myrtle

One of the major sources for the journalists who exposed the Information Scandal was a person code-named 'Myrtle'. In fact, without Myrtle, the full details of the story would never have been uncovered. In Rees and Day's book *Muldergate*, they refer to Myrtle as a man. But Allister Sparks revealed in his much more recent book, *The Sword and the Pen*, that Myrtle was in fact a woman. Rees and Day had agreed that they would change her sex to harden her cover.

Apparently, she was named Myrtle after a character from a children's book called *Myrtle Turtle*. As Day claimed, 'her cover was strong and she could keep her head down'.[25] Sparks, who tracked Myrtle down after nearly forty years, asked her if she would allow him to reveal her identity. She answered by saying, 'My life wouldn't be worth living if people found out.' And Sparks, true to his word, took her identity to the grave. The name of this incredible woman, who knew every detail of Rhoodie's work and life, now seems unlikely to be uncovered. What is more, no woman with access to that kind of information appears in Rees and Day's story, nor in Sparks's. In his book *The Real Information Scandal*, Rhoodie seems to have had no doubt in his mind that Myrtle was a 'he', so – whoever Myrtle was – her cover was indeed very strong. It seems a great shame that the true hero of the tale is a woman whose identity will never be known.

Somewhat ironically, Sparks's secretary at the *Rand Daily Mail* turned out to be an apartheid agent. She relayed almost everything Sparks knew to the infamous BOSS, except for the identity of Myrtle, who was only ever referred to by her code-name.

CHAPTER 9

THE SMIT MURDERS

Wickedness in High Places

1977

'I have enough men to commit murder if I tell them to kill.
I don't care who the prey is.' – 'Lang Hendrik' van den Bergh[1]

Dr Robert Smit and his wife Jeanne-Cora with their children.

A murder most foul

On the morning of 23 November 1977, Daniel Tshabalala knocked on his employers' front door. It was just seven days before the general election, which would surely see his boss elected MP for Springs. Receiving no answer and finding the door unlocked, Tshabalala let himself in. Only a few paces from the entrance lay Robert Smit's body, riddled with bullet holes. A few metres away, slumped over the telephone in the lounge, was Jeanne-Cora Smit's bloodied corpse. Without taking in too many of the gory details of the executions, Tshabalala ran outside to alert a neighbour.

The Smit murders sent shock waves through apartheid-era South Africa. This was a hit carried out against an up-and-coming National Party politician, apparently on the orders of someone at the top of the Afrikaner establishment. Even today, there is no clarity on who was responsible or what the exact motive was. 'Up until that point Afrikaner Nationalism had been a united family,' says *Politicsweb* editor James Myburgh, 'but now you had a situation where members of the family were prepared to go so far as to brutally murder one of their own ... and his wife.'[2]

The morning after the night before

The only small saving grace was that the Smits' children were at the family home in Pretoria that night. Robert and Jeanne-Cora had been staying in a rental house in Springs in order to be to closer to his constituents in the final straight of the election campaign.

The scene that greeted police that November morning was straight out of a horror film. Robert had taken three gunshot wounds (two to the head and one to the chest) and a stiletto knife was plunged into his back. Jeanne-Cora had been killed by one of two gunshots, but her body had been further mutilated by fourteen stab wounds. The letters RAU-TEM (some think the second word might have been 'TEN') were sprayed, in red paint, across the kitchen walls, fridge and freezer. Apart from Robert Smit's briefcase, nothing was missing. The neighbours hadn't heard or seen anything.

Although there's little hard evidence either way, Myburgh says that if he 'were to put money on it', he'd guess that '[t]he person who carried out the hit was not necessarily the same person who did the writing and stabbing … Someone came in afterwards to make it look like it was done by a lunatic.'[3]

One of the National Party's brightest stars, Smit was never a member of the Broederbond. He attended Oxford on a Rhodes Scholarship and held a PhD in economics. He served as Treasury adviser to the minister of finance, Nico 'Dr Gold' Diederichs, for many years before landing a gig as South Africa's ambassador to the International Monetary Fund (IMF) in Washington between 1971 and 1974. When this posting was coming to an end, Smit wrote to Gerrit Viljoen (then chairman of the Broederbond, and who stars in Chapter 12), who helped to find him a job as MD of a mysterious front company called Santam International, which was set up to find ways around trade sanctions to acquire 'international products of a strategic nature for South Africa'[4] – mainly oil and weapons.

Santam International was 'a wholly private concern',[5] writes Hennie van Vuuren, which was backed by the Broederbond's insurer of choice, Santam (which had a 46 per cent share), and Merca Bank (with a 24 per cent share), a little-known financial institution known to extend credit to shady oil traders. The remaining 30 per cent was split between Robert Smit and senior Broederbond member Carel van Aswegen, the firm's chairman. According to Van Vuuren, Van Aswegen wasn't just 'accustomed to the dark arts of finance'; he was also closely linked to the 'clandestine world of arms trading'.[6] He sat on the board of Armscor (the arms agency of the Department of Defence) for many years, and in 1977 he was granted a seat at Armscor's four-person executive committee, whose job it was to deal with top-secret orders, including nuclear components. While no one will say exactly what Smit got up to at Santam International, it certainly wasn't your average financial institution. Curiously, Van Aswegen claimed only a 'slight' recollection of his business partner when asked about Robert Smit in the 1990s.

When Smit was murdered, he was just days away from making an 'honest' living as a Nat politician. His seat as member of Parliament for Springs was virtually assured, and the talk was that at only forty-four years of age he may even be appointed finance minister.

The day of the murder

Robert Smit spent the day of 22 November at his election office in Springs. He had lunch with friends and spoke to a journalist in the afternoon. Smit's receptionist later testified that she took a call from a man named McDougall (a pseudonym Smit had used since his Oxford days) at 3.15 p.m. 'He told me that he would like to speak to Dr Smit about politics and asked whether it would be possible to see Dr Smit tonight...'

At 6.10 p.m. Jeanne-Cora was driven home by Tshabalala. At 7.14 p.m. (some accounts say 7.40 p.m.), Jeanne-Cora Smit phoned her husband's receptionist and asked her to tell him his guests were waiting for him. 'As she put the phone down,' writes Myburgh, 'she sensed something behind her and instinctively put up her hand. She was shot in the back of the head at close range, then in the chest and in the right thigh.'[7]

Not long after his wife had been murdered, Robert Smit walked out of his offices with a Springs town councillor, Danie Joubert. In a statement at the inquest, Joubert said Dr Smit had been carrying two attaché cases. He saw Smit's car pull away just before 8 p.m.

When Robert Smit got home, he was shot in the neck from a few paces, and collapsed to the ground. He was then shot, at close range, in the head, back and chest. Husband and wife had been shot with different calibre guns.

Who pulled the trigger?

Over the years, a number of names have been associated with the case, but seeing as our focus here is corruption, not whodunnit, we will explore only a few of the theories. Most of the rumours concur that regardless of who actually carried out the hit, it was likely authorised by our old pal Lang Hendrik van den Bergh, a man who once told a government commission, 'I have enough men to commit murder if I tell them to kill. I don't care who the prey is.'[8]

(As an aside, the rumours of Lang Hendrik's involvement in the murders are said to have originated on the playgrounds of Menlo Park High School, 'a posh Pretoria school attended by the children of senior officials and members of the Broederbond'.[9] Which just goes to show – all the unmarked firearms and fake identity documents in the world don't count for a thing if you can't keep your mouth shut around the kids.)

In 1997 and again in 2006 *Beeld* publicly named three suspects, all members of various sinister apartheid-era police squads. Dries Verwey (who took to the bottle shortly after the murders) and Phil Freeman (who was known to use the pseudonym McDougall) were both dead by the time

'Lang Hendrik' van den Bergh

the first story came out. But the third suspect mentioned in the newspaper articles, Roy Allen, is (as far as we can tell) still alive and well, and living in Australia. No charges have ever been brought against Allen, who vehemently denies involvement in the crime (while readily admitting many others). Allen, however, has his suspicions about Freeman and especially Verwey:

> At the time I had wondered, could it have been Col Dries Verwey – my commander at the Police Special Task Force?… My suspicions that Verwey could have been involved are NOT founded on any clues at all … rather just a well-developed gut feeling/sixth sense …
>
> In his special room at Special Branch HQ he had silenced weapons of many different types and calibres, poisoned bottles of exotic Portuguese liquor that were popular in Mozambique/Angola at the time, Zambian police officer uniforms and cell keys, and transistor radios that were 'loaded' with deadly explosives that would blow up anyone switching them on.
>
> There were also parcel bombs made in seized copies of Mao Tse-Tung's 'Little Red Book'. These bombs were made with surgical precision, with the Pentolite poured into the hollowed out inside in molten form … The way the pages were surgically cut and glued, the placement and affixing of the micro-switch and the arming device, was like looking at the innards of a Swiss timepiece …

This was typical handiwork of Phil Freeman, who was a perfectionist. When Verwey and Freeman had both been at BOSS, they had worked very closely together, as well as in the Security Police, long before the inception of BOSS.[10]

But this is just one theory.

The fact that the crime took place in the Smits' home and involved the killing of both husband and wife has led many to believe that foreign assassins may have carried out the hit. No other apartheid-era assassination deliberately killed a family member of the target (as far as we can tell). And various former BOSS operatives have said that the crime scene did not bear the hallmarks of a BOSS hit.

One theory is what Joe Trento described in the 24 February 1980 edition of Delaware's *Sunday News Journal* as 'a hit team of Cuban terrorists' used to carry out the murders.[11] Trento's article was primarily concerned with a Cuban death squad's links to assassinations carried out by General Pinochet's notorious Dirección de Inteligencia Nacional in Chile (which often killed married couples). But it also mentioned, almost in passing, that the squad's victims included a 'South African economist and his wife, who were shot to death in their South Africa home in November 1977'.[12]

Predictably, one of the Cuban hitmen whose name has been linked to the murders denies involvement. According to a news report in 2012,

Two days ago, the former fugitive, Virgilio Paz Romero, with ties to the Cuban Nationalist Movement and now living in Miami, spoke out for the first time in an exclusive e-mail interview with the *Cape Times*.

He admitted involvement in another killing, but categorically denied involvement in the Smit murders, saying: 'I'm not hiding from anyone. I did my time for the conspiracy I was involved in. I'm sure that if I had been a suspect of the South African government for whatever reason, they would have found a way, through the American government, to find me.'[13]

Although it's hardly surprising the crime was not solved while the Nats were in power, the case is one of very few from that era that remains completely unsolved. Even today there are many among the older generation of Afrikaners – not to mention the Smits' children, who were fifteen and thirteen when their parents were killed – who would love to get to the bottom of it. Liza Smit has spent much of her life publicly grappling with her parents' murder, submitting reams of evidence to the Truth and Reconciliation Commission and even publishing a book that details the fallout of the murders and tries (and fails) to solve the crime.[14] The National Prosecuting Authority has confirmed that the case remains open.

What did Smit know?

'There was little doubt that the secrets in Robert Smit's brown briefcase held the key to the mystery,'[15] wrote journalist Chris Karsten. Shortly before his murder, Smit apparently told friends and family that 'once he was in parliament, he would reveal a big scandal that "will make Watergate look like a Sunday School picnic"'.[16]

In a 1979 interview with *Rapport*, Smit's brother Iaan said that Robert had confided in him that '[t]hings are not right. There are things on the go that are improper ("*onbehoorlik*") and that will shock our people. I am sorry, but at the right time I am going to go public with them.'[17]

Robert Smit seems to have known that his life was in danger. On his way to a restaurant in Johannesburg with a friend, he 'insisted on walking in the middle of the street rather than on a crowded pavement. He told his companion that he believed he was under surveillance and that either American or Israeli agents might try to assassinate him. He even went to see a Hervormde Kerk pastor to discuss his fears.'[18]

Given Smit's roles at Treasury, the IMF and Santam International, there is a general consensus that what he'd uncovered involved the misappropriation of funds. Many have suggested that this was to do with one of the apartheid government's secret foreign bank accounts. Many fingers have been pointed at one man – Nico 'Dr Gold' Diederichs.

Martin Welz wrote: 'For some weeks before his assassination in October [*sic*] 1977, Smit had hinted to close friends that he had made a very troubling discovery involving the Minister of Finance Dr Diederichs.'[19] In his thousand-page tome *South Africa's Brave New World: The Beloved Country Since the End of Apartheid*, R.W. Johnson went one step further, saying, '[I]t seems clear that [Smit] was murdered at the behest of the State President, Nico Diederichs, who as Finance Minister had creamed off millions into a Swiss bank account which Smit was about to expose.'[20]

Another theory is that the briefcase contained a document destined for Prime Minister Vorster himself, purportedly to do with the clouds gathering around the Department of Information. What this might have revealed is anyone's guess, but the Smit murders were, in Myburgh's opinion, 'the unanswered question that ran through the Information Scandal' which ultimately resulted in Vorster's resignation in 1978.

Eschel Rhoodie saw it otherwise. Rhoodie, of course, had plenty of reason to absolve himself and his department of blame in the murders. But his close association with Diederichs and Van den Bergh nevertheless makes him an important source. In an interview that was secretly recorded in America in 1987 and published by *Noseweek* three years after his death in 1993, Rhoodie stated that he believed that Smit – being a proud Nat – would have supported 'most, perhaps not all'[21] of the Department of Information's secret projects to enhance South Africa's international reputation.

Instead, Rhoodie believed that Smit had unearthed massive irregularities in the so-called Special Defence Account, which had been established as a way to get around the UN Security Council's arms embargo on South Africa. Rhoodie's issue was not that the fund was used to buy weapons on the black market (that would have been totally fine!), but rather that, year after year, the government seemed to be paying way more than it should have for these weapons. (This, as we have seen with everyone from Van der Stel onwards, is one of the oldest tricks in the corruption book.) Together with Lang Hendrik van den Bergh, who had also smelt the same rat, Rhoodie said that he

figured out that, even with all the markups which one must have when buying in secret, even allowing for third parties who are always involved in the process of covering your tracks, allowing for excess commissions and bona fide fruitless expenditure, that about R200 million [R6.8 billion today] too much was going out each year. That was just a guestimate. But even if we were way off by R50 million a year, there could be a fund sitting out there amounting to a billion or two. If not, our buyers have been milked to the point where they are the biggest suckers in the world. And I don't believe our people are that stupid or unqualified ...[22]

The Special Defence Account, Rhoodie noted, was administered by the minister of defence, who at the time was P.W. Botha. 'The only minister he might have had to consult was the Minister of Finance [Diederichs].'[23]

Rhoodie thought that Diederichs and co. might have been squirrelling the money away to support a government in exile if or when the shit hit the fan and the apartheid regime was forced to flee South Africa. This may sound far-fetched, but Rhoodie did have a point:

> I understand how people in South Africa will feel about what I have just said. But during the Second World War there were several governments in exile and huge amounts of money were moved secretly, in time, to help sustain them. What makes you think that the South African government has not taken out insurance? The government thought themselves under an all-out onslaught; in the midst of a revolution. It seems to me to be precisely the time to think of all possibilities.[24]

And, as we saw a few chapters ago, even Oom Paul Kruger – the founding father of Afrikanerdom – had done a very similar thing with his gold when his time in the Transvaal sun came to an abrupt halt.

Stranger than fiction

After fleeing South Africa and building a new life for himself in Atlanta, Georgia, Eschel Rhoodie used his newfound free time to write a novel based on the Smit murders. At the time, he mentioned the project to Allister Sparks: "'It will lead to a lot of speculation,' [Rhoodie] said with a grin, "but only those who read it will know if it's true."' The book was never published, but when, years later, Sparks stumbled upon a copy of the manuscript, he could not resist the urge to read it.

> It was a racy book, laced with sex, glamour and political intrigue ... His main character, not very subtly named Robert Smit, had stumbled upon an immensely wealthy but shady Costa Rican businessman who had done a deal with a small Afrikaner super-elite, more exclusive and secretive even than the Broederbond, calling themselves The Puritans ... Rhoodie's manuscript names the hired assassins as two Swedes who entered South Africa through Swaziland posing as businessmen under the names of Sven Halforsen and Olaff Flaggstad. They brought with them a .38 Webley revolver and a .32 Beretta with specially adapted small silencers. He links the assassins to a West German terrorist group called the Red Army Unit Ten (perhaps explaining the spray-painted 'RAU-TEM' slogan) that had killed two German financiers ... some years before.[25]

A tale of two funerals

But getting back to reportable fact ... The same Hervormde Kerk pastor whom Robert had visited before his death led the Smits' funeral, says Martin Welz, who attended the service as a young *Sunday Times* reporter. Welz has never forgotten the strange text he chose to read:

> Put on the whole armour of God, that ye may be able to stand against the wiles of the devil ... For we wrestle not against flesh and blood, but against principalities, against powers, against the rulers of the darkness of this world, against spiritual wickedness in high places.[26]

Speaking of wickedness in high places, Nico Diederichs would not last much longer than the Smits. At his funeral the following year, a familiar face would take to the pulpit. Anton Rupert had come a long way since the '*hoes vir die volk*' days, even going so far as to label the Broederbond an 'absurdity'. But this would not stop him from eulogising his old pal Dr Gold as 'a man for all seasons'[27] – a curious reference to Thomas More, who in 1551 had written an almost pre-Marxist book titled *Utopia*, which stated that the social order was a 'conspiracy of the rich'!

As Allister Sparks put it, '[A]ll the principal figures involved [in the Smit murders] are dead or disappeared, but the mystery itself remains alive.'[28] A stark reminder that the members of the Broederbond were perhaps even prepared to resort to murder to prevent their corrupt secrets from being revealed.

CHAPTER 10

THE BROTHERS MATANZIMA

Corruption's Homeland
1964–1988

*'What is wrong with ministers of state taking shares
in public and private companies?' – **Kaiser Matanzima**[1]*

George and Kaiser Matanzima, keeping corruption in the family

THE SIGNS WERE NOT GOOD for the Transkei from the moment the National Party started to make real its long-held dream of separate development. The concept of dividing South Africa into racial denominations had been an obsession in the clandestine meetings of the Broederbond in the 1930s. But the idea itself, of 'self-governing' Bantustans, where 'Blacks' could live out of sight and out of mind, had been a long time coming – in 1894, none other than Cecil John Rhodes had passed the Glen Grey Act, which was, in his own words, designed to 'keep the minds of the natives occupied'.[2]

The vast majority of black people – including Nelson Mandela, Walter Sisulu and Oliver Tambo, all from the Transkei area – were vehemently opposed to the idea of apartheid, campaigning instead for a unified South Africa where all races were equal. But the prospect of power (and the money that would surely come with it) was enough to convince one Transkei chief that the Bantustans were actually a wonderful idea. Chief Kaiser Daliwonga 'K.D.' Matanzima (variously, Kaizer Matanzima and Kaiser Mathanzima) was, as Jeff Peires puts it, 'a true believer in the policy of territorial apartheid, [a man] who once declared that "Dr Verwoerd was sent by God to liberate the black people of South Africa"'.[3]

It should come as no surprise then that he was elected chief minister of the newly formed Transkeian Legislative Assembly in 1963. The apartheid regime had cunningly 'set up the system so the democratic element could be nullified to guarantee the result,' says sociologist Roger Southall.[4] K.D. then went on to nominate his brother, Chief George Matanzima, as the Bantustan's first justice minister. But then, while not ideal, this kind of nepotism has long been commonplace in politics, South African or otherwise.

What made Chief George's nomination especially contentious was the fact that less than six months previously, he had been struck off the roll of attorneys for the misappropriation of trust funds. Justice F. van der Riet of the Grahamstown Supreme Court also found that Chief George had made a false statement to the Court.

When, thirteen years later in 1976, the Transkei finally achieved the full 'independence' the chief Broederbonders Diederichs, Meyer, Cronjé and Verwoerd had yearned for, the Matanzima brothers would once again take centre stage. K.D. became prime minister and good old Chief George was still meting out justice. But back to 1963 ...

When the story of Chief George's sticky fingers was reported on by the *Sunday Times*, his older brother, K.D., accused the paper of 'acting maliciously and of

B.J. Vorster and K.D. Matanzima sign the documents
giving Transkei its independence while George looks on

meddling in the affairs of the Transkei'. Mr Daan de Wet Nel, the apartheid
government's minister of Bantu administration and development, was more
forceful still in his defence of Chief George, bemoaning the 'mean press campaign' against him and saying that Chief George 'had paid back his last penny of
debt and not a single person has suffered any damage'.[5]

Even Chief Victor Poto, the leader of the Transkeian opposition Democratic
Party, seemed resigned to the appointment, saying: 'Chief Kaizer had to find work
for his brother.'[6]

Just two months later, a now newly virtuous justice minister George
Matanzima warned 'against bribery and corruption and other such evil practices
in general administration'. At the swearing-in ceremony of sub-chief Mlingo
Salukupatwa, Chief George explained that for the new leader 'to win the support
and love of his people, he would have to be fair and incorruptible in administering his district; to refuse any form of bribery and always show the people he
was prepared to be fair and unbiased even when cases concerned people who

were opposed to him personally'.[7] This unabashed self-delusion could have come straight out of our friend W.A. van der Stel's *Korte Deductie*!

In 1980, Barry Streek and Richard Wicksteed described the trust account affair as 'the great disaster in Matanzima history' (admittedly, they hadn't watched all the way to the end of the Matanzima biopic). Bantu Holomisa, who would ultimately force Chief George to resign his position as prime minister in 1987, did not mince his words when we interviewed him for this book: 'George only got where he was because of his brother ... In another country he wouldn't have been made justice minister after being struck off the roll.'[8]

What's in a name?

'Why Kaizer? To understand how I was given my first name, you have to remember that it was at the time of the First World War. My parents, simple people from the deeply carved valleys of my birthplace, far away from the holocaust in Europe, were not unaware of the leaders striding the world scene in those momentous times. So, I was duly christened Kaizer after the Emperor of Germany. For his part my younger brother, George, the present Minister of Justice, was named after King George V of Great Britain.'[9]

Born with it

K.D. Matanzima was born at Qamata on 15 June 1915 to regional chief Mhlolo Mvuzo Matanzima Mtirara and his wife Mogedi. Three years later, George, his only brother, came along. Despite the fact that their dad had only completed Standard 4 and their mom had no formal education, the boys easily obtained their Junior Certificates from the prestigious Lovedale Missionary Institute, before going on to study at the University of Fort Hare, where K.D. did a BA in Roman law and politics and George a BSc.

Fort Hare in the 1930s was a hotbed of political activism, where future leaders of the ANC, including Nelson Mandela (the Matanzimas' uncle) and Oliver Tambo, forged their beliefs. But the Matanzimas did not allow student politics to concern them overly much, having only a brief dalliance with the All-Africa Convention (ironically, given what was to follow, this radical organisation urged 'non-collaboration' and called for 'universal franchise and equal rights irrespective of race, colour and sex'[10]) and avoiding the ANC altogether.

Matanzima and Mandela

As members of the Thembu royal house, Nelson Mandela and K.D. Matanzima grew up together. Technically speaking, Mandela was Matanzima's uncle, but with K.D. being three years older than Mandela, their relationship was more like that between cousins. They were, in their younger years, apparently inseparable, living in the same Methodist hostel at Fort Hare and playing on the same sports teams. They even went so far as to fancy the same girls, with both vying for Winnie Madikizela's hand in marriage. Not for the last time would K.D. have to settle for the consolation prize – he was Mandela's best man at the wedding.

Their relationship soured spectacularly when K.D. came out in support of the Bantu Authorities Act in the 1950s. As Mandela put it in his autobiography, 'It was especially painful to me that in the Transkei, the wrath of the people was directed against my nephew and one-time mentor K.D. Matanzima.'[11]

In 1979, K.D. even dreamed up a scheme where (his cousin and enemy) Sabata Dalindyebo and Winnie Mandela would use their influence to persuade Nelson Mandela – who was serving a life sentence on Robben Island – to agree to take up a senior position in the Transkei government. On these terms, Matanzima was pretty confident he could get Pretoria to agree to Mandela's release. While the scheme would have been a massive PR coup for both Matanzima and the apartheid government (Mandela would have had to cut all ties with the ANC for it to work), it was doomed to fail.

Dalindyebo refused to have anything to do with it and Mandela made it very clear that Matanzima could never visit him on Robben Island. Madiba would later describe his nephew as 'a sell-out in the proper sense of the word'.[12]

While a student at Fort Hare, write Streek and Wicksteed, K.D. Matanzima was 'studious and anxious to absorb all he could ... Student flirtations with radicalism and liberalism were not for him. Others could talk on the campus of the realignment of racial forces, of the emergence of the sleeping black man. He remained a conservative with his interests centred on the chieftainship waiting for him at Qamata.'[13]

As it turned out, K.D. was a shrewd operator who was able to secure much more than a mere chieftainship for himself. Within twenty-odd years he would have conjured up an entire nation (well, sort of) for himself and his dishonest younger brother to share.

K.D. began his legal articles in 1940, but was soon distracted by the puppet

The first Transkei cabinet, featuring George Matanzima,
K.D. Matanzima and Stella Sigcau (seated in the middle),
and Winnie Mandela's father, Columbus Madikizela (back left)

show that was the Bunga – the half-arsed Transkeian Council System overseen by Pretoria. In 1948 he was eventually admitted as an attorney, although he never practised law. Seven years later, he returned to the Transkei's Bunga 'with the object of killing it', as he had recognised that the Bantu Authorities Act (1951) 'laid the foundation for the eventual independence of the African people'.[14] It is perhaps worth considering here that the quotes above are from Matanzima's *Independence My Way*, a narcissistic 1976 autobiography bankrolled by the apartheid government's Foreign Affairs Association.

Chief George, meanwhile, completed his legal articles soon after graduating and began practising law in 1952. After an uneventful decade as a country attorney, he was – as we have already seen – struck from the roll in 1963 for abusing trust funds.

Birth of a 'nation'

1779–1884: The concept of the Transkei (the northern side of the Kei River) and the Ciskei (south of the river) was born during the nine Frontier Wars fought between the land-coveting European settlers and the Xhosa. By 1870, writes Patrick Laurence, people who lived on the Cape side 'had been brought under control of white magistrates', while those in the Transkei 'still lived in more or less independent chiefdoms'.[15]

1885–1894: By 1885 things had changed and the Transkei was annexed by the Cape Colony as a native reserve, thus transforming the 'subsistence, pastoral, pre-capitalist economy into a reservoir of cheap labour'.[16] But there was a problem: the increase in black landowners (who were allowed to vote back then) influenced the results of the 1888 election, with at least five members of the assembly owing their election to the African vote.

1895–1962: This most unfortunate (if you were white) situation was remedied by our pal Cecil John Rhodes's 1894 Glen Grey Act, which, you might remember, made it much harder for 'natives' to vote. Instead, Transkeians were fobbed off with the Transkeian Council System (known as the Bunga, after the building in Umtata where the council met), which had the stated aim of 'assisting the inhabitants of the Transkei to advance in knowledge and prosperity'. If you've learnt one thing about Rhodes, you will recognise this as a bald-faced lie. Then, the Natives Land Act of 1913 determined that Africans were unable to own or rent land that was not located inside designated reserves.

1963–1975: Using Rhodes's law as their blueprint, the apartheid government started drawing up its Bantustan policy in 1959. By 1963 they were ready to roll the Transkei out as the first Bantustan to achieve the right to self-government. It should come as little surprise that the chief minister of the Transkei Legislative Assembly was K.D. Matanzima.

1976 onwards: In 1976, Transkei became the first homeland to be granted full 'independence' (the fledgling nation's only embassies were in South Africa – go figure!). The paramount chief of the amaMpondo, Botha Sigcau (more about his daughter later), became the first state president of the Transkei and K.D. Matanzima its first prime minister. After Sigcau's death in 1978, Matanzima took over as president.

The cousin who wouldn't go away

What sets K.D. Matanzima apart from some of the other rogues in this book is that he played a pivotal role in the invention of the 'country' he would eventually bleed dry. One of the easier ways to appreciate his political expediency is through the lens of his lifelong feud with his cousin Sabata Dalindyebo. Dalindyebo was everything Matanzima was not – unscholarly, belligerent and fiercely opposed to the apartheid government. Thanks to his royal lineage, he was also a much bigger tribal cheese than K.D. could ever hope to be.

In 1954, Dalindyebo was installed as paramount chief of the Thembu – the big boss of the region where K.D. was a minor chief. It's not hard to understand how Matanzima, a go-getting attorney, might be pissed off at being beaten to a promotion by a high-school dropout thirteen years his junior. But a man who staked his entire existence on the sanctity of Xhosa traditions should have been able to allow Xhosa tradition to run its course. As Streek and Wicksteed put it, Matanzima was 'visibly angered whenever Dalindyebo [was] referred to as King of the Thembus ... which [was] strange for someone who appear[ed] so wedded to the upholding of traditional values and systems'.[17]

Ever the technocrat, K.D. Matanzima worked with the apartheid government to outmanoeuvre his arch-rival and cousin, inventing the title of Paramount Chief of the Emigrant Thembu for himself and getting Pretoria to cede lands traditionally administered by anti-apartheid Dalindyebo to Matanzima the pliant stooge. 'This provided Matanzima with the power base he needed in Transkei and established a pattern of support for him as apartheid's expedient champion,' write Streek and Wicksteed. 'For Matanzima, his brother, and many of his political colleagues, the material rewards of collaboration have been great.'[18]

Dalindyebo did not take this affront lying down. And by 1963, when the apartheid government handed over 'self-government' to the Transkei, K.D. and Dalindyebo would go head-to-head. In the lead-up to the landmark 1963 elections, Dalindyebo's ancestral lands in Engcobo and Umtata were the sites of some serious violence. He openly supported Victor Poto's opposition party and even called the Matanzima brothers 'spies and good boys for the South African government'.[19]

Given that Matanzima had the full backing of Pretoria, the vote that took place in the Bunga was surprisingly close. K.D., the good boy, edged out Poto by fifty-four votes to forty-nine, thanks to the fact that tribal chiefs significantly outnumbered elected officials.[20]

In 1979 Dalindyebo went further, telling a rally that 'the Transkei President visited Pretoria at the insistence of the Boers and accepted independence on terms dictated by them … the President [K.D.] has an abundance of the necessities of life whilst his people have to live on excreta'. Later that year, he (rightly) described the Transkei passport as 'a useless piece of paper'.

On the back of these comments, Dalindyebo was charged with 'subverting the sovereignty of Parliament and the constitutional independence of Transkei, and for violating and injuring the dignity of the State President'. In a trial held at Port St Johns (far away from his raucous home base), Dalindyebo was found guilty on the latter charge and ordered to pay a R700 fine or serve eighteen months in prison.

Angered by the lenient decision (you've got to hate an insufficiently impartial judiciary), K.D. stepped in to depose his cousin and superior. Five days later, on 11 August 1980, Dalindyebo fled the 'country' for good. After a thrilling escape via Swaziland, Transkei's last outspoken critic of the brothers Matanzima died in exile in Zambia in 1986.

Dalindyebo and Matanzima: Each cousin thought *he* had seen the light

A fight beyond the grave

Dalindyebo's story does not end with his death. In keeping with Xhosa tradition, Dalindyebo's remains were repatriated so that he could be buried in his ancestral home. The great king's funeral would have attracted tens of thousands of Xhosa people from all over the country had it not been done under the watchful eye of K.D.'s army and police force. As the *New York Times* reported, Matanzima saw to it that the funeral was a small and 'tawdry affair':

At a Burial of African, Bitterness

They buried King Sabata Dalindyebo here today under a jacaranda tree.

Among the tough young men with Uzi submachine guns, there were mourners, perhaps 350 in all. The King's family mourned too. But they were not invited to stand by the simple grave.

By heritage, Sabata Dalindyebo was the paramount chief of the Themba [*sic*] people, who form the majority of those who live in the Transkei, a nominally independent, so-called homeland on the south-eastern coast of South Africa. Chief Sabata never wanted it that way. Instead, he spoke vigorously for a multiracial South Africa, where each person had one vote regardless of skin colour.

Even in death, the bitter politics of race intruded upon Chief Sabata. Despite a court ban and the wishes of his family, Chief Sabata's most bitter enemy, Chief Kaiser D. Matanzima, Transkei's first President, smuggled the King's body from a funeral home in the early morning hours and under heavy military and police guard brought it here to be buried in the 'Great Place,' the burial ground of kings.[21]

Still, the feud lived on.

Three years after Dalindyebo's funeral, the Transkei's new leader Bantu Holomisa, in close consultation with the ANC, arranged for Dalindyebo's remains to be exhumed and a reburial to take place. According to Holomisa's biographer Eric Naki, mourners came from all over the country to attend the funeral, which 'took place in a dignified manner, following both traditional and Christian rituals and befitting a king. The calibre of speakers at the funeral clearly signified the power Dalindyebo wielded and the respect he commanded in the ANC ... Every major newspaper reported on this major challenge to the Verwoerdian dinosaur.'[22]

A lifetime and two burials later, Dalindyebo would have the last laugh. Neither of the Matanzima brothers would end up having a hero's funeral, and the concept of separate development would also die a pathetic death.

The spoils of independence

But we digress. Let's get on to how the Matanzima brothers used the private Wild Coast fiefdom they had carved out to enrich themselves.

It is telling that Streek and Wicksteed wrote their evisceration of the Transkei experiment, *Render unto Kaiser: A Transkei Dossier*, in 1980, seven years before the big scandals that would ultimately result in the Matanzimas' ousting. But already in 1980 Streek and Wicksteed had enough evidence to publish a 378-page book on the topic of corruption in Transkei.

Two months *before* independence, K.D. and Chief George had moved onto farms near Queenstown that had been bought by the Bantu Trust from a white farmer for R400 000 (R16.9 million today) as part of the homeland consolidation plan. The farms, which occupied some of the best land in the whole of South Africa, were supposed to be the centrepiece of an ambitious Transkei government cattle-ranching project. But no one could work out how the brothers had come to occupy them. Even the secretary-general of Matanzima's own party told the *Sunday Tribune*, 'It's a little bit awkward. I don't know how he got it. We'll just have to wink at it.'[23]

Because independence was still a few weeks away, the South African government should have been able to provide some clarity on the situation, but Pretoria was characteristically opaque. The official line was that the brothers were merely occupying the farmhouses, but it soon become clear that – following the fine example set by W.A. van der Stel and Lord Charles Somerset before them – they were farming the government-owned land for their own profit. Chief George, meanwhile, foreshadowed Grace Mugabe by proclaiming that the land had 'been grabbed by British robbers and allocated to British settlers free of charge'.[24] Just why the Matanzimas in particular deserved it was never explained.

Mr J.Z. Kobo of the opposition party summed up the zeitgeist:

> The acute shortage of land in the Transkei and the poverty, hunger and suffering that goes with it should make the Matanzima brothers ashamed of grabbing everything for themselves. When they clamour for more land for the Transkei, they want that land for themselves and their friends. The people must be aware that what is involved is self-glory for the brothers.[25]

The Matanzimas continued in the same vein after independence in 1976. The fact that civil servants enjoyed salaries far beyond the comprehension of the rest of the Transkeian population should have removed the temptation for corruption. New prime minister K.D., who was gifted a R315 000 (R13.2 million today) palace and a R16 000 (R674 000 today) American limousine by the South African government, should have been especially immune to temptation. But, alas, his newfound wealth seems only to have enhanced his desire to stick his fingers in the till (nothing unique about that, to be fair).

In the first few years of independence, scores of Transkeian government officials used their positions to get first dibs on properties which the South African government had purchased from white owners to pave the way for Xhosa independence. What made these deals even more shady were the bargain-basement prices they paid.

One particularly lucky official, a Mr Mgudla, paid R2 300 for a house that had been bought by the South African government for R44 000 just two years prior. When it was reported that K.D. Matanzima himself was negotiating deals for two of the most desirable homes in Umtata, he promptly ordered the city's deeds office off-limits to the public and 'especially to journalists'.[26]

To find concrete evidence of how the Matanzimas were the beneficiaries of similar schemes we have to venture a little further from the capital of Umtata. Companies featuring the brothers as major shareholders got great deals on a number of rural hotels. The Cofimvaba Hotel, which had been bought by the South African government for R31 193, was sold to one of the brothers' companies for R8 000.

In his personal capacity, K.D. bought two plots in Cofimvaba for R300 each – twenty times less than the price the South African government paid for them. Luckily for the brothers, the system also worked in reverse. When K.D. sold half of his portion of the family farm, he somehow managed to find a buyer who was willing to pay R10 395, despite the fact that the entire property had been valued at a mere R2 313 a few years earlier. To further sweeten the deal, the buyer also gifted him a R60 000 (R2 million today) farm in another part of the Transkei. When all was said and done, K.D. still owned the other half of the family farm.

The sums don't add up

In their keenness to make the Transkei experiment work, the South African government gave the homeland a very generous annual allowance. The analogy with a spoilt teenager is apt, because no matter how much the South African

Pretoria paid for brand-new government buildings in Umtata

government threw at Transkei, it was never enough. In 1976, the first year of independence, Transkei was propped up to the tune of R134 million (R5.65 billion today). By 1980, after frequent flirtations with bankruptcy had forced a succession of Transkei finance ministers to go cap in hand to Pretoria, the homeland was receiving R231 million in pocket money every year.

Given the high salaries for civil servants (all 30 000 of them), administrative incompetence, pervasive corruption and profligate government spending (in 1980, R2.5 million was spent on government cars, the same year that the old fleet was sold for a mere R29 000), the shortfall is easy to understand. Perhaps the most memorable justification for departmental overspend came from one Mr B. Pukwana, the deputy secretary for foreign affairs:

Well, sometimes the department gets a directive and it comes from the Prime Minister [George Matanzima] that he should be given so much, and it is not easy for the Department to say 'no' if the Prime Minister says he must be given so much.[27]

Eventually, even the apartheid government began to grow tired of bailing out its increasingly demanding problem child. Luckily, a misfit shoal of international 'sharks' (Bantu Holomisa's word) were happy to plug the gaps. To be the proper nation K.D. Matanzima dreamed of, his Transkei would need an international airport and a deep-water port. But who would pay for them?

The K.D. Matanzima Airport in Umtata had already been upgraded (and renamed) shortly after independence, so it was only natural for President Matanzima to focus on the need for a port. Finding a suitable spot on the notoriously treacherous coastline was the first challenge. After contracting the services of a French firm to initiate the project, a team of experts wasted little time in identifying the mouth of the Umngazana River, twenty kilometres north of Port St Johns, as the ideal candidate. The fact that there were no road or rail links to the site did not seem to bother anybody.

In February 1978 it was announced that the same French firm would be completing the project, in conjunction with a mysterious financier, Dr Edmond Panigel. Suddenly, Dr Panigel and his enigmatic and ever-present shadow Mrs S.E. Strydom were everywhere. One minute they were supervising the proposed construction of new hospitals, the next they were setting up *The Voice of Transkei*, a state-sponsored magazine designed to counter the scurrilous anti-Matanzima stories.

In their desire for a mouthpiece, the Matanzimas were in good company: Van der Stel, Rhodes, Somerset, the Broederbond and, later, Zuma's beloved Guptas all tried similar tricks.

You've probably deduced by now that Panigel and Strydom were taking the Transkei for a ride. The contract which K.D. eventually signed (on the bonnet of his bakkie) was, in the words of Streek and Wicksteed, 'a straight rip off'.

> The Panigel-Strydom partnership was to net 6% as project coordinators, another 8.5% as coordinating contractors and a fee equal to the minimum paid to the various specialists. This would have meant that on the extremely conservative estimate of R125 million [for the construction of the port], they would have earned ... a minimum of R25.6 million [R874 million today].[28]

Construction on the Umngazana Port never got much further than the glorious artist's impressions that adorned the only two issues of *The Voice of Transkei* ever published. By October 1978, Dr Panigel was declared persona non grata in

Transkei. No one will ever know quite how much cash Panigel, Strydom and the Matanzimas (both of whom served on the board of the company that had been set up to build the port) got out of the brief but passionate tryst. The (non-existent) benefit to the people of Transkei is much easier to quantify.

After this highly public and embarrassing affair (the press was awash with stories and the issue featured prominently in Transkeian parliamentary proceedings), one might have thought the Matanzimas would put their harbour plans on ice. Instead, they supersized them.

At the same time that the Panigel plan was unravelling, another, even more ambitious one was gathering steam. In April 1978, 'Transkei's highly-paid Middle East representative, Salim El-Hajj, suddenly announced spectacular plans to build an R800-million harbour complex in Transkei which would include tourist facilities, casinos, an international airport, an oil refinery, hotels, housing and roads. Finance for the projects would come from his companies and Arab and European concerns.'[29]

With the stroke of a pen, El-Hajj and his 'team of experts' (another must-have in the world of kickbacks and shady deals) moved the proposed harbour from Umngazana to Mazeppa Bay. Before construction could begin, however, they would need a down payment from the Transkei government.

Just a few months later, finance minister Columbus Madikizela (father of Winnie Mandela; Winnie hated the fact that her old man had sided with someone Nelson Mandela termed a 'turncoat'[30]) announced, with his tail firmly between his legs, that the government had cut ties with El-Hajj. He simultaneously applied for an additional R9 million (R307 million today) to be added to the budget to cover their losses in the episode. 'It has been our fear,' he said, 'that El-Hajj is one of the international crooks who have been swindling our state from time to time by making unfulfilled promises to assist the country in return for huge sums of money.'[31]

There's no hard and fast evidence that the Matanzimas benefited from the El-Hajj affair. It's all so amateurish that one almost finds oneself hoping that they did. Why bother otherwise?

Brothers at arms

After the second harbour debacle, the Matanzimas seem to have realised they were going to have to dial down their aspirations a little and return to their tried-and-tested methods. Who needed fancy airports and harbours when there were easier, and far less conspicuous, ways of making a quick buck? Like fudging housing contracts, extorting gambling rights and siphoning government tractors away from small-scale farmers ...

Besides, they had loads of other things to get on with. Much like W.A. van der Stel, Lord Charles Somerset and the Broederbond, they would go on a campaign of silencing, imprisoning and banishing critics. And like the apartheid government, a little bit of 'international' military interference was also on the cards. In 1987, George Matanzima would orchestrate a (failed) coup against a fellow 'homeland' when he attempted to overthrow the Ciskei's president Lennox Sebe in the hopes of creating a united Xhosaland. Perhaps most challenging of all, the Matanzimas would also take to walking an extremely wobbly ideological tightrope which saw them attempting to voice their support for both Pretoria and the ANC.

But forget these extraneous distractions. The biggest bump in the road would be the brothers' own relationship.

K.D. plays God

In 1978, K.D. Matanzima took the extraordinary measure of banning the Methodist Church – to which he owed much of his education – in the Transkei. Since 1975, K.D. had been uneasy about rumours that the Black Consciousness Movement was gaining traction in the dorms and dining halls of St Bede's Mission (Heaven forbid!). But the final straw came when, at its annual conference in 1977, the Methodist Church of Southern Africa resolved to stop sending Christmas messages of goodwill to the leaders of Bantustans.

Incandescent that his own church did not recognise Transkei's independence, K.D. banned the buggers (and sent the security police to arrest ministers who ignored the ban). His creation of the government-backed Transkei Methodist Church sent a clear message: freedom of religion had serious caveats in the Transkei. The *Cape Argus* compared the move to that pulled by Henry VIII, who, in 1534, broke away from the Catholic Church and declared himself 'Supreme Head on earth of the Church of England'.

Notwithstanding his many sins, K.D. does seem to have been a fairly close approximation of a proper politician. As the trust account scandal attests, his *boet* was an entirely different kettle of fish. 'Chief George was too careless,' laughed Holomisa in our interview.[32] In their book, Streek and Wicksteed euphemistically discuss his 'entrepreneurial' streak. But the most damning assessment comes from Jeff Peires: 'The notorious corruption of both Matanzima brothers has been extensively documented but, whereas Kaiser had maintained a modicum of discretion, George threw all caution to the wind. On one occasion, for instance, he took delivery of R500,000 in a cardboard box in exchange for a housing contract.'[33]

Despite these fundamental differences in character, the brothers managed to maintain a positive relationship until the mid-1980s. 'Although the brothers will sometimes say disparaging things about one another in private, and although there have been conflicts, they have rarely been publicised and, in the final analysis, the survival of each depends on the support he can give the other,' observed Streek and Wicksteed in 1980.[34]

Looking into their crystal ball

This remarkably prescient prediction was written by Streek and Wicksteed seven years before the brothers' downfall:

Whenever Kaiser Matanzima fades from the scene, the process of succession will be traumatic and complicated. Without Kaiser to back him, George Matanzima's power base will disappear – and it is unlikely that he could ever exercise the same hold over the party or the government. He certainly does not enjoy the same legitimacy in the eyes of Kaiser Matanzima's key support groups, such as the chiefs, the party, the army and the police. What this means is that in the process of succession, a new leadership with very different policies and interests could develop. It could even be that some form of military and/or police coup will be the only way to establish initial stability.[35]

As predicted, 'the wheels began to come off in February 1986, when Kaiser Matanzima's term of office as president of the Transkei expired, leaving effective power in the hands of the prime minister, his brother George'.[36] K.D. was succeeded by Tutor Ndamase as state president but, in his hands, the role became largely ceremonial. It might come as a surprise that a man as ruthless as K.D. respected such banalities as presidential terms of office. Term limits don't generally mean much to the tinpot dictators of banana republics, but K.D. was shrewder than most. After ten years of the brothers' corrupt ways, a number of important players across the Transkeian hierarchy had had enough. And K.D., at least, could see the writing on the wall.

True to form, 'Careless George' played a central – and comical – role in setting in motion the dung ball that would eventually see George imprisoned and K.D. banished. There are two contrasting accounts of how George came to authorise the commission(s) of inquiry that would lead to their downfall, but neither paints Chief George in a particularly flattering light.

JEFF PEIRES'S TAKE – A SLIP OF THE PEN

Some time in 1985 Jiyana Maqubela, the Auditor-General, slipped a motivation for a Commission of Inquiry into a pile of routine papers which George Matanzima unthinkingly signed. The first Commission of Inquiry, into the Department of Commerce, Industry and Tourism, began to hear evidence in February 1986. It was a slow-burning fuse, but it led inexorably first to George, and then to Kaiser himself.[37]

ERIC NAKI'S TAKE – A STAGGERING MISJUDGEMENT

Ironically the Van Reenen Commission was approved by George Matanzima and came at a time when the two brothers had become sworn enemies. Chief George was hoping that the commission would expose his elder brother's involvement in corruption, but, unfortunately for him, it was to reveal his own shady dealings and he would serve a long jail term as a result ... when Pretoria came with the idea of a commission, Chief George was jubilant. He believed that he had never been tainted by the graft that happened under his brother's watch. He was wrong.[38]

'A government of drum majorettes'

It is no coincidence that the Alexander Commission of Inquiry (later known as the Van Reenen Commission after Advocate Alexander was called away from Umtata) kicked off in February 1986 – the very month that President K.D. Matanzima chose to slip from centre stage. Besides, as a paramount chief, he remained an ex officio member of the Transkei legislature, and a vocal critic of his brother's leadership. Eric Naki writes:

K.D. denounced George's administration as weak and castigated his brother for not being as tough as he was in dealing with Transkei's 'enemies'. He had on occasion reduced George to tears for his inept handling of matters of state.

He once described George's government as 'ceremonial' and a 'government of drum majorettes' (urhulumente wamagubu), referring to his habit of organising drum majorettes to be present at official ceremonies. K.D. often accused his younger sibling of being a 'womaniser' instead of caring about the development of the country.[39]

Within months of relinquishing the presidency, K.D. attempted a political comeback by nominating his own slate of candidates for the September 1986 Transkei elections. But 'the electorate, preferring the easier master, chose George'.[40]

K.D. wasn't done yet. Early the following year, he and forty of his loyal followers walked out of the congress of the Transkei National Independence Party (which K.D. had formed twenty-four years earlier) and formed a new party, with the intention of taking over the government. His reasons were predictable: his brother's administration was corrupt, he said.

Chief George was having none of it. On 7 May 1987, the Speaker in the assembly prevented K.D. from bringing a motion of no confidence in his brother's

Chief George and P.W. Botha share a rare light moment

government on the grounds that his new party was not registered. According
to a report by the Institute of Race Relations,

> The following day Chief George Matanzima introduced the Republic of
> Transkei Constitution Amendment Bill, which was rushed through all three
> readings, signed by the state president, and gazetted in one day. In terms of
> it any former state president of the Transkei was prevented from sitting as an
> MP in the national assembly. Chief Kaiser Matanzima was the only living
> former state president.[41]

But it got better. Three days later, following British colonial and apartheid 'best
practice', George banished K.D. from Umtata and he was placed under house
arrest at Qamata Great Place. K.D. was defiant, saying that he would continue
his efforts to topple his brother's administration, as 'bribery and corruption
flourished in its ranks'. The embezzlement of funds, K.D. argued baselessly, had
only started after his retirement with the arrival of 'white vultures' on the scene.
But the white vultures had been there all along ...

Dad's army and the Ciskei coup

It wasn't just the judiciary that was *gatvol* of the Matanzimas; the army had also had
enough of them. Established a year before 'independence', the Transkei Defence
Force (TDF) was always supposed to be a blacks-only army (even if the officers were
all trained in South Africa). However, in 1981 K.D. fired the three most senior black
officers and placed a group of white ex-Rhodesian Selous Scouts at the helm.

'The Selous Scouts provided Kaiser with security, but they were disliked by
their black subordinates,' writes Peires. 'The sharpest critic of the Selous Scouts
within the TDF was its second-in-command, Brigadier Bantu Holomisa, who was
detained on 21 January 1987 for complaining that the Selous Scouts used TDF
facilities for their private security operations.'[42]

In September 1986, at Chief George's request, the Rhodesian-led TDF launched
a daring coup attempt in neighbouring Ciskei. In the first phase of the campaign,
the white mercenaries simultaneously freed Charles Sebe (brother of Ciskei's
president Lennox Sebe – family feuds were all the rage in the Bantustans) from a
maximum-security prison and kidnapped Kwane Sebe, Lennox's only son. With
the two Sebes in the bag, they launched an armed assault on Lennox's presidential
palace. But phase two didn't go according to plan.

'The attack was a failure,' writes Peires, 'and one TDF soldier was killed. The Transkeian officers were furious, partly because they disapproved of the entire project, but mostly because George Matanzima attempted to evade his own responsibility by placing the blame on them.'[43]

This farcical incident played a huge role in paving the way for the bloodless coup a year later. While Chief George was roundly hated by just about everyone in the army, K.D. remained popular in certain quarters – most notably with Craig Duli, who masterminded the Transkei coup, and Bantu Holomisa, who led it.

Give George enough rope ... and he'll hang himself

In the end, K.D. didn't have to do anything to topple his brother from his lofty perch.

Things came to a head in September 1987, when the public gallery of the Harms Commission of Inquiry (set up to investigate 'cross-border' crimes committed in South Africa) was treated to the evidence of Mr Herman Visser, a housing developer from Port Elizabeth. Before then, reported the Weekly Mail, 'whenever evidence had strayed too close to them, the hearings quickly became in camera [in the private chambers of a judge, with the press and public excluded]'.[44] In this manner, George had managed to keep the findings of the previous Van Reenen Commission of Inquiry secret for months. But his luck was about to run out.

Visser testified that his construction firm had paid Chief George lobola – the isiXhosa term for a bride's dowry, which in this case also translated as 'bribe'– of R1 million (R10.2 million in today's money). The payment had been made in two instalments. Visser had personally given Chief George a cheque for R500 000. He had also arranged for a cash payment of R500 000 that was presented to Chief George in a tattered cardboard box by Visser's brother-in-law (whom Visser paid an additional R100 000 for his 'hospitality' in doing the deed.)

Visser also listed various bribes (often referred to as icuba, or 'tobacco money') to other government officials. 'These people do not say directly: "If you do not pay, this and this and this will happen to you", but you know that there is pressure on you to pay,' Visser testified.[45] After paying the bribe, his firm was duly awarded a R30-million contract to build 800 houses in Umtata.

Visser's testimony opened the floodgates and prevented Chief George from concealing Van Reenen's findings ('a bulky document which [was] merciless in its documentation of the Matanzimas' corruption'[46]) any longer.

Laundry list[47]

The various commissions into corruption in the Transkei amassed thousands of pages of evidence. Some of the dicey dealings they catalogued included:

- Kaiser Matanzima's bid to gain control of the entire petrol market in Transkei. The unsuccessful ploy would have earned Kaiser some R400 000 (R6.5 million today) a year.
- The case of Umtata motor firm Nduli Motors, in which Chief George had a major share. The company owed the Transkei government some R500 000 when it went into liquidation.
- Housing contracts in Butterworth and Umtata worth R68 million awarded irregularly to JALC Holdings and its subsidiary, Temba Construction. On the directives of the Matanzimas, no tenders had been called for, despite advice to the contrary by officials. The contract price on one of the housing projects had increased from the original total of R17 million to R54 million, and that on another from R9.1 million to R14.7 million. The housing projects had been carried out even though housing was not in demand and the ground was unstable. The Alexander Commission found that the role of Mr Chris van Rensburg (the 'C' in JALC) had been 'ubiquitous' and his close relationship with Chief George had become apparent.
- How K.D. received amounts totalling R274 000 from the establishment of the Transkei's only casino, the Wild Coast Sun at Mzamba Beach. Curiouser still, Holiday Inn (owned by none other than hotel tycoon Sol Kerzner) gave the casino rights to a company that was wholly owned by Mr Monde Sihele, a nephew of the Matanzima brothers, before buying them back from him for R500 000.
- How Chief George had instructed the Transkei Development Corporation to sell its 25 per cent shareholding in the Wild Coast Sun, worth between R12 million and R15 million, for R50 000 to a Transkeian company in which Chief George apparently had interests. Chief George also ordered the TDC to sell its share in a brewery for R650 000, losing the government R6.3 million in the process.

Once these revelations had come to light, Duli, Holomisa and a few other senior members of the TDF decided they had to intervene. As Bantu Holomisa recalled in our interview, 'The commission didn't mention George by name. They called him Mr X. When we realised it was him, we went to see him, and we said to him, "Sir, there is a lot of anxiety. People are aware that Mr X is yourself." He said, "Yes, my boys, I know it is me." We advised him to step down to allow the commission to handle things its own way. He agreed, he said he would go and inform Pik Botha...'

The newspaper front page reads:

PRICES: WITWATERSRAND & PRETORIA R1.00 (incl. GST) | ELSEWHERE IN SA R1.12 (incl. GST)

THE WEEKLY MAIL

VOLUME 3, NUMBER 38, FRIDAY SEPTEMBER 25 to THURSDAY OCTOBER 1, 1987

THE PAPER FOR A CHANGING SOUTH AFRICA

Iron-man George Matanzima flees T'Kei

Weekly Mail Reporters: EAST LONDON

AN army coup toppled Transkei Prime Minister George Matanzima yesterday. Matanzima has fled and eight ministers are under house arrest.

An interim government has been set up after the bloodless and unopposed coup, led by Transkei Defence Force chief Major-General Bantu Holomisa.

Reports of a coup come in the wake of commissions of inquiry into alleged massive government corruption. Transkei troops have put up roadblocks in an attempt to seal off the "homeland".

Matanzima, involved in a corruption probe, is believed to be hiding in Port Elizabeth.

Among ministers under house arrest are Reverend GT Viks (deputy prime minister and minister of agriculture and forestry; Digby Koyana (justice and prisons); Tshepo Letlaka, (commerce); M Lujaba (interior, manpower utilisation and planning; S Xaba (transport); HB Tsengwa (local government and land tenure); MZ Ngceba (deputy minister of agriculture); WT Nomvalo (deputy minister of health.

The official, who refused to be named, said Transkeian troops had turned up at the ministers' homes on Wednesday night and forced them to

- Military coup topples Transkei Prime Minister
- Troops set up interim cabinet
- Eight ministers house arrested

THE NAPOLEON OF THE TRANSKEI, FOR THE FULL STORY OF HOW GREED BROUGHT DOWN THE MATANZIMA EMPIRE, TURN TO PAGES 10 AND 11

Chief George finds himself on the wrong side of justice (*Weekly Mail*, 25 September 1987)

Chief George, Holomisa continued, 'had to agree to our terms. His back was against the wall. But after a week he still hadn't come back from Pretoria. We began to panic. We thought of everything, even that he might have asked Pretoria to arrest us. When a week became two weeks, we decided we had to act.'[48]

With Chief George still nowhere to be found, on 23 September 1987 armed TDF officers compelled a number of ministers and other officials who had been implicated by the report to sign letters of resignation. 'None of them resisted and all put their signatures on the document that was to seal their fate.'[49]

Chief George remained in exile, with reports saying that he was staying in a Port Elizabeth hotel under the name of 'Mr Smith'. After a period of limbo, George eventually relayed his resignation telephonically. At some point, he left PE and went to Austria to hang out with his buddies at the tractor factory.

Before the Arms Deal …

… there was the Austrian Tractor Deal.

The Van Reenen report described how the Transkei had been persuaded to buy 1884 Steyr tractors from Austria, resulting in an exchange loss of up to R30 million. Of these tractors, 224 had not been accounted for and some had been sold at bargain prices to the Matanzimas and their friends. The tractors were wholly unsuited to the Transkei's terrain and no plans had been made for their maintenance. The tractor deal was 'almost exactly the same as the arms deal,' says Holomisa. 'But at least the tractors did actually come!' This explains why you can still find working 1980s Steyr tractors scattered across the platteland, and why George Matanzima fled to Austria, of all places, after the coup.

While Holomisa was put under great pressure to assume the leadership of the Transkei there and then, he insisted that the party elect a new leader democratically. Stella Sigcau (daughter of pro-Pretoria Botha Sigcau, Transkei's first president) was duly elected the first and only female prime minister of Transkei (and, for that matter, any other part of South Africa). Her leadership was, Holomisa says, a breath of fresh air. She ordered the arrest of K.D. Matanzima and she was even spied dining with the Matanzimas' arch-enemy Lennox Sebe over in Ciskei.

But then, eighty-six days later, advance findings of a(nother) commission into gambling rights implicated Sigcau in wrongdoing and the military was left with no option but to take over. 'We realised that this basket was full of rotten apples,' says Holomisa.

Everything the Sun King touches

At midday on 31 December, Holomisa led an entirely bloodless coup which was greeted with jubilation on both the streets of Umtata and in the hallways of the Union Buildings in Pretoria. The apartheid government, who had grown sick of the Matanzimas' corruption, were thrilled to have the problem taken off their hands.

But Stella Sigcau – who was building sandcastles on a Durban beach at the time of the coup – was not as enamoured of the move. '"Why do you do this to me," she shouted over the phone. "Why did you not inform me about this … What you have done is foolish, boys."'[50]

But the 'boys' had evidence that Sigcau had taken a R50 000 bribe from none other than the Sun King, Sol Kerzner.

In December 1986, the virtuous South African hotelier and casino owner had ordered his lawyer (David Bloomberg, an esteemed former mayor of Cape Town) to pay George Matanzima R2 million in exchange for exclusive gambling rights within a 100-kilometre radius of Umtata. This despite the fact that Transkei's constitution expressly forbade the granting of 'exclusive' rights.

In an attempt to cover their tracks, the cash was transferred – according to the *1988/89 Race Relations Survey* – 'into the account of an Ugie farmer, Mr J Gouws, whereafter it [was] used by Chief George Matanzima to purchase Mr Gouws' farm for R1,4m and to pay amounts of R50 000 each to various influential Transkei personalities', including K.D. Matanzima and Stella Sigcau.[51]

After initially denying the claims completely – he even went so far as to take out full-page newspaper adverts to this effect – Kerzner ultimately admitted paying the bribe. 'Under undue pressure from then prime minister George Matanzima, R2m of the funds available were ... paid into the account of Mr G J Gouws for the ultimate benefit of Prime Minister G Matanzima. I accept responsibility for this jointly with Mr Bloomberg,' he said in an affidavit.

Sigcau, for her part, told the commission that she had believed the R50 000 from Chief George was a gift and had accepted it in good faith. She was, she insisted, 'the only recipient who openly announced the fact of her gift immediately, telling friends, family and the church that she had the money'.[52]

K.D., somewhat less convincingly, told the commission that he had been unaware of the R50 000 deposit Chief George had made into his account in January 1987 as he 'did not have time to look at his bank statements'. Advocate Alexander noted that K.D. had been an extremely bad witness and that he was not satisfied that he had been told the truth by him. 'I am left with a grave suspicion that the monies he received were for favours improperly rendered by him,' he said.

Discussing the entirety of the evidence uncovered by the report, Advocate Alexander described 'a grotesque pattern of corruption in high places' and urged all beneficiaries to 'disgorge their ill-gotten gains'. Mr W.Z. Yako, the Transkei's auditor-general, said in an interview that he estimated that 'about R200m had been stolen or misappropriated between "independence" in 1976 and March 1986 ... There has been a complete disregard for treasury instructions and Tender Board regulations over a number of years.'[53]

Under Holomisa's leadership, George Matanzima was 'charged with nine counts of corruption, and alternative charges of bribery involving thousands of rands in the awards of building contracts for housing schemes in Butterworth and Umtata between 1985 and 1987'.[54] He was found guilty of corruption and sentenced to nine years in prison. He served almost three years before receiving a pardon. K.D. Matanzima was never charged with a crime, as 'he knew how to make sure there was nothing on him,' Holomisa told us, laughing.

Christo Nel, the attorney-general of the Transkei, also charged Kerzner with corruption, but the hotelier made it clear he would not appear voluntarily in a Transkeian court and Pretoria blocked Nel's frequent 'extradition' requests. After 1994, once the ANC had come to power, the charges were formally dropped against Kerzner. Nel maintains this was due to the death of a key witness, but Holomisa remains convinced that it had more to do with Kerzner's R3-million donation to the ANC's election campaign. Corruption, as we have seen all too often, knows no political ideology but its own.

As for the Matanzimas' legacy, Holomisa is quick to credit K.D. with everything he did to advance the Transkei education system. Many of the black accountants, lawyers and doctors in South Africa today are products of that system, he said. 'But the brothers could have done a lot more if they had not been so corrupt,' he added.

There is no denying the Matanzimas had sticky fingers, Holomisa explained, but they didn't become stinking rich either. 'K.D. had a farm in Queenstown, he was involved in a hotel near Coffee Bay. I don't remember any other business interests ... Compared to the ANC comrades today, the Matanzimas don't come close,' he laughed. 'Under the ANC government they talk billions. They don't play around ...'

CHAPTER 11

LUCAS MANGOPE

The Dog of the Boers
1977–1994

'Lead us and we shall try to crawl.' – Lucas Mangope[1]

Lucas Mangope aka the Great Lion
of Bophuthatswana surveys
the savannah for lucrative prey

O N 6 DECEMBER 1977, BOPHUTHATSWANA became the second apartheid-era homeland to achieve 'independence'. The new country and its new president, Kgosi Lucas Manyane Mangope (known as 'Tautona', the Great Lion), were in many ways cut from the same cloth as the Transkei and K.D. Matanzima.

Lucas Mangope, like K.D. before him, was not destined by birth to lead his people. A minor chief of the Bahurutshe boo Manyane, he made a name for himself as a shameless apartheid stooge as early as 1958. If you thought K.D.'s subservience was cringe-making, try this on for size ...

When Bahurutshe women openly opposed the apartheid government by publicly burning their pass books, Pretoria responded by deposing Chief Abram Moiloa (a proud ANC member) and quelling the uprising through brute force. Once the state had re-established control, a more pliant chief was installed. At this new chief's swearing-in ceremony, Lucas Mangope famously implored minister of Bantu affairs Daan de Wet Nel to 'lead us and we shall try to crawl'.

This single cringe-making utterance would establish Mangope as the ultimate 'apartheid good boy' (to borrow the Xhosa chief Dalindyebo's phrase) and made him a shoo-in, as far as Pretoria was concerned, for leader of the newly 'independent' state of Bophuthatswana two decades later. (Verwoerd would later riff on Mangope's baby analogy: 'Black people I am going to give you government ... because you are grown and mature now. You are not children. You are going to be given the opportunity to serve your own people and build your own nation.'[2])

Mangope used those two decades wisely, inventing both a paramount chieftainship for himself (à la K.D. Matanzima) and a glorious unified past for the many disparate factions and groups that would comprise the new nation. Not to mention banishing (there's nothing a South African leader enjoys quite so much as a good banishment) and/or intimidating chiefs who were hostile to his leadership and installing yes-men in their stead.

But this was not the only way in which he borrowed from the Matanzima playbook. In 1961, Mangope was put in charge of the Tswana Territorial Authority by Pretoria. Eleven years later, when the self-governing Bantustan of Bophuthatswana was created, he became its first chief minister. By the time 'independence' was achieved in 1977, his popularity among the chiefs who sat on the legislature meant he did not need the support of a single elected official to secure the role of president. Which is not to say he ever did badly at the ballot box – Tautona's stranglehold on Bop saw him win forty-three out of forty-eight seats in the inaugural elections. And in 1982 he went one better by winning all seventy-two seats available!

Same same, but different

But if there were similarities between Bop and the Transkei, there were also yawning differences.

On paper, the whole concept of Bop – vaunted by the kind folks at Bantu Administration as a place for Setswana-speaking people to feel entirely at home – was absurd. The supposedly united nation was made up of sixteen landlocked islands spread across what are now the North West, Free State and Northern Cape provinces. The newly named capital of Mmabatho (on the outskirts of Mahikeng aka Mafikeng aka Mafeking) was wedged up against the border with Botswana, and there were also enclaves near Upington, Johannesburg and even Lesotho. While some of the 'islands' comprised farms that had long been legally owned by the Bafokeng and other Tswana chiefdoms, others were nothing more than dormitory towns of predominantly Setswana-speaking miners. Taken

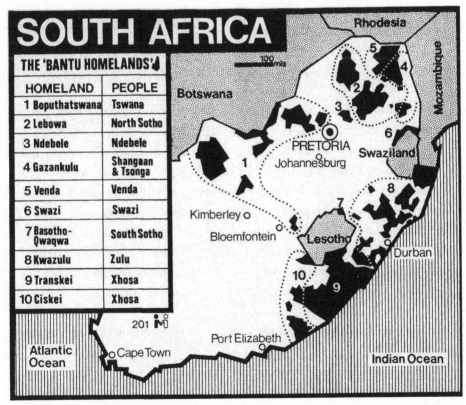

A map showing the absurdity of the homelands system in general and Bop in particular

together, the population of all these bits and pieces came to around 1.5 million – half of whom were not Setswana-speakers. Even Mangope acknowledged this 'territorial credibility gap', and others nicknamed the new country Jigsaw Land.

If the Transkei had the upper hand in terms of geographic and some kind of ethnic cohesion, Bop did have one very big ace up its sleeve. The homeland contained 30 per cent of the world's platinum. And if you're wondering how the apartheid government allowed this little detail to escape their attention, you can rest assured that they did not. The Broederbonders pulling the strings in Pretoria knew exactly what they were doing.

Not long after the discovery of platinum in the region in 1921, it became apparent that most of the very best reserves lay on Bafokeng tribal lands. When the inevitable flocks of 'white vultures' (to use Matanzima's term) arrived to claim their share, the Bafokeng stood their ground, going through the courts to protect their assets. Unlike Lobengula's Ndebele, they would not have their mineral rights stolen from under their noses. However, the high cost of platinum extraction meant that before the 1960s the Bafokeng had not made any serious cash out of the ground beneath their feet.

But this all stood to change when Broederbond-backed Impala entered the fray. As Andrew Manson and Bernard Mbenga explain,

In 1968, Impala Prospecting Company, a subsidiary of Gencor, entered into certain Notarial Prospecting Contracts with the Bafokeng. Prior to this, Anglo-American Platinum (Amplats) had been the major platinum-producer in South Africa. These two companies broadly represented the interests of English and Afrikaner capitalists, Gencor [being] an initiative of the National Party government to empower an Afrikaner capitalist class. A major shareholder in Gencor is Sanlam, in turn controlled by the Rembrandt group, both bastions of Afrikaner economic power and control. With the acquisition of leases on Bafokeng-owned land, moreover, Impala positioned itself to become the second largest producer of platinum in the world.[3]

The Bafokeng stood to make a mint out of the agreement. Or at least they thought they did.

Once in power, Mangope would waste no time in pouncing on the unsuspecting Bafokeng and their platinum royalties. Over the ensuing decades, he teamed up with the Broeders at Impala to systematically squeeze his tribal rivals out of what was rightly theirs, using court orders, banishments and even violence to achieve his aims. His argument was that, as president of Bophuthatswana, the mineral rights actually belonged to him – and who was Impala to disagree?

But the Great Lion would also find other lucrative prey in the arid scrubland of his new fiefdom. By stacking his cabinet with yes-men (and appointing himself to no fewer than five cabinet positions), he was able to do pretty much as he pleased. The problem, say Michael Lawrence and Andrew Manson (who both taught at the University of Bophuthatswana during the bad old days), was that 'Mangope had a profound sense of his entitlements, but little sense of his obligations'.[4]

Mangope and South African prime minister B.J. Vorster

The Lion's share

Once he'd ridden roughshod over his opponents to become president of the fledgling nation, Mangope had the temerity to declare Bophuthatswana a 'place for all' and 'a haven of non-racialism'. He wheeled out a gleaming new constitution and a glittering Bill of Rights which protected the rights of all individuals. Or that was the theory. In practice,

[t]he very last Section (18.1) in the Bill of Rights specified that other laws could override the provisions of the Bill. These laws included the Internal Security Act and the Security Clearance Act, which were used increasingly to suppress political opponents and organisations.[5]

Mangope didn't only persecute political opponents. Non-Tswanas (who made up more than half of Bop's population) were routinely denied work permits, citizenship and pensions. Many were reclassified as 'squatters' so that they could be kicked off the farms and homes they rightfully owned more easily.

Despite what was really happening on the ground, Mangope's lofty proclamations caught the attention of the international community, with some gullible souls believing that Bop truly was a place for all. While historian Manson points out that 'for a brief moment in time Mangope did offer an alternative to apartheid and the education system was generally better than Bantu education in South Africa with many Tswana parents choosing to send their kids to school in Bop',[6] most of the foreigners drawn to Mangope's honeypot had impure intentions. When it came down to it, Bop was a Place for all Scoundrels.

Sol Kerzner (yes, him again) first set his sights on Bop long before independence. It must have come as a real blow to the Sun King when, in 1965, justice minister B.J. Vorster (of Ossewabrandwag fame) announced that gambling would be outlawed in South Africa. Clutching his Bible, Vorster passionately argued that Afrikaners 'should combat the evil of gambling', for it 'undermines the morale of any nation'.[7]

Luckily, another piece of apartheid legislation would come to Kerzner's rescue. The 1971 Self-Governing Territories Constitution Act, which gave Bantustans powers to write their own laws, presented him with the opportunity to 'undermine the morale' of some brand-new nations. Kerzner wasted no time in hatching his plan to 'establish casino resorts in Bophuthatswana, Ciskei and Transkei and dominate the casino trade in southern Africa,' writes Nicola Sarah van der Merwe. 'Bantustan independence freed Kerzner not only from the restrictive Gambling Act, but also from the South African trade unions and the wearisome ways of "democracy".'[8]

Bophuthatswana's proximity to Pretoria and Joburg made it especially attractive to Kerzner. In 1976 he signed a deal with Mangope which would give his company exclusive gambling rights in Bop. In that same year construction commenced on the 100-room Mmabatho Sun in the new capital. The hotel's opulent

Pik Botha and Mangope sign documents incorporating Mafeking into Bop
(in the process changing its name to Mafikeng)

Presidential Suite was continuously reserved for Mangope at an outrageously preferential rate of R20 (R840 today) per night, and another block of rooms was reserved for members of his cabinet at R10 a night.

But this was small fry compared with the dreams Kerzner had for his Sun City resort – if he could only find the money he needed to make them come true. Luckily for Sol, he would find government investments from both Mmabatho and, of all places, Calvinist Pretoria to build his hedonistic Sin City.

The company behind Sun City was jointly owned by the Bophuthatswana government and Sun International (which in turn was heavily funded by South African Breweries), with Kerzner's company holding a controlling interest of 50 per cent. The South African government, however, footed much of the bill for wider infrastructural developments, without which the resort could never have been developed. Pretoria, for example, chipped in R800 000 (R27 million today) towards the construction of a new tar road to the resort and a further R10 million (R340 million today) for other infrastructure. As if this wasn't enough, they also gave a virtually interest-free loan of R8 million for other upgrades in and around the town of Heystekrand, where Sun City is located.

The first sod was turned at Sun City on 15 July 1978, with 1200 people (mostly poor locals) working to a gruelling schedule. Under drill-sergeant Kerzner, the first phase of the resort was completed on 7 December 1979, only eighteen months after the site had been selected.[9] By 1983, according to *Time* magazine, Sun City's 'slot machines, roulette wheels and befeathered chorus girls [would] attract as many as 50,000 visitors a day, mostly well-to-do whites who make the two-hour drive from Pretoria and Johannesburg'.[10] The same *Time* magazine report goes on to say that

[u]nlike most of South Africa, homelands like Bophuthatswana allow blacks and whites to mingle openly. Still, South Africa is in such bad odour because of apartheid that Kerzner has to pay platinum-plated premiums to get American entertainers like Linda Ronstadt and Kenny Rogers to brave possible censure for having performed at Sun City. Two years ago, Kerzner paid Frank Sinatra $2 million for nine shows over seven days, charging up to $85 per seat. Although such prices create a kind of economic apartheid at the resort since most blacks cannot afford admission ...[11]

Lucas Mangope and Sol Kerzner enjoying the lion's share of the profits

What *Time* magazine did not note was that the road they drove to reach Sun City had been paid for by the Broederbonders and NG Kerk-goers who publicly denounced Kerzner's hedonistic playground as worse than Sodom and Gomorrah combined.

But this wasn't even the half of it. Later in 1983, it was discovered that Pretoria had actually 'advanced Southern Sun a maximum sum of R12 million [R409 million today] towards the building of the hotel and casino complex itself [in return] for a 9% stake in the company', according to Van der Merwe, who goes on to explain:

> This information was leaked by the South African media in 1983, which reported that the 'conservative and morally [abhorrent]' apartheid govern-ment had an indirect 9% interest in the 'hedonistic playground' just across the border with Bophuthatswana, where gambling and pornography proliferated. A deal was reached, and the IDC [Industrial Development Corporation of South Africa] divested their stake in Sun International, selling the shares to private entities. Kerzner had managed to play both sides of the coin and reap the benefits from both the government of Bophuthatswana and South Africa.

But King Sol would not stop there. In 1984, Bop's finance minister Leslie Young agreed that any investment by Sun International 'that marketed apartheid South Africa internationally would be tax deductible in Bophuthatswana'.[12]

'(Ain't Gonna Play) Sun City'

As we've already seen, the only foreigners who took Bophuthatswana's independ-ence seriously were those who stood to gain from it. But the 'country' didn't only attract white supremacists, arms dealers and property sharks. In the 1980s, literally hundreds of musicians (including Cher, The Beach Boys, Rod Stewart, Queen ... the list goes on.) and sportsmen broke the cultural boycott of South Africa to play at Sun City.

'We've thought a lot about the morals of it a lot,' said Queen's guitarist Brian May at the time, 'and it is something we've decided to do. The band is not political – we play to anybody who wants to come and listen.' Of course, 'morals' was really a code word for 'money'. No one knows how much Queen was paid, but as we have seen, Frank Sinatra received $2 million (R95 million today) for nine shows.

It wasn't just musicians who were lured by south by Sol's lucre. Dozens of important international boxing matches were held at Sun City's 'Superbowl', including a heavyweight world title fight in which white Afrikaans-speaking boxer Gerrie Coetzee (who would later receive $800 000 for losing yet another fight at the Superbowl) was knocked out cold by the African American Mike Weaver. And, in 1981, on a course designed by Gary Player, five of the world's best golfers (Jack Nicklaus, Lee Trevino, Seve Ballesteros, Johnny Miller and Player himself) lined up for the first-ever golfing tournament to boast a million-dollar purse.

Given what we've learnt about human nature over the course of this book, it's probably more surprising that some artists and sportsmen refused to tarnish their reputations by playing at Sun City. Stevie Wonder, Ella Fitzgerald and Tony Bennett are all known to have refused offers in excess of a million dollars. In 1985, Steven van Zandt (of E Street Band fame) brought together fifty-four musicians (including Bruce Springsteen, Bob Dylan, Miles Davis, Bono, Run-DMC and Keith Richards) under the banner of Artists United Against Apartheid to perform a jaunty protest song called 'Sun City', which highlighted the injustices of the homelands system and black people's ineligibility to vote, and raised over a million dollars for the anti-apartheid cause.[13]

In 1987, Young levied a 50 per cent tax on entertainers who earned more than R26 000 per annum in Bop. But the Bop government were so in bed with Kerzner that they then returned 90 per cent of the funds raised through this tax to Sun International. In practice, this meant that the huge sums spent on bringing international artists out to Sun City were being subsidised by the Bop government (which, in turn, was funded by Pretoria). While Kerzner had had to foot most of the bill for early visitors like Dolly Parton and Frank Sinatra, later acts like Queen and Elton John were effectively brought out to South Africa at the expense of the government. Talk about having your cake and eating it.

Twenty years later, in newly democratic South Africa, the reason for Young's willingness to appease Kerzner was revealed. A document dated 1987 (the same year the crazy tax scheme described above was implemented) was uncovered, which showed that Mangope had asked Kerzner to personally subsidise a R20 000 (R203 000 today) salary increase for none other than finance minister Leslie Young. The deputy chairperson of Sun International responded to Mangope's request in writing:

We would certainly be prepared to contribute to the augmentation of Mr. Young's salary ... Upon receipt of the amount required each year and the desired manner of payments we will make the necessary arrangements.[14]

It was later discovered that Impala (the platinum-mining company) had also been augmenting Young's salary.

Bop TV puts 'whites on the wrong side of apartheid'

Anyone who was subjected to the SABC's puritan programming choices in the 1980s will remember the excitement when Mangope launched Bop TV in 1984. After years of Calvinist propaganda, the line-up of popular American shows was positively hedonistic. If, as the *New York Times* reported, you could manage to wangle a signal:

'If you are lucky you can find one decent program an evening to watch on South African television,' said Steve Roos, an activist campaigning for greater access in South Africa to Bop-TV. The new channel, by contrast, he said, 'tries to please 90 percent of the people 90 percent of the time,' mainly offering American comedies and series such as *Gimme a Break* and *Falcon Crest.*

Overnight, in areas where the Bop-TV signal spilled out beyond its black target areas, white viewers like Mr. Roos began erecting forests of broad-band antennae to improve their reception of the new station, settling in comfortably each evening to watch news programs that were not as self-censored as those on South African television and entertainment programs they had never seen before.

The South Africans struck back, gradually refining the Bop-TV signal until it reached only its target areas among blacks and did not spill over into white areas. 'I spent about R350 on four new antennae,' Mr. Roos said, 'but I can't get the signal properly anymore ... This is segregation the other way round.'[15]

A KGB double agent enters the fray

As the friendship between the dictator and the hotelier blossomed, Kerzner introduced Mangope to a number of his business associates. Most colourful among them was Shabtai 'Kal' Kalmanovich, a Lithuanian-born Israeli whose 2009 obituary in the *Baltic Times* described him as 'a short man with long hair, a heavy smoker, non-drinker of any alcoholic beverages and a passionate admirer of young women' and 'probably the most controversial Lithuanian'.[16]

Taking their lead from Pretoria's alliance with Tel Aviv (former Nazi sympathiser Prime Minister Vorster famously visited Israel in 1976 and South Africa was Israel's biggest arms customer), all of South Africa's Bantustan leaders made pilgrimages to the Promised Land in the early 1980s. While the Ciskei's Lennox Sebe was known to have visited Israel on at least seven occasions, quantity should not be confused with quality. As Arianna Lissoni points out, 'the relationship between Bophuthatswana and Israel not only outlasted those with all other Bantustans, it also was by far the most lucrative and pervasive of the lot'.[17]

This was thanks in no small part to Mangope's burgeoning friendship with Kalmanovich. When the Mangopes visited Israel in 1983, writes Sasha Polakow-Suransky, Kalmanovich 'chauffeured Mangope's wife around Tel Aviv in a black Mercedes flying Bophuthatswana's flag'.[18] On that same trip, Kalmanovich was appointed Bop's trade representative in Israel, a role that he took extremely seriously. The following year, he helped to set up Bophuthatswana House, which, although not an official diplomatic mission, was prominently positioned in the same sought-after street as the British embassy. After extensive renovations, paid for by Mangope's government and lovingly supervised by Kalmanovich, the building was finally fit for the Great Lion.

The glitzy edifice featured loads of marble, glass and aluminium, not to mention an 'uncorrupted' view of the ocean. Kalmanovich's office took up the entire sea-facing portion of the first floor, while the second floor housed a central dining room and kitchen and three hotel-style suites. Facing the sea on the third floor, writes Lissoni,

> was the Presidential Suite which included a bedroom, a study, a dressing room and two bathrooms ... On the same floor were a gym (complete with sauna) and two rooms with conveniences intended to service the president's family or personal guests. 'High-quality' Italian furniture was especially imported [and additionally taxed!] to furnish the building.[19]

While Bophuthatswana's sovereignty was never officially recognised by Israel (Israeli phone books did, however, list both Bop and Transkei in their 'international dialling codes' section), Bophuthatswana House may as well have been an embassy. It wasn't just the only building outside of South Africa to fly Bop's flag, it also issued Bop work permits and provided information for would-be investors.

With Kalmanovich's help, Mangope succeeded in opening two other trade mission offices in Frankfurt and Rome. It should come as no surprise that the men Kalmanovich picked to head up these satellite offices had dubious credentials. 'Entertaining local political and financial figures for the purpose of "furthering the Bophuthatswana cause" seems to have been a favoured [tactic],' writes Lissoni. 'In the year 1984 alone Italian representative [Roberto] Scio claimed 45 million liras [R22.5 million today] in expenses for private parties and receptions held at his villa in Rome.'[20] In 1992 the Bop government bailed out one of Scio's Italian hotels to the tune of R13 million (R66.5 million today) for no discernible reason other than to help out an old friend.

But this was all chicken feed compared to what Kalmanovich and Israel were able to squeeze from the homeland. Between 1984 and 1985 it was reported that seventy-nine business projects had been submitted to the Bophuthatswana government by Israeli firms and/or individuals. According to Lissoni,

> These ranged from housing projects, the construction of the [football] stadium, the opening of a tennis centre in Mmabatho, irrigation projects, security systems, television programming, the purchase of tractors [there's always a tractor deal], aviation, diamonds manufacturing, a shoe factory, a meat-processing plant, and the establishment of a crocodile farm near Sun City.[21]

Kalmanovich's most obvious legacy is the Mmabatho Independence Stadium, a 60 000-seater monstrosity featuring a 'unique design' (that's one way of describing the floating stands, which resemble a wind-strewn deck of cards) that concentrated 75 per cent of fans at either end of the pitch. While this strange layout was the official reason for FIFA overlooking it for the 2010 World Cup, the oblique view of the action was by no means the biggest issue facing spectators: 'Sitting in the stands you feared for your life,' remembers Manson. 'It was terribly built, a complete death-trap.'[22]

The stadium was designed by the Israeli architect-engineer duo Israel Goodowitch and Ben Avrhan and (nominally) built by Kalmanovich's construction firm LIAT, whose 'main contribution' to Bop's 'economic development', writes R.T. Naylor, was to win public contracts, sublet the actual work to other companies whose own bids had been lower, then kick back part of the profits to the president. To make sure he got paid [Kalmanovich] also arranged for "Boph" to borrow abroad, specifically from Kredietbank in Belgium, the institution through which South African intelligence financed its European espionage activities.[23]

Suffice to say, Kalmanovich would have got on famously with all of the heroes of this book. Once the stadium was completed, he set up a coaching academy that was staffed not by an Italian, Brazilian or English coach but by a very well-paid Israeli. It should come as no surprise that the Bophuthatswana Professional Soccer League which followed shortly after was sponsored by none other than Sun International – to the tune of R500 000 per year!

The R3-billion power plant that never produced a watt

The Great Lion seems to have had a peculiar predilection for elephants of the white variety. While the most famous member of the herd is undoubtedly the Independence Stadium, the power plant that never generated a single watt of electricity takes the prize for most spectacularly epic fail.

Ignoring the vehement objections of Finance Minister Young and the fact that Bop had had no issues with electricity supply (how times have changed), Mangope went ahead with plans to build a R177-million (almost R3-billion today) power plant in secret. He teamed up with minister of economics Ephraim Keikelame and his old Italian buddy Roberto Scio (who had, conveniently, been granted sole rights to sell coal in Bop) to carry out a scheme that, according to Peris Jones, 'was totally lacking in viability with no research or project planning done'.[24] Although unit one of the project was completed, the plant was never finished and ended up being sold for scrap in the 1990s. This led Jones to openly wonder in his PhD thesis what motivated them to go ahead with the project:

The plant epitomised the concept of the prestige project and was intended to demonstrate Bophuthatswana's capacity to generate electricity independently of South Africa. This badly misplaced and flawed effort can be interpreted as misguided and driven by ideological considerations. An alternative explanation suggests possible mass fraud by the three signatories, Mangope, Scio and Keikelame.[25]

But the power plant was not the only example of such a project. Mmabatho's dusty streets are littered with the skeletons of white elephants. Take, for example, the R25-million 'international' airport with only one scheduled daily flight: the forty-five-minute flip to Jozi. (You will be relieved to know that the airport was put to some good use by the weapons smugglers at Armscor.) Mangope also built a new legislative assembly, a 'massive' convention centre, a fancy opera house, a state-of-the-art recording studio and, ironically, no fewer than three Supreme Court buildings. In his quest to improve education, writes John Seiler, a gleaming 'International School was constructed at a cost of R64 million, providing unmatched facilities for secondary school students, many of whom [came] from Botswana and Zimbabwe, but few from [Bop] because the charges [were] so high'.[26]

Better still was the fact that none of the projects above were ever put out to tender because, in Mangope's own words, 'a number of companies had proved themselves capable'.[27] As Karl Magyar wrote in the *Financial Mail*,

> Since being forced into early retirement from my position as Economic Adviser [to Mangope] in 1982 [he was kicked out for standing up to Kalmanovich], I have observed sadly that nothing is really developing in Bophuthatswana – except the government offices, houses, cars and the roads for the elite to drive around on. Mmabatho as a capital must surely rival the ancient pyramids as a monument to its ruler.[28]

Beyond the soccer stadium, Israel also provided Bop with other expertise. Israeli doctors stitched up the gaping wounds in Bop's hospital system, Israeli lecturers padded the hallowed hallways of the University of Bophuthatswana (UNIBO), and Israeli architects ensured that Mmabatho's skyline would leave an indelible mark on the savannah. It goes without saying that philanthropy was not a key motivational driver for any of these acts.

And then, like a Kalahari dust storm, Kalmanovich was gone. As rumours swirled about just how much cash he'd been able to siphon out of the soccer stadium and into his own pocket, he hightailed it to Sierra Leone, whose blood-stained diamonds had caught his eye. Using his trademark charm, he was able to persuade President Joseph Momoh to grant his company LIAT an international marketing monopoly on the country's stones. Not content with the profits he was making from this dicey enterprise, he also used the Sierra Leone contract to smuggle South African diamonds into the international market.

In 1987, his luck would finally run out. Lissoni writes:

Kalmanovich was arrested for fraud he had committed in the US while travelling in London. He was then extradited to the US, only to be released on bail (towards which Mangope apparently contributed) and allowed to return to Israel, where he was charged with being a KGB agent and sentenced to nine years in prison.[29]

After his release (he ended up serving only five years), Kalmanovich moved to Moscow, where – true to form – he got involved in the Russian mafia. His life came to an end in 2009, when he was gunned down on the streets of Moscow in an apparent contract killing.

Same coup, different result

In the early hours of 10 February 1988 – barely a month after Bantu Holomisa's successful coup in the Transkei – residents of Mmabatho were disturbed by the sounds of a brief battle between loyal and rebel factions of Bop's defence force. Once Mangope had been located (rumour had it that he and his mistress were found in a suite in one of Kerzner's hotels), the president and his closest associates were rounded up and dragged to Mmabatho's Independence Stadium.

At 4.30 a.m. Radio Bophuthatswana was seized and the announcers began reading a prepared statement that bemoaned Mangope's corrupt autocracy and made specific mention of Kalmanovich and the stadium contract. President Mangope, the statement continued, had been ousted and power had been entrusted to Rocky Malebane-Metsing, the leader of one of the homeland's two official opposition parties. By 7.20 a.m., hundreds of students had gathered on the UNIBO campus, shouting slogans like 'Tyranny is out!' and 'Now we can enjoy freedom!'

Their jubilation was short-lived. At 4.15 p.m., three SADF Puma helicopters started circling the stadium and a strong force of SADF troops entered the city by road. An hour later, according to a Black Sash report, 'a force of 34 South African paratroopers staged a dramatic rescue mission of the President and his coterie'.[30]

Later that evening, South African president P.W. Botha addressed the nation. 'Well, we have had these problems [but] we are back in full control.' He then hastily corrected himself. 'The President of Bophuthatswana is in full control.' When asked why his government had not intervened in the Transkei coup, P.W. uttered a curious statement. The coup, he said, could not be compared '*in any way*' to the Transkei uprisings.[31]

Mangope would go on to lead the country for six more years, but his embarrassment at being held hostage there meant that the stadium was never again used for official events. The Great Lion saw to it that 143 rebels were found guilty of treason and sentenced to between two and eighteen years in prison. Kgosi Edward Patrick Lebone Molotlegi, the king of the Bafokeng (who just happened to be kicking up a massive fuss over platinum royalties), was accused of backing the coup and both he and his wife were banished from Bop.

Rocky Malebane-Metsing, who had taken advantage of the chaos to flee Bophuthatswana, would later star in another of South Africa's most curious political developments when he teamed up with, of all people, Louis Luyt to form the Federal Alliance.

Mangope and the Afrikaner right wing

At first it seems odd that the leader of a seemingly independent black nation would turn to a bunch of white-supremacist thugs in his time of need. Looking at the bigger picture, however, it becomes clear that Lucas Mangope enjoyed a life-long codependency with the Afrikaner *volk*. In fact, as a young man, Mangope had worked as an Afrikaans teacher.

But his bond with the Afrikaners ran deeper than this. After his inevitable post-independence land grab (we've spared you the details), Mangope and other land-owning members of Bop's elite teamed up with the *boere* on the fringes of the homeland to establish commercial farms which ensured that the rich got richer and the poor, supposedly liberated masses remained as disadvantaged as ever. All this in a region where the Afrikaners and the Tswana had competed for land for centuries, sometimes going so far as to launch deadly attacks on one another.

As early as 1852, the Bahurutshe chief Moiloa, who had had enough of the Afrikaners' intense demands for tax and labour, complained that he had become nothing more than a 'dog of the boers'. Moiloa's words were, of course, laced with spite. But Mangope would embrace the term to become the boers' prize poodle.

The big ass massacre of 1983

In 1983 the Great Lion ordered the massacre of some 20 000 donkeys. (The law truly is an ass.) While the party line was that an unprecedented drought meant that cattle had to be given first dibs on scarce fodder, word on the street was that first lady Leah Mangope's car had narrowly avoided ploughing into a family of donkeys and this had turned her hubby 'against the entire species'.[32]

Donkeys, which were introduced to Bop by English missionaries in 1858, had acquired a curious political importance in the region, as poor farmers relied on them but richer cattle-owners (i.e. Mangope and his *boere* buddies) despised them. There had been several regulated donkey culls over the years. But according to American academic Nancy Jacobs, who interviewed residents of nearby Kuruman in her memorably named academic paper 'The Great Bophuthatswana Donkey Massacre: Discourse on the Ass and the Politics of Class and Grass', for many local people the events of 1983 were 'the most traumatic experience of apartheid'.[33]

Bop soldiers and policemen arrived in Hippos, 'the troop carriers that would become infamous patrolling black urban townships during the 1980s,' explains Jacobs. The soldiers

> did not explain the procedure or count the assembled animals but simply opened fire ... After shooting the gathered donkeys, soldiers fanned out across the veld. Searching the streets, the river valley, and grazing areas, they shot the donkeys they saw ... There is strong consistency in the interviews about the brutality of the shootings and how it provoked revulsion: 'The soldiers did not take aim, but shot animals anywhere, as often as it took to kill them.' Every interview indicated that these were inhumane killings. 'We were very disturbed about the actual way in which the donkeys were killed because they were not put to death – they were savaged. Others were shot in the eye, different parts of the body, and the feet, and this made the actual killing gruesome because they had to suffer too much pain.'[34]

Uniquely for a homeland leader, Mangope stacked his cabinet (or at least those positions he himself did not occupy) with whites. Minister Rowan Cronjé explained that this was because '[t]he president [Mangope] has realized from the first day that to run the complicated business of a government is not yet within the grasp of his people'.[35] As we've already seen, a bunch of these whites seem to have been in it mainly for the money. But others had more sinister ulterior motives.

Cronjé (who had served in Ian Smith's racist Rhodesian government for

Mangope on his cattle farm (not a donkey in sight)

thirteen years) washed up on Bop's shores in 1985 with dreams of establishing a *volkstaat* for Afrikaners. He had tried (and failed at) a similar tactic in the Ciskei, but in Mangope he found a kindred soul. Before long he'd been appointed minister of defence, minister of state and minister of aviation and had become 'the [second] most important man in Bop'.[36]

In the early 1990s, as the wheels began rapidly to fall off the apartheid regime's Casspir, Mangope had to dream up a way of remaining relevant in a new South Africa, which would soon be dominated by his bitter rivals, the ANC. He came up with a cunning plan to rival Baldrick's finest. On 23 March 1992, several hundred Bop government officials, academics (from UNIBO and Potchefstroom University), farmers and businessmen got together to discuss what *The Star* described as a 'Tswana-Boereland superstate'. The Southern African Tswana Forum (SATSWA), to give it its official name, would comprise

most of the then Bophuthatswana, large portions of the Orange Free State (including Bloemfontein), and parts of the Northern Cape (including Kimberley and Upington) ... Provision was also made to incorporate the farming areas ... of Ellisras, Thabazimbi and Nylstroom in the north-western Transvaal ... The aim of SATSWA was 'to promote a "greater Bophuthatswana", which would incorporate and guarantee white farming interests, against an envisaged centralist state'. The population of the area was projected to be about 6.3 million inhabitants (56% Tswana speaking). It would have a Gross Geographic Product of R239 billion, derived from mining (60%), commerce and industry (11%) and agriculture (3%).[37]

As Mangope stated in his pitch-perfect Afrikaans:

In tye van nood en gevaar moet ons mekaar se hande vat en saam die toekoms aandurf. Ek glo dat nou, meer as ooit tevore, die tyd aangebreek het dat die Afrikaner en die Batswana in die westlike gebiede van Suider Afrika mekaar se hande moet vat en met moed en geloof aan 'n nuwe toekoms werk. [In times of need and danger we must take each other's hands and embrace the future together. I believe that now, more than ever, the Afrikaner and the Batswana in the western part of southern Africa must take hands and work towards a new future with determination and conviction.][38]

While the idea of the Tswana-Boereland did not last long, the concept of homeland leaders aligning with right-wing Afrikaners gathered steam with the formation of COSAG, the Concerned South Africans Group. This group brought together a curious ménage, with the Afrikaner Volksfront and Conservative Party on the one hand, and the Inkatha Freedom Party and the governments of Bop (represented by chief negotiator Rowan Cronjé), KwaZulu and Ciskei on the other.

As the *New York Times* reported, Bop came out fighting:

Bop officials said that even though they are attending the multi-party transition talks, they have no intention of having their 'country' participate in next April's scheduled non-racial elections. And if the South African government or the ANC tries to take Bop by force, they said they were willing to fight back with their tiny armed forces, which include helicopters and a brigade of trained soldiers – setting the stage for a possible confrontation over the future of the defiant homeland.[39]

When interviewed by the *Chicago Tribune*, Cronjé was even more blunt, warning that invading Bop 'would be the beginning of civil war in South Africa'.[40]

By March 1994, a month before the first free and democratic elections in South

Mangope inspecting the troops with Brigadier Jack Turner, head of the Bop Defence Force

Africa, Mangope and Cronjé's stance had become increasingly unpopular in Bop. A huge cohort of civil servants and policemen had downed tools in protest and the homeland was in chaos (the president's son, Eddie, was even taken hostage at one point). Backed into a corner, Mangope phoned a friend: General Constand Viljoen, former chief of the SADF and now leader of the Afrikaner Volksfront.

On 11 March (by which time Mangope had fled his fiefdom in a helicopter), a large and well-organised Afrikaner Volksfront militia gathered at the Mmabatho Air Force Base under the leadership of Commandant Douw Steyn. Excited at the prospect of what one member would later refer to as a '*k*****skiet piekniek*', the Afrikaner Weerstandsbeweging (AWB) also descended on the homeland.

In Mangope's defence, he made it clear to General Viljoen from the beginning that Eugene Terre'Blanche and his radical AWB would not be welcome in Bop. But by that stage no one was listening to the Great Lion any more. After a heated argument between Steyn, Terre'Blanche and Jack Turner, the leader of Bop's defence force, an angry column of armed AWB paramilitaries, who'd refused to remove their swastika insignia and serve under Steyn, left the airbase. Instead of returning directly to South Africa as agreed, the AWB column made a detour to

Mafikeng, where they randomly shot at blacks. They ended up killing at least forty-two innocent people.

But this senseless massacre was not what made the headlines. The most publicised event of the conflict was the killing, while the news cameras rolled, of three wounded AWB members by Bop police constable Ontlametse Bernstein Menyatsoe. AWB militia members Alwyn Wolfaardt, Nicolaas Fourie and Jacobus Stephanus Uys had been shooting at houses along the road from their clapped-out blue Mercedes-Benz, when members of the BDF returned fire, hitting the driver in the neck and injuring both passengers too. Wolfaardt lurched out of the car waving a handgun but was swiftly disarmed by a Bop police officer. After confirming that the men belonged to the AWB, Menyatsoe shouted, 'Who do you think you are? What are you doing in my country?' – and shot the three men dead at point-blank range with his government-issue R4.[41]

A *Sunday Times* story titled 'Sheer Bloody Murder' focused mainly on the deaths of the AWB men. *Rapport* went even further, using the tear-jerker head-line 'Is my pappie dood?' – a reference to the pleas of Wolfaardt's eight-year-old daughter as she watched the footage on TV.

Winners and losers

Thankfully, the civil war Cronjé had longed for did not materialise and order was swiftly restored in Bop. Mangope was deposed and, unlike most of the other members of COSAG, he refused to participate in the 1994 elections. By the following year he'd had a change of heart, and the Great Lion moved to form the United Christian Democratic Party (UCDP). It is no coincidence that the ANC chose to release the Skweyiya Commission of Inquiry's 'Final Report into Corrupt Practices and Irregular Use of Public Funds in Government Departments and Parastatal Departments in Bophuthatswana' in the same week as the UCDP's inaugural conference. The report stated explicitly that Mangope should face criminal charges for enriching himself to the tune of R22 million.

Lovers of justice were given a brief moment to celebrate in 1998, when Mangope was found guilty on 102 counts of theft and fraud totalling R3 543 685. Despite the severity of the crimes, however, he received only a two-year suspended sentence and was ordered to repay his victims: to his Bahurutshe boo Manyane chiefdom, R1 184 343 (plus a fine of R250 000); to the Bophuthatswana

State Security Council, R907 865 (and a R150 000 fine); and for the illegal transfer of funds to a Jersey bank a fine of R1 000 000 was imposed. Only failure to pay back the money would see him go to jail.[42]

While the sentence was passed 'in the spirit of reconciliation', it was still 'scandalous' for the people who had lived under Mangope. As Andrew Manson recalls, 'We were all so disappointed.'[43]

Mangope (or one of his wealthy *tjommies*) obviously forked out the cash, because Mangope's UCDP would go on to contest the 1999 elections, claiming a paltry 9 per cent of the provincial vote and 0.78 per cent of the national vote. A little bit of a comedown from the 100 per cent he had once garnered in Bop's 'national' elections.

The devil is in the details

The Skweyiya Commission 'uncovered an extraordinary web of corruption and misuse of public money by Lucas Mangope and top government officials'. Some of Mangope's misdeeds included:

- Spending R4.5 million (R17.5 million today) of government funds on improvements to his personal residence.
- Illegally farming government land since 1985 and using a salaried government employee to run a commercial dairy venture for his personal benefit. (This scheme will be very familiar by now.)
- Siphoning a total of R2.6 million in chrome mining royalties away from the Bahurutshe and directly into his pockets.
- Using R10.4 million of State Security Council (SSC) money to fund his Bophuthatswana Christian Democratic Party.
- Getting J.J.A. Esterhuizen of the SSC to make an illegal transfer of R1.3 million into a foreign bank account in Mangope's name. (Esterhuizen, it turned out, only deposited R800 000.)[44]

Mangope's cabinet didn't fare too well either: Advocate Skweyiya recommended that
- Rowan Cronjé should face criminal charges for accepting an unaccounted-for cash gift of R75 000 from the SSC.
- Jerry Reid, director general of the Information Service, should be made to repay approximately R300 000 he'd spent on government credit cards or be indicted for fraud.
- J.J.A. Esterhuizen, of SSC fame, should face criminal charges unless he testified honestly in all criminal cases relating to misuse of SSC funds.

By contrast, 1999 was a good year for the Bafokeng people, who won a landmark case against Impala Platinum Mining. As a result, Impala was forced to increase the mining royalties due to the Bafokeng from around 15 per cent to 22 per cent. The judgment also granted the Bafokeng one million shares in Impala Platinum and guaranteed them a seat on the company's board. The judgment irrevocably changed the relationship between South African landowners and mining companies, ensuring that the 'days of the Bafokeng [being] ripped off were over'.[45]

Ironically, the Bafokeng used some of their windfall to build the state-of-the-art Royal Bafokeng Sports Palace. One can only imagine Mangope's anger when the stadium was selected as one of the official venues for the FIFA 2010 World Cup.

The Great Lion, meanwhile, was expelled from his own ailing party in 2012 after being accused of autocracy (fancy that) and failing to attend his disciplinary hearing. He died in 2018, aged ninety-four.

Old King Sol's merry old ending

As apartheid crumbled, Mangope quickly became a pariah (some might argue he had always been one), but Sol Kerzner's sun continued to rise – thanks in no small part to his burgeoning friendship with Nelson Mandela. Just two weeks after his release from prison in 1990, Madiba praised the 'young Jewish man ... creating thousands of jobs out in the African countryside'. (It seemed to have escaped his attention that (a) Kerzner was fifty-four years old and (b) the tycoon had a reputation for exploiting black workers and quashing trade unions.) Four years later, Kerzner, one of the greatest beneficiaries of territorial apartheid, 'was given the honour of hosting Mandela's presidential inauguration reception at Sun City'.[46]

In the interim, Sun International bought the rights to host the Miss World pageant at Sun City, a move that legitimised the resort as a key international attraction within the new South Africa. The once-spurned Million Dollar Golf Challenge was also widely embraced by the international golfing community. Like the ace gambler that he was, Sol had once again come up trumps. As Van der Merwe notes,

Sun City was no longer in exile, but a member of the emerging South African democracy ... Kerzner succeeded in his plans, whilst Mangope failed. The hotel tycoon went on to secure a working relationship with Nelson Mandela as well as casino licences in the new South Africa. Sun City [remains] an iconic South African venue despite the tumultuous history, bribery, and staff exploitation.[47]

CHAPTER 12

WOUTER BASSON

And the End of History
1981–1993

'Public officials felt they were missing out if they were not helping themselves.'
– Judge B. de Villiers Pickard[1]

Wouter Basson: a wink in the face of death

B Y THE LATE 1980S, the apartheid regime was dog-tired of fighting wars both externally and internally, hot wars, cold wars, culture wars, sanction wars and sporting boycotts. And then there was corruption – that fuel-syphoning hosepipe in the tank. Apartheid was done, finished, kaput, its coffers were nearly empty, and its friends had flown the coop. There was, perhaps, just enough fuel left for the plane out of here. But hey, better make sure *you* had the parachutes …

As the political scientist Francis Fukuyama claimed in his influential book *The End of History and the Last Man,* 1989 and the fall of the Berlin Wall had summoned in, as his title suggested, 'the end of history'. By this he meant that history as theorised by the philosopher Hegel was now over. Hegel had claimed that history was the clashing of one thesis against its antithesis, or, in the late twentieth century, democracy clashing against communism. But with the fall of the Berlin Wall, Western democratic free-market capitalism was the victor and you either got on board or you were left behind at a soon-to-be-disused airport to fight over Russian bread made from sawdust while men in faded safari suits played *jukskei.*

But the truth was that the end of apartheid's history had slightly earlier roots. The rot had started to set in long before the late 1980s. The B.J. Vorster gang, the direct inheritors of Verwoerd's group of Broederbonders, had been swept out by a new broom in the form of the polished and shiny dome of P.W. Botha,

P.W. Botha: Krokodil at the Rubicon

but there was no real reform. Instead, one bunch of corrupt, secretive, money-laundering, murderous racists had taken over from another. The only significant difference was that where Vorster had relied on the police and the Bureau of State Security, P.W. Botha would create his own almost identical networks with his friends in the military and what would be called, somewhat bizarrely, the Civil Cooperation Bureau (CCB).

To be fair, personal enrichment and the jet-setting lifestyles of the likes of Eschel Rhoodie were not P.W. Botha's cup of rooibos. Die Groot Krokodil he may have been, but fashionable 1980s designer crocodile-skin accessories were certainly not to his or his wife's tastes. P.W.'s group paraded in cheap, dark suits and 1950s black fedoras that were neither ostentatious nor fashionable. Botha's versions of Eschel Rhoodie and Lang Hendrik were plodding, thuggish enforcers. They were equally (if not more) murderous and corrupt, but with none of the flared trousers or fascist dreams. The young, charismatic vision of Rhoodie had been replaced by the beaten and hangdog demeanour that was defence minister Magnus Malan.

A special account of secrets

But whatever this new breed of apartheid overlords was made of, they would not get caught out in another Information Scandal. In fact, to this day, very little is known about just how they used that famous secret Special Defence Account, although there is some pieced-together information of how it did get used. What *is* known is that during the height of the 1980s arms embargo, when no nation should have been selling South Africa military equipment, planeloads of contraband arms and military hardware arrived month in and month out.

Certain companies *were* caught illegally selling arms. In 1978, the American Olin-Winchester Corporation pleaded 'no contest' in a Connecticut court on a charge of violating the UN arms embargo. That was, as US professor of security studies Michael T. Klare writes, 'for conspiring to ship 3,200 firearms and 20,000,000 rounds of ammunition'. The famous ammunitions manufacturer was ordered to pay by the American court '$510,000 [$2 million today] to local charities as "reparations" for the firm's illegal arms deliveries to South Africa'.[2]

When you add this to the fact that the assassinations of many anti-apartheid activists, including Ruth First (killed by parcel bomb in Mozambique), Matthew Goniwe (abducted and murdered by the security police outside Port Elizabeth) and Dulcie September (shot dead outside the ANC's office in Paris), were almost certainly financed via the Special Defence Account, the corruption surrounding it seems in some ways of secondary importance. But the murders were in many ways a symptom of a broader disease.

Interestingly, the Special Defence Account still exists today. In fact, it was at the centre of the infamous Arms Deal. How's that for an apartheid legacy?

There is little doubt that between the murdering that occurred on the Angolan border, in the townships, in suburban homes, in police stations or at the infamous apartheid hit-squad farm Vlakplaas, huge bribes were paid. In an interview a few years before his death, Eschel Rhoodie told Martin Welz:

The so-called Defence Special Account was established for the purchase of weapons abroad after the UN imposed an embargo on South Africa. The law removed these funds from scrutiny, even by the Auditor General ... Over the past 15 years [up to 1987] they probably totalled R3-billion. One day General van den Bergh remarked casually: 'Given the known facts about the black market, we seem to be paying two or three times more than we should'. We figured ... about R200 million or more was going out unaccounted for each year.[3]

And some people, somewhere, in some country like Israel or Taiwan or the USA or France or Germany or the UK, were getting filthy rich on apartheid's failed attempt to stave off its enemies. Sadly, we just don't know who benefited. One of the reasons for the lack of information is that South African arms manufacturer Armscor was involved in one final secret project, code-named 'Masada'. (This was named after the ancient fortification built by King Herod which was set alight by its Jewish inhabitants once besieging Roman legions had entered it. What's more, all the citizens of Masada were said to have committed suicide.) It was a project that literally laid waste to a massive quantity of documentary records detailing the South African government's vast money-laundering networks. As Hennie van Vuuren put it, the destruction of information was on an 'allegedly biblical proportion'.[4] It should be noted, though, that the top brass at Armscor did not replicate the suicides of the original Masada – they and those that followed them would live to 'fight' another day (see Chapter 13).

Martin Welz relates that in Operation Masada, 'documents once held by Armscor and Absa Bank (successor to the original Volkskas Bank), at the SA Reserve Bank and at South Africa's embassies in Paris and Tel Aviv, had been either shredded or burned'.[5] When one considers that in 1988 the defence expenditure was estimated to be around 28 per cent of the government's annual budget, you can just imagine what kind of cover-up there was. The apartheid government were spending about R15 billion a year (R133 billion today) on arms and secret projects.

One auditor-general by the name of Peter Wronsely did try to get his head around what was going on with this spending near the end of apartheid. What Wronsely discovered was that in 1990 only 1.4 per cent of the R12 million (R82 million today) spent by the CCB (the SADF's clandestine death squad) went towards the cost of operations. The rest was spent on salaries, cars, housing and other perks. Extrapolate that figure across the entire defence budget and weep ...

A Wouter of confidence

Perhaps one of the most bizarre, corrupt and morally abhorrent stories to come out of the 1980s and early '90s is apartheid's chemical and biological weapons (CBW) programme. The programme would hit the headlines in 1997, when Dr Wouter Basson was arrested as he stumbled, fully clothed and soaking wet, from an impromptu dip in Walkerspruit.

Before attempting to avoid arrest by leaping into the stream in the tranquil suburban setting of Magnolia Dell Park, Pretoria, the good doctor had allegedly just sold a bag containing 1 027 capsules of Ecstasy for R60 000 (R200 000 today) to a police informant.[6] More about this in a moment. In the days that followed, Wouter Basson was introduced to the broader South African public, not as a drug dealer, but as the man who had headed apartheid's clandestine CBW programme code-named 'Project Coast'. After these revelations, he became known to most people simply as 'Dr Death'.

The history of Basson's involvement in CBW began in 1981, when minister of defence Magnus Malan approved a programme that would develop and research the use of chemical and biological weapons. Malan and the SADF decided that they would use 'private' (but government-funded) front companies in order to pass the buck if the project was discovered. The surgeon general then placed a young SADF medical doctor by the name of Wouter Basson at its head.

Basson seems to have slotted almost perfectly into the shady and morally abhorrent world of CBW. Despite the fact that he was not a chemical or biological scientist, Basson was seen by the apartheid regime as the perfect fit for a CBW project that would break medical ethics and violate human rights on a massive scale. An apparently highly intelligent and talented cardiologist, Basson was deemed a charismatic and even charming character. Married to two different women at the same time, Basson openly admitted in court that

Dr Fred du Plessis, chairman of Trust Bank, hands a R15-million investment in National Defence Bonds to Magnus Malan, 1978

he 'was a good source of stories – and you need good stories to launder funds'.[7] Whether that was a good trait for heading up a chemical and biological weapons programme is another story.

What was more, 'Dr Death' was close to many of the leading lights in apartheid's securocrat inner circle. Basson even served as P.W. Botha's personal physician. But perhaps more importantly, he was close to Magnus Malan. Malan's nephew Dr Philip Mijburgh not only served under Basson in an army medical unit, but he would also go on to become the managing director of one of the main front companies of Project Coast, Delta G Scientific. Mijburgh was also the director of another front called Medchem Consolidated Investments, at whose offices in Centurion Basson was regularly spotted.

In fact, as Chandré Gould and Peter Folb put it, the whole of Project Coast was 'built on personal relationships and informal networks'.[8]

The project's (tactically and morally) offensive programme began with the authorisation by Magnus Malan of the fronts Delta G Scientific and Roodeplaat Research Laboratories (RRL). Delta G's hi-tech research and production plant was built in Midrand, north of Johannesburg, at the cost of about R30 million (R460 million today). The project's biological wing, RRL, was developed on 350 hectares of land near the Roodeplaat Dam Nature Reserve, a mere twenty-six-minute drive from the Union Buildings in Pretoria. A R40-million (about R570-million today) complex of sophisticated laboratories, testing and production facilities, and even an animal centre for testing their products, was built there over several years and was run at a cost of about R10 million per year.

In total, and within the space of about five years, the SADF put R418 226 509 (about R4 billion today) of taxpayers' money into Project Coast, of which R98 million went into RRL and R127 million was expended at Mijburgh's Delta G.

The agonies and the ecstasies

RRL was mainly focused on the biological component of the project. There, as its clinical pathologist Dr Daan Goosen revealed, they genetically modified E. coli organisms that potentially could have killed millions of people if introduced into a food or water supply. RRL was also said to have begun to investigate a female infertility medication that might be secretly administered to black women with the aim of controlling black population growth. Just what happened to this idea is not known, but it seems that it was never practically conceived and remained an apartheid-era wish-fulfilment fantasy. But, as Goosen admitted,

> [t]he scientists assembled there [at RRL] had the potential of developing really new and fancy biological weapons. But it was never done. When we got to the point that we should have produced, there was no support for the scientists to produce.

As Goosen would go on to say in the same interview, the poisons used against anti-apartheid activists were 'crude off the shelf products, and that is my point, and this was the sort of thing that worried me, that they were not interested in proper sophisticated products'.[9] Dr Peter Folb, the Truth and Reconciliation Commission's (TRC's) scientific advisor, went further, saying that despite the expensive facilities at RRL, 'the science involved in Project Coast was pedestrian'.[10]

But if Goosen and Folb's suggestions that the biological project achieved very little, the chemical project at Delta G accomplished a great deal, although not, strictly speaking, in its specified field. Perhaps the most sophisticated product it produced was a potent form of tear gas called CR that was perfectly legal and hardly groundbreaking. Delta G also produced vast amounts of illegal recreational drugs, including Mandrax and MDMA (known then as Ecstasy). According to the scientist who manufactured the MDMA at Delta G, Dr Johan Koekemoer, Wouter Basson ordered him to produce 912 kilograms of the world's favourite rave drug, claiming that it was for the SADF. As Basson would assert in court, the MDMA was made with the idea that it might be deployed against crowds to calm the confrontational and fervent effects of the toyi-toyi.

In the mid-1980s, the head of the SADF, General Constand Viljoen, had certainly been looking for something that could 'neutralise the offensive spirit' of angry crowds. But the idea described by Basson and Mijburgh – that Ecstasy could be used as a 'calmative' to 'pacify' and 'incapacitate' crowds – is nonsense. Firstly, one only needs to consider that the rave culture of the 1990s used Ecstasy as a stimulant to energise and heighten emotions, not calm them. And although Ecstasy famously manufactures amorous emotions, having a crowd that professes love could be as intimidating to the oppressor as one that expresses hatred, as was proven by the anti-Vietnam protests in the US, where protestors placed flowers in the barrels of soldiers' guns, or indeed Gandhi's peaceful satyagraha methods. Secondly, there was absolutely no scientific evidence that MDMA put into aerosol cans and shot at crowds would have any effect whatsoever. As forensic scientist Dr David Klatzow said, '[I]f this is the best you can come up with after spending R100 million on research, then you are dealing with intellectual Neanderthals.'[11]

Nevertheless, 912 kilograms of MDMA was produced at Delta G (at a staggering 98 per cent purity, no less) at a cost to the taxpayer, according to Mijburgh, of R840 000 (R4.3 million today). But this was only the tip of the iceberg. At the end of apartheid, the SADF wrote off their budget a figure of R21.7 million worth of drugs, including Mandrax, MDMA, cocaine and PCP. Most of this was seemingly created at Delta G. It seems highly coincidental that Basson's charge sheet after his dip in Walkerspruit included possession of MDMA, Mandrax and cocaine.

The TRC's chief legal officer, Hanif Vally, put the street value of Delta G's MDMA at between R600 million and R1 billion. Basson, however, claimed that the SADF drugs were written off after he personally dumped the lot out the back of a plane off the coast of Cape Agulhas in January 1993. But as the *New Yorker*'s William Finnegan wrote, there were rumours that the drugs had not been dumped but had 'ended up in the hands of Basson and his cronies'.[12]

And one of Basson's chief cronies at the time was Magnus Malan's nephew, Philip Mijburgh. According to Dr Koekemoer, the chemist who produced the MDMA, he was ordered by Basson to deliver the 912 kilograms of MDMA not to the SADF, but instead to Mijburgh's rented offices at Medchem Technologies in Centurion. During testimony given at the TRC, Hanif Vally grilled Mijburgh on just what had happened to the MDMA. His responses are testimony to the tangled web of deceit and obfuscation that both Basson and Mijburgh were involved in.

Mijburgh admitted that Delta G had sold the MDMA to a company called Kowalski International, of which Mijburgh was a director. He qualified this by saying that the drugs had never been delivered to the company as it was only a 'paper transaction' done for tax purposes. Vally was suitably puzzled by this.

MR VALLY: So, when we say that Kowalski International, of which you were director, possibly were the final recipients of the Ecstasy, it was all just a paper transaction for tax purposes?... You mentioned Kowalski International wasn't a front company, but a private company, that was used in paper transactions to conceal actions of the front companies, including for the drugs. Do I understand you correctly, maybe I'm tangling myself a bit, let me start again. Kowalski International as a

private company of which you were director is the final recipient of
Ecstasy, purely for the purposes of VAT?

DR MIJBURGH: No, it was not the final recipient, there was a transaction
via Kowalski International to Medchem Technologies.

MR VALLY: And they were involved ... regarding the drug Ecstasy?

DR MIJBURGH: For the paper transaction, yes.

MR VALLY: I see. How would you mix private companies and front companies
like this, wouldn't that be a major security risk? Wasn't Dr Kowalski a
foreign citizen?

DR MIJBURGH: He was, yes.

MR VALLY: So, what about the security risk?

DR MIJBURGH: There was no security risk, Mr Vally.

MR VALLY: Dr Mijburgh, you're concerned about being prosecuted for this
substance, you actually write [to the surgeon general] and ask for an
indemnity, you have a foreign doctor who is a director of a company, you
have Ecstasy [...] being manufactured on a large scale by a Government
institution, and you tell me there's no security risk. Is that logical?[13]

There was a lot that wasn't logical or even understandable in this exchange.
It's not at all clear where the drugs were moved and just why this Dr Kowalski
allowed Mijburgh to use his company for a deeply dubious 'paper transaction'
for the purposes of committing tax fraud. And the only proof that the MDMA,
possibly worth hundreds of millions of rands on the street, was thrown off the
back of a plane in 1993 is a single insubstantial and factually incorrect piece of
SADF paperwork – and Basson's word.

Certainly, the MDMA was never made into gas or inserted into canisters for
the SADF. One of Mijburgh's employees at Medchem Technologies submitted an
affidavit to the TRC stating that Mijburgh had ordered him to put the MDMA
into ingestible capsules. Hanif Vally went on to suggest there was some evidence
that around a million of these capsules had in fact been produced for the MDMA.

And one can't but forget that Basson was arrested for (allegedly) selling 1 027
capsules of Ecstasy to a police informant in 1997. When one considers that Ecstasy
was almost never produced in capsule form in the 1990s, the mystery of just
where the drug produced by the government at Delta G ended up is perhaps
solved. In fact, a bottle of the same MDMA capsules had been discovered the day
before Basson's arrest in 1997 at Delta G's premises.

The wisdom of Wouter

One of Basson's main tasks as head of Project Coast had been to manoeuvre around sanctions and the embargo on military-related equipment. Although Basson was required to provide financial records of his expenditure, the famous Special Defence Account meant that the auditor-general had no clue what these amounts were really spent on. As Stephen Burgess and Helen Purkitt put it, 'Basson's unsupervised activities would lead Project Coast into a morass of corruption.'[14]

According to Hennie Bruwer, the Office for Serious Economic Offences (OSEO) auditor who conducted a ten-year investigation into Basson's financial transactions, from 1 March 1987 to 28 February 1993 Project Coast was allocated R340 million. Out of this, Bruwer calculated, R37 million (R253 million today) was misappropriated by Basson and his cronies.

As we have seen in Philip Mijburgh's TRC testimony, money and 'paper transactions' (and perhaps even drugs) were liberally and deceitfully being shuffled from one company to the next. And Basson would set up a truly staggering number of companies both locally and abroad. These fronts included an international company called WPW set up in the Cayman Islands – supposedly named after (W)outer, (P)hilip Mijburgh and (W)ynand Swanepoel, the directors of Delta G and RRL[15] – and a local one named Wisdom, where, as we will soon see, wisdom was in very short supply.

We would need far more than one chapter to unpack just what these companies and their subsidiaries did. Suffice to say, Basson and his *maatjies* set up an elaborate network of secret accounts in various parts of the world, through which SADF money could be funnelled to procure embargoed materials, set up businesses, pay foreign collaborators, and bribe foreign officials in order to facilitate the transfer of materials and equipment to South Africa. Mijburgh, for one, was a director or shareholder in a truly staggering number of companies – of which many held contracts with the SADF, which his uncle just so happened to oversee.

Basson's story in court, however, was that he wasn't just laundering money for the SADF, he was working with a group of arms dealers, or what was referred to by journalists as the 'Chemical and Biological Warfare Mafia'. As he would claim, he laundered money for them all as part of his patriotic duty to apartheid South Africa. Whether these people were just a part of Basson's storytelling is impossible to say, but they must have been a haplessly gullible and naive bunch if they did really exist. According to Basson, he convinced this group of hardened and crooked arms dealers, while using his own identity (which could have been easily checked), that he too was an international dealer in CBW. These East German, Libyan and Russian arms dealers (all from countries that were enemies of apartheid South Africa) supposedly took Basson into their trust and personally asked him to launder $250 million (R9.5 billion today) for them.

Et in Arcadia ego

The trial that commenced after Basson was arrested for dealing Ecstasy not only implicated him in gruesome apartheid-era murders in which he allegedly supplied assassins with poisons, but also in several counts of fraud.

No one knows quite what Basson did with hundreds of millions of rands' worth of taxpayers' money that came to him via the Special Defence Account, but what is certain is that Basson's name appeared on bank accounts around the world and on transactions for aeroplanes, houses, cottages in the UK, Swiss drug companies, travel agencies, farms and, perhaps most bizarrely of all, on a deal for the cash-strapped Tygerberg Zoo.

According to Basson, he bought the Tygerberg Zoo in 1989 for R711 928 (R5.7 million today) for two reasons. One was to have access to wild animals for experiments for Project Coast. The second, which he seemed to think was perfectly consistent with the first, was the clearly absurd claim that he bought the zoo so that millionaire foreign arms dealers could take the lion's share of its burgeoning profits. Basson also never quite reconciled just how experimenting with chemical and biological weapons on animals (and presumably killing or disfiguring them) is good business practice for a zoo intent on making money as a place of public recreation.

The real reason for Basson's purchase is easier to understand, albeit equally crooked. The zoo was owned by his uncle, Cyrus Steyn, and had for many years been held together by rusted wire and broken biscuits. After Basson bought it, Steyn continued to run it as it lurched along in a state of near total collapse. In 2012 it was finally put out of its misery and closed.

Many of Basson's financial deals and purchases ended in huge losses. A potato farm lost R3 million, but finally ended up in the hands of his sister and brother-in-law. And then there was the case of Merton House, a property Basson acquired in 1990 in the highly sought-after area of Arcadia in Pretoria. According to reports from the trial, Basson embarked on a renovation that would end up costing over R10 million (R68 million today). He went as far as buying the house next door and knocking it down to make space for parking. Merton House was, in fact, never lived in and was eventually sold to the Zimbabwean government in 1994 at a R4-million (R17-million today) loss. Basson would of course claim that this money was not misappropriated government funds but belonged to the very same mysterious millionaire arms dealers who had bought his uncle's ailing zoo. Just how these (fictitious or otherwise) mafia figures felt about Basson's financial bumbling has not been established.

Basson's indictment claimed that he had defrauded the SADF of R36 million and stolen at the very least another R10 million. As Marléne Burger and Chandré Gould stated,

> The prosecution was confident that seasoned forensic auditor Hennie Bruwer's 379-page report would be the court's guide to the paper trail snaking through Switzerland, Luxembourg, Lichtenstein, Belgium and Croatia to England, via the Channel Islands, New York, Orlando (Florida), Canada and the Cayman Islands.[16]

What's your poison?

Sadly, this was not the case. In a trial that lasted from 4 October 1999 until 22 April 2002, where 153 people appeared for the prosecution and only Basson appeared in his defence, the apartheid-era judge Willie Hartzenberg (brother of the extreme right-wing politician Ferdi Hartzenberg) found him not guilty on all forty-six counts of murder, fraud and dealing drugs.

According to both journalists and the state prosecutors, Judge Hartzenberg had made it clear throughout the three-year trial that he did not believe any of the charges brought against Basson. Basson was, he claimed, the victim of a witch-hunt. In his opinion, 153 people had lied in court, while Basson was the only man capable of telling the truth. At the sentencing, which everyone knew was a fore-gone conclusion, Magnus Malan appeared in the gallery, seemingly there to support one of the darlings of apartheid's most criminal endeavours. Basson would state that the verdict was a victory for our 'hard-gained democracy'. One can't help but wonder if his English had failed him. Perhaps what he meant to say was that he had gained a victory over the democracy he had fought so hard against.

The poisoned pants of Reverend Frank Chikane

Project Coast cost the South African taxpayer nearly R4 billion in today's terms. It also ended up costing hundreds and perhaps thousands of people's lives, including those who were poisoned and infected with diseases that allegedly came out of Delta G's and RRL's laboratories. In 2007, Adriaan Vlok, the erstwhile minister of police and a 'born-again Christian', became the first senior politician to be convicted of an apartheid crime. Vlok admitted to having ordered the killing of Rev. Frank Chikane, the well-known anti-apartheid cleric and secretary-general of the South African Council of Churches. CCB agents had laced Chikane's underpants with poison on two occasions. In the second instance, he was on a trip to the USA when he fell gravely ill and was hospitalised with a mystery illness. US doctors discovered that he had been poisoned with organophosphate. The poison used by the CCB had allegedly come from Project Coast's laboratories. Vlok was given a suspended sentence after he pleaded guilty. In a suitably bizarre moment in South African history, Vlok asked for Chikane's forgiveness by washing the reverend's feet in the biblical manner. He didn't go near his underpants.

But the story of Project Coast had a further poisoned sting in its tail. When the ANC was unbanned and Nelson Mandela released, Basson and his cronies came up with privatisation schemes for the front companies that had realisable assets, including RRL and Delta G Scientific. Delta G was valued at R20 million (R136 million today), but Basson persuaded the government to hand it over to Mijburgh and his mates at a 40 per cent discount. After some wheeler-dealing, it was finally agreed in Magnus Malan's offices in April 1990 that Philip Mijburgh would receive the new privatised Delta G with R15 million in hand (R103 million today).

Finance minister Barend du Plessis, who oversaw the deal in Malan's office, claimed that he was not aware at the time that Mijburgh was Malan's nephew, nor that Basson, who was in the meeting, stood to gain from the deal. A few years later, Mijburgh's Delta G (a company into which the South African government had poured hundreds of millions of rands) was sold to the chemical giant Sentrachem for a rather pathetic R3 million. Without his uncle's contracts, it seems that Mijburgh's Delta G simply could not sustain itself and was bordering on worthless.

The final fall

But Basson and Mijburgh were certainly not the only ones involved in questionable dealings. *Au contraire*, the stench seeped all the way up to P.W.'s cabinet. One case that hit the news in 1989 was the sacking of minister of manpower and public works Pietie du Plessis. Du Plessis was forced to resign when the police stumbled upon proof that land deals had taken place between his department and a company he owned with his son. Minister du Plessis, who, like Eschel Rhoodie and Nico Diederichs, had a farm in Hoedspruit, was actually convicted of fraud and served three years of a nine-year sentence in Pretoria Central. Some years later, Pietie's son, Johan du Plessis, was found guilty on fifty-eight counts of fraud and one of corruption, involving around R30 million.

Du Plessis and his son were trailblazers for people like Schabir Shaik and Jackie Selebi who form that elite class of South African political figures to have actually done hard time for corruption. Another one of Minister du Plessis's National Party colleagues, Peet de Pontes, also served time in jail in the early 1990s. With overtones of the Guptas' South African citizenship debacle and also Jackie Selebi's relationship with Glenn Agliotti, De Pontes had helped the mafia's Vito Palazzolo get into South Africa by organising him a Ciskeian passport (for what those were worth).

De Pontes was no doubt kicking himself when Palazzolo rocked up at his trial and testified against him. Or, as the *Mail & Guardian* put it, 'Palazzolo helped the prosecutors prove that De Pontes had assisted in the illegal immigration of an Italian financier (himself).'[17] De Pontes was convicted of bribery, theft and forgery for assisting Palazzolo with his passport. His defence – that Palazzolo was very much part of the National Party furniture – did not go down well with the judge. But this did not change the fact that Palazzolo was a generous financial donor to the National Party. De Pontes claimed that he had worked with Palazzolo in the 1980s on sanctions-busting deals to import submarines and fighter jets.

More familial tales

As apartheid wound down, and F.W. de Klerk brought a slightly newer broom to proceedings, more and more corruption was uncovered. Commissions of inquiry into the Department of Development Aid and the Department of Education and Training (DET) revealed that corruption was rife within apartheid's bureaucracy.

Judge Pickard, who was tasked with looking into the corruption in the Department of Development Aid, discovered a nest of dishonesty. The department, which had replaced the infamous Department of Native Affairs some years before, was designated to fund the supposedly 'independent' homelands. With an annual budget of around R6 billion (R41 billion today), which was at the time around 11 per cent of central government's total expenditure, there was certainly some room for the manoeuvring of money. Pickard had been appointed to lead the inquiry after a parliamentary budget committee discovered that R50 million (R342 million today) from the department's budget had been misappropriated by officials and outside contractors.

As Pickard stated in his findings:

Public officials felt they were missing out if they were not helping themselves ... many of these public officials had become disillusioned by their futile efforts to serve the apartheid ideology of administering the removal and resettlement of thousands of black people. (They) have developed a syndrome of a lack of enthusiasm to the extent sometimes of apathy and the huge amounts of money made available to the department became too tempting to resist for some officials.[18]

Dishonesty in the department, Pickard discovered, was rife and had been so since the mid-1980s. In one case, officials in the department had been paid for work while they were on a deep-sea fishing trip. In another, contractors who were close to the department were paid out for houses they had never built.

In yet another case, a tender had been put out by two officials in the department for portable toilets. The two manipulated the specifications of the tender so they could only be met by a company that they owned. (Sound familiar?) The tender for these portable toilets also mysteriously increased from R2 million to R14 million without being referred back to the tender board that had awarded it. Thousands of portaloos were, by all accounts, then sent out around South Africa. Unused and unwanted, they dotted the landscape in some of South Africa's most desolate places. And then there was the inevitable case of nepotism involving the daughter of the deputy director who was promoted up the ranks of the department without the requisite qualifications.

Pickard's final report was not published until May 1992. In the end, six cases were finally brought to trial but all of the accused were acquitted. Pickard, in an almost biblical pronouncement, stated that the Department of Development Aid should be

> physically dismantled, their staff transferred to all ends of the public service earth, and their functions distributed over as wide a spectrum as possible, to as many other appropriate bodies as possible, the better.[19]

The man who had been in charge of the department over many of those years (and who had been chairman of the Broederbond) was the round-faced Charlie Chaplin lookalike and former university rector Gerrit Viljoen. But Viljoen, who gained the nickname 'Minister of Toilets' in the English press, refused to take any responsibility for what had happened on his watch. According to one commentator, he is said to have suggested that 'a minister in South Africa was not expected to pay for any contraventions in his or her department, even if it had been serious'.[20] And if you, dear reader, pause for one moment, you might just hear the sound of Zuma's old cabinet ministers crowing with approval.

According to June Goodwin and Ben Schiff, the reality of the corruption in Viljoen's ministry, which had assigned huge contracts to Afrikaner firms, was starkly revealed on TV. They showed that what should have been the construction of schools and outhouses [i.e. toilets] in planned townships ... turned out to be vacant fields where blacks were to be deposited under the Group Areas Act. The 'towns' remained empty, though millions of rands had been spent on construction. School buildings were condemned and unusable even before they were completed. And outhouses stood derelict.[21]

Whatever the outcome of Judge Pickard's report, he took an absolutely withering view of the department:

'The Minister of Toilets'

I am satisfied that management is not up to its task; that controls and control systems are grossly neglected; that personnel are inadequate in numbers and often quality; that planning is inadequate; that dishonesty and abuse are rife, and that attitudes generally fall short of what is required of a huge organization of this nature. It goes without saying that I do not share the alleged 'appreciation and confidence the Cabinet has in the expertise and high quality of service which officials of the Department of Development Aid has [*sic*] rendered'.[22]

The Van der Heever Commission into the Department of Education and Training, which controlled the funding for black education, discovered that a similar rot had set in. It too discovered nepotism, with the deputy director general favouring his son's company and attempting to cover up this favour. Expressing her complete disbelief at the state of the department that had seemingly gone out of its way to fail an already unequal black education system, Justice Van der Heever was quoted in the *Financial Mail* as saying, 'It is difficult to believe that so many irregularities could take place within one department ... without the knowledge of the deputy DGs, the DG, the Treasury, the Auditor-General ... Why was it left to the press to open this Aegean stable?'[23]

Once again, the buck should have stopped with Gerrit Viljoen, whose ministerial oversight included the DET. But once again, 'Minister of Toilets' Viljoen refused to flush. As Constanze Bauer put it,

> Concerning the issue of ultimate political responsibility, the then responsible Minister, Gerrit Viljoen, was simply allowed to retreat from the whole sordid affair without having to account for the actions of his subordinates. Such action was possible because in South Africa the system functioned in such a way that people who are accused are allowed to continue at their posts, move to another department, or merely slide into retirement.[24]

Not much can really be said to have changed.

History repeats itself

And with all of this in mind, it is perhaps worth casting one's eye over a document the ANC published in 1992 after the revelations of the Pickard Commission.

FROM MURDER, CORRUPTION AND MISMANAGEMENT TO DEMOCRACY, JUSTICE AND GOOD GOVERNMENT

Corruption

In early May the report of the Pickard Commission was released disclosing extensive corruption in the Department of Development Aid involving billions of taxpayers' money. These disclosures were the tip of the iceberg. Indications are that virtually every arm of the central apartheid state have [sic] been deeply implicated in theft and corruption, including DET, Defence, Law and Order, Health and Welfare, Finance, Foreign Affairs, Justice and Correctional Services. (See Sunday Star 10/5/92) This cesspool of corruption extends far beyond the central apartheid state, to Bantustans, regional and local government. Mangope, Gqozo, De Klerk and others whose insistence on regionalism/ Federalism is partly motivated by their desire to hang on to these freedoms, to perpetuate their hold over resources and entrench their ill-gotten gains ...

Our demands on corruption and mismanagement:

1. The setting up of an independent commission into corruption and state expenditure – at all levels of government – which would ultimately come

under the direction of the Transitional Executive Council. This Commission should have full access to all government Departments and records.

2. The dismissal and, where appropriate, prosecution of all Ministers and officials implicated in the misappropriation of public funds. This would involve most senior Ministers in the current government.

3. The seizure of assets of those implicated in the theft of public funds.

4. In addition to acting against those responsible for corruption, we should demand the renegotiating of the allocation of public funds. For example, the R5 billion allocated to covert projects should be reallocated to compensate victims of the violence, and to finance reconstruction.[25]

Fast-forward thirty years and it would seem fair to make almost identical observations (and demands) of the ANC.

Fukuyama's 'end of history' claim discussed at the beginning of this chapter theorised that, following Hegel's philosophy, after the clashing of thesis and antithesis ended, humans would enter an almost Arcadian state of self-conscious freedom. And perhaps we did briefly enter this wondrous prelapsarian Mandela-induced state. Those who lived through it might recall that the going seemed pretty good for a while on the surface of things. But, sadly, even in Arcadia (in both the Pretoria iteration and the bucolic rolling hills of Nkandla), lives the presence of 'Dr Death' – both figuratively and literally.

PART FOUR
THE END OF
THE RAINBOW

Nelson Mandela's election in 1994 filled South Africans with hope of a new dawn. But the last twenty-five years have proved that the sun never sets on corruption.

CHAPTER 13

JACOB ZUMA

The Case Against Accused Number One
2009–2018

'Me? Well, I don't know, I must go to a dictionary and learn what a crook is. I've never been a crook.' – Jacob Zuma

Out of the frying pan and into the firepool

No one can deny that the rise of Jacob Zuma to the position of 'Number One' was one of the most earth-shattering events to befall South Africa. The internet, South African archives and bookshelves are now filled with the details of the dizzying acts of corruption and state capture that occurred while JZ was at the helm. The chapters of this book are in no way intended to diminish the impact Zuma and his *chinas* have had on our democracy and our economy. Zuma has dealt a devastating blow to our country, and the poorest and most marginalised have inevitably borne the brunt of his actions.

The ANC and others BZE (Before the Zuma Era)

'This rot is across the board. It's not confined to any level or any area of the country. Almost every project is conceived because it offers opportunities for certain people to make money. A great deal of the ANC's problems are occasioned by this.'
– Kgalema Motlanthe, 2007

In focusing on JZ, we should bear in mind that corruption certainly did not stop during the Mandela and Mbeki eras. Many people might have hoped for a government that would focus on a more equal distribution of resources, but unfortunately it was corrupt politicians, bureaucrats and those in their patronage circles who instead became 'more equal' than others.

- In 1992, a letter written by Winnie Mandela to her lover Dali Mpofu (now of the Economic Freedom Fighters) found its way into the press. In it she claimed to have given Mpofu R160 000 of allegedly misappropriated ANC funds. She also stated that she was worried that the ANC was going to investigate the accounts of its Department of Social Welfare, which she ran. The ANC did indeed lead an internal investigation, resulting in Winnie's dismissal as head of the department in May 1992.[1]
- In August 1995, Nkosazana Dlamini-Zuma's Department of Health awarded a R14.3-million contract to Mbongeni Ngema (who, it was claimed, was her 'good friend') to produce a sequel to the hit musical *Sarafina* to create awareness around HIV/AIDS. As entertainment it didn't come close to her later hit, 'When People Zol', and AIDS experts described some of the *Sarafina 2* dialogue as dangerously misleading. As the *New York Times* put it, 'As a musical, it closed quickly. As a story of Government bungling, it [was] still running six months later.'[2] The allocation exceeded the Department of Health's entire expenditure for provincial AIDS education. An investigation by the Public Protector

uncovered a deeply flawed tender process, finding that Ngema had provided 'a defective service' and that Dlamini-Zuma had misled Parliament.[3] Two years later, in another scandal, the Department of Health released figures showing 'that more than $1 million [around R25 million today] had been stolen from feeding schemes in South Africa's nine provinces'.[4]

• In 1996, Mac Maharaj's Department of Transport awarded a R265-million contract for drivers'-licence provision to a consortium that included a company in which Schabir Shaik had a stake and French arms company Thomson-CSF (later rebranded as Thales). Both Shaik and Thales would later become embroiled in the Arms Deal. According to the *Sunday Times*, companies linked to Shaik made personal payments to Maharaj and his wife at the time that he was transport minister.[5] Although this sparked a furore in the press, Maharaj and his wife have consistently denied that they accepted any bribes and have never been charged in connection with corruption.

• In 1998, the Arms Deal saga began. At the centre of a great deal of the wheeling and dealing were minister of defence Joe Modise, brothers Schabir and Moe Shaik, Thomson-CSF and, of course, JZ himself. In 2003, Mac and Moe, in what might have been an attempt to divert the scrutiny away from Zuma, accused the head of the National Prosecuting Authority (NPA), Bulelani Ngcuka, of being an apartheid spy. When Judge Hefer's commission of inquiry looked into this charge at the end of that year, Hefer found that Mac's evidence was 'most unconvincing', 'entirely unsubstantiated' and 'ill-conceived'. Ngcuka, Hefer found, was almost certainly not an apartheid spy. But it was Ngcuka who would find himself having to step down from the NPA a few months later after being accused of political meddling. The Mac, however, would return to favour in 2011 when he was appointed as Zuma's official spokesperson.

• In 1999, Reverend Allan Boesak, a famous anti-apartheid activist, was convicted of stealing R1.3 million that had been donated by American singer Paul Simon and various Scandinavian foundations to aid black children and voter education. Boesak, who had broken another of the Ten Commandments by having an adulterous affair with an Afrikaans TV presenter, would then break a third by claiming he was innocent of the charges. He was backed up in this by Nelson Mandela. As a result, Mandela and his government were accused of attempting to cover up corruption, engaging in political cronyism and undermining the course of justice.[6]

• In 2000, National Party member Abe Williams, the minister of welfare in Mandela's government of national unity, was found guilty on forty counts of fraud, theft and accepting bribes amounting to R600 000. Branded in the press as 'Dishonest Abe', Williams was sentenced to three years' imprisonment, but ended up spending little more than a year in Pollsmoor Prison – with apparently positive effects on his waistline.[7]

- In 2003, ANC stalwart and snappy dresser Tony Yengeni was convicted of corruption after it was found that he'd received a large discount on the purchase of a Mercedes-Benz 4x4 from a firm bidding for an arms contract. He served just under five months of a four-year sentence.[8] More recently, in a classic case of pot and kettle, Yengeni told President Ramaphosa he should step down, claiming that his election campaign had been corrupt.

- In 2005, Schabir Shaik was found guilty on two counts of corruption and one count of fraud. Judge Squires stated that there was 'overwhelming' evidence of a corrupt relationship between Shaik and Jacob Zuma. On 8 June 2005, Schaik was sentenced to fifteen years' imprisonment. Four years later, in 2009, he was released on medical parole after serving two years and four months.[9] Zuma still stands accused of pocketing millions of rands' worth of bribes from Thales. The trial continues...

- In 2005, businessman Brett Kebble was gunned down in what was referred to in the *Guardian* as a Robert Smit–like 'professional "hit"'. Barry Sergeant, a journalist and Kebble's biographer, referred to Kebble as 'one of the sharpest confidence tricksters the South African investment community has ever hosted'.[10] Kebble, financially and physically corpulent, became famous for sponsoring the arts, as well as the lifestyles of several ANC politicians.

- In 2007, the NPA issued a warrant of arrest for national police commissioner (and Thabo Mbeki ally) Jackie Selebi on charges of corruption. As a result, NPA head Vusi Pikoli was suspended by President Mbeki. During Selebi's trial, convicted drug smuggler Glenn Agliotti admitted to paying Selebi over R1.2 million in bribes. Agliotti also stated that he channelled nearly $100 000 to Selebi from Brett Kebble. In 2010, Selebi was sentenced to fifteen years' imprisonment.[11]

- In 2019 it was revealed at the Zondo Commission of Inquiry that Bosasa, a company owned by the politically well-connected businessman Gavin Watson, received multiple government tenders between 2003 and 2018 worth around R12 billion. Watson, whose family was linked to the ANC and whose struggle credentials included playing mixed-race rugby matches during apartheid, died in a high-speed car accident in 2019. Bosasa's chief operating officer, Angelo Agrizzi, testified to handing over payments of R300 000 to South African Airways chairperson Dudu Myeni. According to Agrizzi, the cash was intended for Zuma himself.[12]

One of our reasons for writing this book is to show that Zuma's alleged acts were in no way new to our beloved and benighted country. (Almost) everything JZ has done has a precedent, and much of it has already played out in history to an almost laughable degree (and hopefully you did laugh).

However, many believe that Jacob Zuma and the ANC were the first to have committed these crimes. As Cyril Ramaphosa wrote in an open letter in 2020, 'Today, the ANC and its leaders stand accused of corruption. The ANC may not stand alone in the dock, but it does stand as Accused No. 1.'[13]

There is little doubt that Jacob 'Number One' Zuma was foremost in Ramaphosa's mind when he wrote about the smelly Number Two that is government corruption. So, let's assess the charges against Jacob Gedleyihlekisa Zuma in the court of public opinion and see if he really does stand alone in the dock …

ACCUSED NUMBER ONE, YOU STAND ACCUSED IN THE COURT OF PUBLIC OPINION.

You are charged with being the first to misappropriate public funds to build and improve your private home

With Nkandla and its firepool, chicken run, kraal, amphitheatre and visitors' centre so fresh in our minds, it's easy to fall into the trap of thinking that JZ's KwaZulu-Natal bolthole (whose renovations cost the taxpayer over R200 million) was somehow unique. If you've made it to the end of this book, you will have realised that building and/or embellishing one's private residence at government expense is *absolutely* the done thing in South Africa.

Willem Adriaan van der Stel didn't just get the land Vergelegen was built on for free, he also used company labour, materials, seed and livestock to build a grand manor, plant magnificent gardens and set up by far the largest agricultural operation at the Cape. If this wasn't enough, he sold the fruits of all this labour back to the Company at prices he determined!

Sir George Yonge didn't last long enough at the Cape to get into farming, but he did use his time here to deck out his official residence with Moroccan leather and other accoutrements. Lord Charles Somerset, meanwhile, recreated a far less productive version of Vergelegen at Groote Post and built a luxurious mansion for himself in Newlands at His Majesty's expense.

Cecil Rhodes was not one to bother with such trifles as free homes or farms.

Instead, he got the colonial and imperial governments to pay for a railway to serve his business interests. And while Paul Kruger lived in a decidedly modest home on Church Street, he certainly didn't pay for it himself – it was gifted to him by a businessman who stood to gain a lot from being in the president's good books.

Dr Piet Meyer, chairman of the Broederbond and the SABC, managed to sell his family home to the state broadcaster (at a heavily inflated price, of course), while Eschel Rhoodie amassed a veritable portfolio of state-funded properties everywhere from Clifton to Miami and paid for his renovations with government-got cash.

The Matanzima brothers in the Transkei and Lucas Mangope in Bophuthatswana both pulled off the age-old trick of farming state land for personal gain. Mangope was also found guilty of spending almost R20 million (in today's money) of taxpayer funds on improvements to his personal residence. And then, of course, there was Wouter Basson's R68-million renovation to the mansion in Arcadia.

You are accused of being the worst corrupter, because you lived in progressive, democratic times

Some might say that Zuma should have known and done better; that the ANC was elected to promote the interests of the poor, not add to their troubles. It is true that the scales of liberal democracy which we use to weigh Zuma's deeds may not apply to crimes past. But if the *skelms* in this book have taught us anything, it's that in every era of our history there were outraged people who felt very much the same as we do about Zuma. In the preceding pages we have quoted from as many diaries, confessions, letters, commissions, parliamentary proceedings and court cases as possible to allow the voices of South Africans from every era to be heard.

Over 300 years ago, Willem Adriaan van der Stel was described as 'a scourge unto the people of this land'. In 1800, a commission into Sir George Yonge's conduct revealed 'scandals without parallel'; twenty-five years later, a post-mortem of Lord Charles Somerset's reign stated that 'this Government is in a state of total incompetence'. Equally damning statements were made of most (if not all) of our other villains.

But as much as JZ comes from a long line of rogues, Thuli Madonsela, Glynnis Breytenbach, Mcebisi Jonas, Pravin Gordhan, Andrew Feinstein and the journalists at the coalface of the Gupta leaks come from a proud heritage of blowing the whistle and speaking truth to power. Throughout our history, where there are Zumas there are fortunately also Madonselas.

Thuli Madonsela sends Number 1 on the (chicken) run

You are charged with showing unprecedented disregard for the taxman

Strictly speaking, this is 100 per cent true. But it is only because before Mandela came to power in 1994, presidents were not required to pay tax at all (and before 1914, income tax didn't even exist in South Africa). When it comes to taxes, Zuma clearly seems to have thought he was above the law. Thing is, his predecessors *were* above the law.

You are accused of being the first to capture the media

As most of us now know, Zuma and the Guptas tried to control various sections of the media. The Guptas started the *New Age* newspaper and created the television network ANN7, filling these platforms with fake news. Zuma was also seemingly complicit in chief operating officer Hlaudi Motsoeneng's machinations in censoring the SABC. Motsoeneng famously suspended eight SABC journalists for speaking out against censorship at the national broadcaster.

Unprecedented? Hardly. From the very beginning, the media in South Africa (which started during the time of Yonge and Somerset) was either completely controlled by the government or had its presses sealed. And then, of course, there was Rhodes, who secretly owned newspapers that not only lambasted his political opponents but also published political adverts that were deemed by a court of law to have come 'perilously close' to bribery. Kruger too got his buddy Nellmapius to set up a pro-government rag.

After all that there came the Broederbond's almost total control of the Afrikaans press through Nasionale Pers (Naspers, which is still around today) and Perskor. The National Party's Broederbonders also took control of the SABC under their chairman Piet Meyer. And who can forget the case of Louis Luyt and Eschel Rhoodie, who set up the government-front newspaper *The Citizen*?

You are accused of being the most shameless nepotist of them all

You probably knew this myth wasn't true even before you started reading this book. Who in this country isn't bathed in nepotism? We (the authors) both went to schools where an appreciation of the wonders of nepotism was instilled in us from day one.

And there's no denying that Zuma's nepotistic practices were central to the way he operated. His sons were neck-deep in alleged corruption and questionable business connections. In his book *The President's Keepers*, Jacques Pauw fingered the 'fiercely loyal to his dad' Edward and the 'Gupta family's favourite' Duduzane in various dodgy and corrupt dealings.[14] Both have seemingly been protected by their father from the long arm of the law.[15] But Zuma was by no means the first South African leader to favour his own – and nor will he be the last.

Willem Adriaan van der Stel only got the gig at the Cape because his daddy had done such a fine job of ~~feathering his own nest~~ advancing the Colony. Both Lord Charles Somerset and Nico Diederichs threw craploads of cash at their inept sons, and Wouter Basson seems to have done the same for his uncle's ailing zoo. Rhodes's brother Frank and Paul Kruger's son-in-law Frikkie Eloff also made the most of their lofty connections. Rhodes even went as far as to get his mate – and one of the most corrupt figures of Cape politics – James Sivewright a knighthood, while Sir George Yonge created vastly overpaid military positions for his civilian buddies. Then there was K.D. Matanzima's willingness to fast-track his brother's career, despite young Chief George being found guilty of abusing an attorney's trust fund. And these are just a few twigs in the vast family tree of South African nepotism.

You are accused of being the first to benefit from an arms deal

Zuma has been embroiled for decades in allegations and criminal trials to do with the famous post-apartheid Arms Deal. The deal dates back to the final years of the Mandela government and has shaped much of the public discourse concerning corruption in the post-Mandela period. It is clearly a hugely important piece of South African contemporary history. Amazingly, Thales (formerly Thomson-CSF) still stands accused, after twenty years, of agreeing to pay Zuma R500 000 annually for protection from an investigation into a $2-billion arms deal.

But we should not forget that during apartheid, arms deals were ten a penny. While there's no way of knowing which members of the apartheid government benefited financially (the records were conveniently destroyed), they certainly got what they wanted, as did the criminals who sold them the military hardware. And as we've seen, Wouter Basson appeared to be up to his neck in arms deals – they just happened to be of the chemical and biological variety.

But there is another point to be made here. As the academic Jonathan Hyslop states, the 'striking feature of the [Arms Deal] affair is that it demonstrates the emergence of a confluence of interest between new and old elites, in this case between the military-industrial complex of the old regime and the leaders of their former guerrilla opponents'.[16]

BKS, an engineering company that had 'impeccable Broederbond heritage', according to *Noseweek*, and African Defence Systems (ADS), the leading military electronics firm of the P.W. Botha era, were involved in the deal. During the mid-1990s, ADS was sold to Thomson-CSF, which had links to Schabir Shaik's Nkobi Holdings.

The Arms Deal also had another link to apartheid. As Paul Holden and Hennie van Vuuren point out, the Auditor-General's Act of 1995 'incorporated the original apartheid legislation' known as the Special Defence Account Act.[17] With this legislation in place, both the apartheid government *and* the post-apartheid government were able to censor any report by the auditor-general.

At its core, the Arms Deal involved paying too much for things South Africa didn't really need and receiving kickbacks and bribes in return. Using this definition, there are dozens of similar examples strewn across the pages of this book that don't include arms. Sir George Yonge was paid millions to turn a blind eye to the illegal importation of slaves, and Somerset 'sold' horses at inflated prices to people who wanted free land from his government.

Rhodes, of course, wore the shoe on the other foot and bribed engineers, members of the electorate and politicians in order to get land, win elections and have his railway built. And with his stadiums and power plants, Lucas Mangope was the kickback king. The Matanzima brothers' Austrian tractor deal was almost a carbon copy of the Arms Deal, but at least the tractors arrived and were put to some use!

You are accused of being the first to hand his tjommies an Eskom coal deal

When it was revealed that Zuma's favourite family, the Guptas, had essentially been gifted a huge coal contract with Eskom, the country was shocked. Eskom's decision to give Gupta-linked Tegeta R659 million up front for 'the sale' of coal not yet produced or delivered so that they could buy out Glencor (which held the Eskom contract) will hopefully end up in court one day.

But as we've discovered, the Broederbond also made a habit of handing Eskom coal contracts to their mates, so the Tegeta affair was no light-bulb moment for Zuma. To be fair to all parties, though, the apartheid government did oversee Eskom's total generating capacity increase from 1217MW in 1945 to 3297MW in 1959 – a growth of 170 per cent in fourteen years. Under Zuma, Eskom's output capacity declined from 239108GW in 2008 to 221936GW in 2018, a lot more than can be said of Lucas Mangope's power plant, which never produced a watt!

You are accused of being the only one to capture the state

Allegations revealing Zuma's systemic capture of state organs may be one of the most shocking tragedies to befall our nation. During Zuma's reign, the NPA, the South African Revenue Service (SARS), the Directorate for Priority Crime Investigation (Hawks), the SABC and Eskom all appear to have come under the collective control of Zuma's patronage circle, known as the Zuptas.

But in our country's history there have been some other pretty good attempts at state capture. Van der Stel and Somerset were blessed to live in an era with fewer checks and balances and were almost gifted their Cape fiefdoms, although even they, all those centuries ago, would have their comeuppance.

A protester holds a banner showing Atul Gupta (with a horned Zuma in his pocket)

Rhodes certainly attempted state capture with his old chum Sivewright, and he was continually scheming with Hofmeyr and then Sprigg in attempts to create an ascendant parliamentary majority. He also had many politicians in his pocket. What got in the way of his plans were people like James Rose Innes and the fallout of the Jameson Raid, which wrecked any chance of his controlling Parliament and the state.

Kruger's close relationships with businessmen like Marks, Nellmapius and Lippert resulted in the Oom's critics talking about a so-called third Volksraad – an informal 'parliament' comprising Kruger's preferred business buddies. But as Richard Mendelsohn points out, Kruger (unlike Zuma) was always his own man, and the power of his wealthy friends had limits.

The South African state *was* effectively captured during the peak of the Broederbond years. The Broeders shifted government contracts to their mates, packed the courts with their judges, changed the Constitution to serve their needs and ran bogus commission after bogus commission, the findings of which were not worth the polyester safari suits of the men who wrote them.

The NPA, SARS and the Hawks may all have been headed by Zuma allies, but during apartheid very much the same could be said of all the same kinds of institutions, which were all run by apartheid stooges who did the government's bidding. One just needs to remember that Colonel 'Lang Hendrik' van den Bergh arrived to investigate a common burglary at the 'harmless cultural organisation' called the Broederbond, and that the SABC's main radio service was interrupted by the selfsame Broeders when a simple *dominee* said he no longer wanted to be a member of said harmless cultural organisation.

Going further back, under Somerset there was 'Dog Dan' Denyssen, seemingly an early version of Shaun Abrahams (dubbed 'Shaun the Sheep' in the media due to the widespread criticism of his leadership of the NPA). And in Leyds, Kruger had his own obedient fiscal.

If there is a difference between Zuma's cohort and the others, it is perhaps that along with his capture of these institutions came total dysfunctionality. But it is also worth remembering that while we may have load-shedding today, during the period of state capture under apartheid most South Africans lived *in* a load of sheds without a snowball's chance of electrification. To suggest Zuma's state capture was worse than that under apartheid is very much a matter of perspective and debate. It is true, however, that the Broeders remained a little more in touch with the needs of their voter base. No one can claim that Zuma did.

You are charged with avoiding jail time for corruption

That others would have gone to jail for what Zuma has done is one of the biggest nonsenses of all. In all of our research, the only top-tier leader (if you can call him that) to serve jail time for corruption was Chief George Matanzima, and even he was released after serving three years of his nine-year sentence. Eschel Rhoodie was initially found guilty and sentenced to six years, but he was let off in the stacked Appeal Court. Something similar happened with Lucas Mangope, who was allowed to avoid jail despite being found guilty on 102 counts of fraud and theft. Wouter Basson must have been in a state of pure ecstasy when he was found not guilty on forty-six counts, including murder, fraud and drug trafficking.

But really, these men who faced prosecution are the outliers. Most of our corrupt leaders get to live out their days either in wealthy disgrace (Van der Stel, Somerset, Yonge) or, better still for them, as national heroes (Rhodes, Kruger).

You are accused of not 'paying back the money'

When Public Protector Thuli Madonsela's 'Secure in Comfort' report detailing Jacob Zuma's Nkandla misappropriations was released, calls of 'pay back the money' resounded from every corner of South African society. Eventually, Zuma (or one of his billionaire friends?) paid back R7.8 million of the R246 million in taxpayers' money that had been spent on *Extreme Home Reno: Nkandla Edition*.[18] But thinking that JZ was the first to drag his feet and refuse to cough up would be a mistake.

When Willem Adriaan van der Stel was kicked off Vergelegen, 'the delinquent was not even compelled to make good to the Company the amount which he had defrauded it of'.[19] There was never a chance that the perpetually bankrupt Sir George Yonge would pay anything back either. Just being rid of him was prize enough. After Lord Charles Somerset was dragged kicking and screaming to Britain, he first refused to hand over his accounts and then was pretty damned peeved at having to hand some of it back: 'The Auditors have come to the subject of my salary,' he sniffed. 'I think I have managed badly. I went to Lord Bathurst and the decision is, I am to pay [back] half.' In comparison to Zuma's piffling Nkandla payback, we guess he had a reason to be sniffy.

And if Somerset was annoyed, can you imagine how *gatvol* Louis Luyt must have been when he was forced to pay back an unprecedented 69 per cent of his government 'loan'? Of course, there never seems to have been a question about repayment on the part of Eschel Rhoodie or Wouter Basson, despite both ending up in court.

You are accused of being the first to cosy up to common gangsters

Many people were shocked by Jacques Pauw's uncovering in *The President's Keepers* of Zuma's close connections to hardened criminals. As Pauw put it, 'Nothing can illustrate the moral slippage of President Jacob Zuma [better] than ... his cavorting with the Western Cape's most notorious gangsters.'[20]

But again, Zuma was certainly not the first to have done so. Willem Adriaan van der Stel's landdrost, Beelzebub, was the eighteenth-century equivalent of a West Rand heavy, while George Yonge made a pretty penny out of his close relationships with slave smugglers – the *tik* dealers of their day.

Somerset too was certainly not shy of using spies and strong-arm tactics against anybody who stood in his way. He sided with people who used extortion and bribery within the Colony, as well as with his son, who refused to pay his debts.

Rhodes was more than capable of bribing people to break the law. He set up perhaps one of the world's biggest cartels in the form of De Beers. Worse still, he got his bestie, Dr Leander Starr Jameson, to wage war against any tribe or state he thought might be sitting on gold deposits. As Joseph Conrad wrote in *Heart of Darkness*, this kind of thing 'was just robbery with violence'.

Lucas Mangope had many dubious friends, but none was dicier than KGB double agent Shabtai Kalmanovich, a man who made fortunes out of Sierra Leone's blood diamonds and was killed in a drive-by shooting on the streets of Moscow.

Both State President Nico Diederichs and Prime Minister B.J. Vorster had intimate dealings with the Ossewabrandwag, an organisation that openly engaged in murder and bombings. These men also approved of acts of staggering fraud and engaged in the illegal arms trade. And when you add the torturing and murdering carried out by 'Lang Hendrik' van den Bergh's Bureau of State Security, Magnus Malan and Adriaan Vlok's Civil Cooperation Bureau and Vlakplaas, it does seem to put Zuma's involvement with garden-variety gangsters from the Cape Flats in the shade. As for the Smit murders – which involved the killing of one of apartheid's brightest stars and his wife to avoid the truth coming out – they were about as Mafia as it comes.

Add to this the National Party's links to the Mafia's Vito Palazzolo and there is a healthy slice of humble pie to eat for those who suggest Zuma was the first to have these sorts of unsavoury connections. Apartheid was in many ways the quintessence of a gangster state.

You are accused of wrecking the economy on an unprecedented scale

Bantustans aside, there is some truth to this. Others have come close, though: the apartheid government, Van der Stel, Yonge and especially Somerset ('We are perfect bankrupts, and it is needless to conceal it, as we have not enough money to pay our own salaries'[21]) all gave it a good tonk.

It is certainly a myth worth busting that the apartheid government developed a burgeoning economy. From Rhodes's arrival in Kimberley to 1977, South

Africa ran largely on diamonds, gold and the abuse of labour. But as the political scientist David Welsh put it, the apartheid government created an economic crisis that

> had its roots in the mismanagement of the economy over several decades. The economy had performed poorly since the mid-1970s, low growth had continued through the 1980s, and negative growth had been recorded in 1990 and 1991. Inflation hovered around 15 per cent, business confidence had declined, foreign and domestic investment was sharply reduced, and there had been a substantial outflow of capital that had accelerated in the 1980s.[22]

There is no doubt that Zuma made a particularly bad and malfeasant fist of the economy, but he did have the bad fortune of leading a country that was facing some of its worst challenges in nearly 100 years. This is not to say that he shouldn't take the blame for wrecking our economy – of course he should – but like the Broederbond, Van der Stel and Rhodes, he looked after his own. There are people out there who claim that this made these guys 'lekker okes' and 'jolly good chaps', so why shouldn't some say the same of Zuma?

You are charged with capturing the justice system like none before you

Zuma's attack on the NPA, interference in the duties of the police and what was called his 'Stalingrad approach' in the court cases against him have threatened and hollowed out our democratic institutions. Zuma has often been quoted saying that he desperately wants his day in court, but as Andrew Feinstein told us, 'he has spent untold millions avoiding his day in court or at a commission'.[23]

However, Zuma was not the first to employ such tactics. At the tribunal into his own conduct, Willem Adriaan van der Stel kept track of proceedings from behind a thin door through which 'it was possible to hear every word. When any difficulty arose the commissioners and the prosecutor would step aside, with no attempt at concealment, to consult with the Governor!'[24]

Somerset and his fiscal, 'Dog Dan' Denyssen, were wedded at the waist, while Rhodes had an equally evasive and constipated approach to the handling of evidence in the courts. Kruger barged into his prosecutor's bedroom to shower him with legal opinions and desires (as well as sputum) when he wanted to get his way in the courts.

The apartheid government went further and stacked the courts with their own judges to a degree that makes Zuma look like a novice. At least when Zuma came to setting up a commission of inquiry, he was forced to make it open to the public. When Verwoerd was cornered into setting up a commission, he pushed legislation through Parliament so he could make it a secret one. Not that Zuma didn't have similar hopeful desires ...

When P.W. Botha found out that Judge Mostert's commission looking into the Information Scandal was acting independently, he dropped it like a hot *braaibroodjie*. The Groot Krokodil then set up the Erasmus Commission, which rushed through its work and found largely what P.W. wanted it to find. Paul Kruger, meanwhile, did one better after his controversial victory in the 1893 election, setting up a commission which 'regarded speed as the essence of its task' and took only three days to find in Oom's favour![25]

You are accused of taking the golden handshake (and handcuffs) to new heights

When Jacob Zuma gave national director of public prosecutions Mxolisi Nxasana a R17.3-million golden handshake to make way for Shaun Abrahams, many believed this to be unprecedented. South Africa was also shocked when Mcebisi Jonas revealed that the Zuptas had offered him a set of 'golden handcuffs' (to the tune of R600 million) if he would act in their favour when made minister of finance.

But Zuma was not the first to shower people in gold. When the National Party came to power in 1948, they proffered hundreds of golden handshakes in their (highly successful) quest to rid the government of any trace of liberal thinking. One case in point was the talented, English-speaking head of the railways, Marshal Clark, who at the age of only forty-eight received two R60-million golden handshakes in quick succession from the Broederbond's Nationalists.

For C.J. Rhodes, the golden handcuff was very much his weapon of choice. Many of the Bond's 'wobblers', as they were called, remained loyal to Rhodes even after the Jameson Raid for one reason and one reason only: Rhodes had dished out shares to them.

You are charged with allowing your sexual impropriety to seep into your politics

Zuma's sexual promiscuity has often been linked to his acts of corruption. And, granted, if you can have sex with your friend's daughter, even if you are later acquitted of raping her, heaven knows where else your broken moral compass might take you. But Zuma is not alone in his sexual impropriety. Somerset may well have had an extramarital affair with a person whom G.E. Cory calls the 'woman Doctor' James Barry. Somerset also seemingly had some sort of relationship with at least one slave.

Willem Adriaan van der Stel is said to have had such lax morals that his wife attempted suicide upon hearing of his philandering, while Lucas Mangope had to be hauled out of his mistress's bed to attend to a coup d'état. Of course, sexual deviance is no marker of corruption. In Rhodes's case, despite all the rumours that he was homosexual (the height of deviance at the time), we seem to have drawn a blank. There remains no proof that he ever had an amorous relationship with anybody. And this hardly seems to have helped matters.

THE VERDICT

It hardly seems worth pointing out that Zuma is not South Africa's first corrupt leader and that he most certainly will not be the last. Even if Zuma does go to prison (we're not holding our breath) and Cyril Ramaphosa manages to toss a few rotten apples from the ANC's basket (as Bantu Holomisa put it), you can bet your bottom Krugerrand that the 'scourge unto the people of this land' that is corruption will return in many guises in the decades and centuries to come.

The good news is that it's easier than ever before to trace corruption. Smartphones and laptops mean that almost every corrupt action leaves some kind of digital trace. Whistle-blowing is, as it has always been, a difficult task filled with moral dilemmas and acts of extreme courage. But people still seem as brave as ever in standing up against corruption. Plus, the advent of pesky concepts like freedom of speech, the right not to be tortured, and political accountability, as well as the twenty-four-hour news cycle, make it a more difficult environment for corrupt officials to operate in. Which is not to say they won't keep on trying…

Say my name/change my name

Rhodes's statue at the University of Cape Town (UCT) may have fallen in 2015, but the names of a number of other rogues continue to grace some of South Africa's most prominent landmarks. Here are some interesting ones that came to our attention while writing this book:

'They will hang Mr Rhodes if they ever catch him.' – Mark Twain

Apart from his confiscated statue, Cecil John Rhodes still occupies prominent 'real estate'. Think of **Rhodes University** (which is located on Somerset Street!), the **Rhodes Scholarship** and the still-standing statues in the Company's Garden (an attempt to sever his Achilles tendon with an angle grinder proved unsuccessful) and at Oxford University. At **Rhodes Memorial**, his bust was first subjected to several nose jobs and then a decapitation. While he probably deserves nothing less, the authors discovered that his head was recently repaired by the Friends of Rhodes Memorial in a strange act of agalmatophilia.

Jameson Hall – which proudly celebrated a mercenary for well over a century – at UCT may have finally had its name changed to Sarah Baartman Hall, but there still is a **Jameson Road** in Goodwood.

Cape Town's **De Waal Park**, a place of summer concerts and doggy play dates, still carries the name of Rhodes's corruptee, the 'wobbly' Bondsman D.C. de Waal. His father-in-law's statue – that of 'Onze' Jan Hofmeyr – still stands, legs akimbo, in Parliament Square in the Mother City. An entire suburb of Pretoria is named after **Nellmapius** (which also boasts a street named after Lippert), and **Sammy Marks Square** is another major landmark in our nation's administrative capital.

We couldn't find much named after Willem Adriaan van der Stel, but his almost-as-corrupt daddy Simon more than makes up for this omission. **Stellenbosch** (which Simon named after himself in 1679) wasn't just the scene of Willem's crimes, it is also home to a modern 'mafia' of its own, whose money is linked to the Broederbond.

Somerset West and **Somerset East** might be a thousand kays apart, but they're joined at the hip of corruption and incompetence. That said, the **Lord Charles Hotel** in Somerset West appears to have been forced to shut down due to COVID-19.

Paul Kruger's statue still towers over Church Square in Pretoria, and two of our country's icons – the **Kruger National Park** and the **Krugerrand** – also proudly bear his name. The statue, which recently had the words 'KILLER, KILLER' daubed on its base despite being hidden behind an EFF-proof fence, is in danger of being relocated to a 'cultural park' that many are already referring to as Boerassic Park.

One of Joburg's most important thoroughfares, **William Nicol Drive**, is still named after the theological granddaddy of apartheid and founder of the racist Broederbond.

To this day, the main drag of Ga-Rankuwa just outside Pretoria bears the name of **Lucas Mangope**. More fittingly, Louis Luyt's name adorns a street of scrap dealers and panel beaters, while KD Matanzima still has at least five roads named after him. Sol Kerzner's legacy, meanwhile, is secured by Sun City and scores of other hotels around the world.

A technical high-school named after Nico Diederichs still exists in **Krugersdorp**, and **Nic Diederichs Road** in Roodepoort is, fittingly, an extension of **Paul Kruger Road**. The built-for-purpose apartheid police prison facility **John Vorster Square**, which was a location for detentions, interrogations and torture, had its name changed (and a bust of B.J. removed) in 1997. However, a road in Roodepoort still carries Vorster's name.

ACKNOWLEDGEMENTS

This book would never have been written if we hadn't embarked on an earlier enterprise – which failed dismally – to market and sell a little-known craft rum to the hipsters of Cape Town. About a year into that excruciating escapade, it dawned on us that we were among the most awkward and reticent salespeople on the planet. Working together, however, had been fun, so we decided to give it one more shot, on a venture we were actually capable of pulling off. Having met on the University of Cape Town's Creative Writing programme in 2004, and given our shared obsession with South Africa's wacky and intriguing past, a history book seemed the obvious choice.

We didn't have to think too hard about a topic. At braais, bars and kids' birthday parties, we'd both seen it as our civic duty (it was, admittedly, also quite enjoyable) to correct anyone who made the absurd and all-too-frequent claim that widespread government corruption in South Africa began with the election of Jacob Zuma in 2009. Or at the very least with the African National Congress.

Over a preliminary meeting at Rhodes Memorial tea room (where else?) we realised that while we had read enough about Willem Adriaan van der Stel, Cecil Rhodes and the Broederbond to win an argument, we had barely scratched the slimy surface of South Africa's boldest and oldest *skelms*. We vowed to do some reading and meet again in a month: same time, same place. COVID-19 saw to it that we only had three Rhodes Mem meetings; the remaining dirt had to be dished virtually.

Most of this book was written during lockdown, and there's no doubt the distraction served to keep us both sane. (Our families would dispute this.) As it turns out, nothing takes one's mind off a pandemic better than delving into the financial follies of an eighteenth-century toff.

Writing a book that spans 350 years of history was daunting, and we couldn't have pulled it off without input from the experts who read and commented on each chapter. We owe a great debt of thanks to all those people who took time and much effort to read and comment on our initial attempts. The book quite simply would not have been what it is without them. We list them in order of the chapter they dealt with: Dan Sleigh (whose 1700s comb is of the superfine variety), Bruno Werz, Kirsten McKenzie (we owe her for two chapters, and for being so thorough and generous with her time!), Nigel Penn, Paul Maylam, Richard Mendelsohn, Carel van der Merwe (who even joined us at Rhodes Mem once), Ivor Wilkins, Martin Welz (who also gave us access to his archive), Roger Southall (who was very generous with his library of books on the Transkei), General Bantu Holomisa, Andrew Manson (who provided some great pics of Bophuthatswana), Chandré Gould and Andrew Feinstein.

Then there were the archivists and librarians who, during the Coronavirus pandemic, went the extra mile with and for us. They not only directed us but were also always willing to fact-check and send us scans and information during a very difficult and confusing time in the world's history. Many thanks to archivists Erika Le Roux, Zabeth Botha, Marise Bronkhorst, Sewela Mamphiswana and Lila Komnick, and librarians Ntombiyakhe Gangathela, Marlene Swanepoel and Lungi Banca. To Desmond Louw for his photo edits, Johan Fourie who helped with historical exchange-rate conversions, and Michael Marchant from Open Secrets for sending the relevant documents at a time of complete desperation.

Of course, we cannot leave out the wonderful people at Penguin who took up this project with immense enthusiasm and expertise. We are truly grateful for your support, interest, knowledge and professionalism: Robert Plummer, Alice Inggs, Ryan Africa, Colette Stott, Lisa Compton and Sanet le Roux. And, of course, Marlene Fryer, whose initial email saying how much Penguin wanted the book will go down as among the best we have ever received (certainly from a publisher).

And then to our gentle readers who got through early drafts of the book. To Shelly Dall, who ironed out the bumps in our contrasting writing styles to ensure that the book has one voice; Andrew Feinstein, who offered invaluable general advice; and Michael Dall, who was the first to read it from cover to cover.

Then, there are those most important to us, who suffered through the writing experience in person:

Thanks go to my partner in crime, Shelly, who has always supported and improved my writing and who, despite knowing just how big an impact it would have on my ability to be a husband, father and companion, encouraged me to write a book during a pandemic. To my children, who put up with an even-slower-than-usual response time to their requests for food, fun and homeschooling assistance. To

Matthew, whose knowledge and humour shaped this book into what it is. And to my parents, who never once tried to convince me to get a real job. – **Nick Dall**

I would like firstly to thank Nick for not only getting us through this (I am not a finisher) but also for convincing me that humour, both yours and mine, might make the whole experience an enjoyable one; it did. Thank you too to Grant Quixley for your almost lifelong friendship, and for listening to the constant nonsense that flows from me. To my sister, Sally, and Michael and Emma for the walks and everything else. Then there was Chad, who was a damn decent sort during the whole period. Thanks to Brian Willan, who pointed the way to Rhodes. And to faithful Morgan, who lay on my left foot for large swathes of the writing process. – **Matthew Blackman**

Nick and Matthew grapple with Rhodes's immense and brooding spirit

NOTES

INTRODUCTION

1. Kempe Ronald Hope, Sr, and Bornwell C. Chikulo, *Corruption and Development in Africa: Lessons from Country Case-Studies* (London: Macmillan Press, 2000), p. 18.
2. Hoang Anh Tuan, 'Silk for Silver: Dutch-Vietnamese Relations, 1637–1700' (PhD thesis, University of Leiden, South Holland, 2006), p. 192.
3. H.C.V. Leibbrandt, *Precis of the Archives of the Cape of Good Hope: Riebeeck's Journal, December 1651 – December 1653* (Cape Town: W.A. Richards & Sons, 1897), p. 5.
4. Bruno Werz, *The Haarlem Shipwreck (1647): The origins of Cape Town* (Pretoria: Unisa Press, 2017), p. 129.
5. Eric A. Walker, *A History of Southern Africa* (London: Longmans, 1964), p. 30.
6. Leibbrandt, *Precis of the Archives of the Cape of Good Hope: Riebeeck's Journal*, p. 125.
7. Ibid., p. 171.
8. Ibid., p. 163.
9. Ibid., p. 193.
10. Email correspondence with Dan Sleigh, 14 November 2020.
11. Corruption Watch, 'What Is Corruption: Our Definition of Corruption' (available at https://www.corruptionwatch.org.za/learn-about-corruption/what-is-corruption/our-definition-of-corruption/; accessed 1 November 2020).

CHAPTER 1: WILLEM ADRIAAN VAN DER STEL

1. Leo Fouché and A.J. Böeseken (eds), *The Diary of Adam Tas* (Cape Town: Van Riebeeck Society, 1970), p. 13.
2. H.C.V. Leibbrandt (ed.), *Precis of the Archives of the Cape of Good Hope: The Defence of Willem Adriaan van der Stel* (Cape Town: W.A. Richards and Sons, 1897), p. 69.
3. Fouché and Böeseken, *The Diary of Adam Tas*, p. 255.
4. George McCall Theal, *Willem Adriaan van der Stel and Other Historical Sketches* (Cape Town: Thomas Maskew Miller, 1913), p. 208.
5. Fouché and Böeseken, *The Diary of Adam Tas*, p. 199.
6. Leo Fouché (ed.), *The Diary of Adam Tas* (London: Longmans, Green and Co., 1914), p. 213.
7. Fouché and Böeseken, *The Diary of Adam Tas*, p. 97.
8. Ibid., p. 257.
9. Theal, *Willem Adriaan van der Stel and Other Historical Sketches*, p. 224.
10. Leonard Guelke, 'The Anatomy of a Colonial Settler Population: Cape Colony 1657–1750', *International Journal of African Historical Studies*, Vol. 21, No. 3 (1988), pp. 453–73.
11. François Valentijn, *Description of the Cape of Good Hope with the Matters Concerning It*

– *Amsterdam 1726*, ed. P. Serton, R. Raven-Hart, W.J. de Kock and E.H. Raidt (Cape Town: Van Riebeeck Society, 1971), pp. 115–17.

12. Theal, *Willem Adriaan van der Stel and Other Historical Sketches*, p. 220.
13. Leibbrandt, *Precis of the Archives of the Cape of Good Hope*, p. 52.
14. Ibid., p. 53.
15. Theal, *Willem Adriaan van der Stel and Other Historical Sketches*, pp. 208–21.
16. Ibid., p. 219.
17. Fouché and Böeseken, *The Diary of Adam Tas*, pp. 131–3.
18. Leibbrandt, *Precis of the Archives of the Cape of Good Hope*, p. 54.
19. Ibid., p. 64.
20. Fouché and Böeseken, *The Diary of Adam Tas*, p. 235.
21. Ibid., p. 239.
22. Ibid., p. 241.
23. Ibid., p. 243.
24. Theal, *Willem Adriaan van der Stel and Other Historical Sketches*, p. 21.
25. Leibbrandt, *Precis of the Archives of the Cape of Good Hope*, p. 55.
26. Theal, *Willem Adriaan van der Stel and Other Historical Sketches*, p. 225.
27. Fouché, *The Diary of Adam Tas*, pp. xxvi–xxix.
28. Fouché and Böeseken, *The Diary of Adam Tas*, p. 231.
29. Ibid., p. 231.
30. Ibid., p. 235.
31. Ibid., p. 235.
32. Leibbrandt, *Precis of the Archives of the Cape of Good Hope*, pp. 72–3.
33. Fouché and Böeseken, *The Diary of Adam Tas*, p. 237.
34. Ibid., p. 241.
35. Ibid.
36. Graham Viney, *Colonial Houses of South Africa* (Cape Town: Struik-Winchester, 1987), p. 23.
37. Email correspondence with Johan Fourie, 22 October 2020.
38. Viney, *Colonial Houses of South Africa*, p. 23.
39. Leibbrandt, *Precis of the Archives of the Cape of Good Hope*, pp. 1–54.
40. Theal, *Willem Adriaan van der Stel and Other Historical Sketches*, p. 242.
41. Fouché and Böeseken, *The Diary of Adam Tas*, p. xvii.
42. Kevin Davie, 'A Farmer, the Governor and the Memorial', in *Southern African Muckraking: 300 Years of Investigative Journalism That Has Shaped the Region*, ed. Anton Harber (Auckland Park: Jacana Media, 2018), Kindle edition.

CHAPTER 2: SIR GEORGE YONGE

1. George McCall Theal, *History of South Africa from 1795 to 1872: Volume I* (London: George Allen & Unwin Ltd, 1915), p. 71.
2. Lady Anne Barnard, *South Africa a Century Ago (1797–1801)*, ed. H.J. Anderson (Cape Town: Maskew Miller Ltd, 1924), p. 99.
3. History of Parliament Online, 'YONGE, Sir George, 5th Bt. (1732–1812), of Colyton and

Escott House, Devon' (available at http://www.histparl.ac.uk/volume/1790-1820/ member/ yonge-sir-george-1732-1812; accessed 16 October 2020).

4. Barnard, *South Africa a Century Ago*, p. 109.
5. Theal, *History of South Africa from 1795 to 1872: Volume I*, p. 81.
6. Ibid., p. 81.
7. Nigel Penn, 'The Last Years: Dundas and Yonge, 1798 to 1803', in *Britain at the Cape: 1795 to 1803*, ed. Nigel Penn and Maurice Boucher (Houghton: Brenthurst Press, 1992), p. 238.
8. Barnard, *South Africa a Century Ago*, p. 111.
9. Theal, *History of South Africa from 1795 to 1872: Volume I*, p. 81.
10. Barnard, *South Africa a Century Ago*, p. 111.
11. Ibid., p. 110.
12. Histparl.ac.uk, 'YONGE, Sir George'.
13. Dorothea Fairbridge, *Lady Anne Barnard at the Cape of Good Hope, 1797–1802* (Oxford: Clarendon Press, 1924), p. 241.
14. George McCall Theal, *Maskew Miller's Short History of South Africa & its People*, comp. Thomas Young (Cape Town: Thomas Maskew Miller, 1909), p. 90.
15. Ibid., p. 78.
16. Encyclopaedia of South African Theatre, Film, Media and Performance (ESAT), 'George Yonge' (available at https://esat.sun.ac.za/index.php/George_Yonge; accessed 16 October 2020).
17. Tudor Society, 'The Order of the Bath by Sarah Bryson' (available at https://www .tudorsociety.com/the-order-of-the-bath-by-sarah-bryson/; accessed 16 October 2020).
18. Theal, *History of South Africa from 1795 to 1872: Volume I*, p. 71.
19. Histparl.ac.uk, 'YONGE, Sir George'.
20. Ibid.
21. Barnard, *South Africa a Century Ago*, p. 137.
22. Histparl.ac.uk, 'YONGE, Sir George'.
23. Author interview with Stephen Taylor, 12 May 2017.
24. Theal, *History of South Africa from 1795 to 1872: Volume I*, p. 80.
25. Ibid., p. 82.
26. Penn, 'The Last Years: Dundas and Yonge, 1798 to 1803', p. 235.
27. Ibid., pp. 235–6.
28. Barnard, *South Africa a Century Ago*, p. 144 (footnote).
29. Theal, *History of South Africa from 1795 to 1872: Volume I*, p. 78.
30. Barnard, *South Africa a Century Ago*, p. 144 (footnote).
31. Theal, *History of South Africa from 1795 to 1872: Volume I*, p. 79.
32. Ibid., p. 83.
33. Ibid., p. 83.
34. Ibid., pp. 83–4.
35. Penn, 'The Last Years: Dundas and Yonge, 1798 to 1803', p. 238.
36. Michael Charles Reidy, 'The Admission of Slaves and "Prize Slaves" into the Cape Colony, 1797–1818' (M.A. thesis, University of Cape Town, 1997), p. 33.

37. Ibid., p. 32.
38. Ibid., p. 54.
39. Theal, *History of South Africa from 1795 to 1872: Volume I*, p. 84.
40. Reidy, 'The Admission of Slaves and 'Prize Slaves' into the Cape Colony, 1797–1818', p. 58.
41. Ibid., p. 59.
42. Barnard, *South Africa a Century Ago*, p. 129.
43. Ibid., pp. 129–30.
44. Email correspondence with Kirsten McKenzie, 14 September 2020.
45. Histparl.ac.uk, 'YONGE, Sir George'.
46. Theal, *History of South Africa from 1795 to 1872: Volume I*, p. 79.
47. Penn, 'The Last Years: Dundas and Yonge, 1798 to 1803', p. 239.
48. Ibid., p. 239.
49. Theal, *History of South Africa from 1795 to 1872: Volume I*, p. 80.
50. Ibid., p. 80.
51. Histparl.ac.uk, 'YONGE, Sir George'.
52. Penn, 'The Last Years: Dundas and Yonge, 1798 to 1803', p. 233.
53. Frank O'Gorman, *Voters, Patrons, and Parties: The Unreformed Electoral System of Hanoverian England 1734–1832* (Oxford: Clarendon Press, 1989), pp. 133–34.
54. Oxford Dictionary of National Biography, 'Yonge, Sir George, Fifth Baronet' (available at https://doi.org/10.1093/ref:odnb/30223; accessed 16 October 2020).
55. Wikipedia, 'Sir George Yonge, 5th Baronet' (available at https://en.wikipedia.org/wiki/Sir_George_Yonge,_5th_Baronet; accessed 25 October 2020).

CHAPTER 3: LORD CHARLES SOMERSET

1. Noël Mostert, *Frontiers: The Epic of South Africa's Creation and the Tragedy of the Xhosa People* (London: Jonathan Cape, 1992), p. 408.
2. Jeffrey Butler, *American Historical Review*, Vol. 71, No. 2 (1966), p. 638.
3. Antony Millar, *Plantagenet in South Africa: Lord Charles Somerset* (Cape Town: Oxford University Press, 1965), p. 18.
4. Millar, *Plantagenet in South Africa*, p. 30.
5. Mostert, *Frontiers*, p. 408.
6. G.E. Cory, *The Rise of South Africa Vol. II* (Cape Town: Struik, 1965), pp. 240–41.
7. J.B. Peires, 'The British and the Cape 1814–1834', in *The Shaping of South African Society, 1652–1840*, ed. Richard Elphick and Hermann Giliomee (Middletown: Wesleyan University Press, 1979), Kindle edition, p. 491.
8. *Records of the Cape Colony: Vol. XXIII, Nov.–Dec., 1825*, pp. 176–180.
9. Ibid., p. 494.
10. Ibid., p. 500.
11. Cory, *The Rise of South Africa Vol. II*, p. 242.
12. Millar, *Plantagenet in South Africa*, p. 106.
13. Ibid., p. 13.
14. Peires, 'The British and the Cape 1814–1834', p. 473.

15. Millar, *Plantagenet in South Africa*, p. 151.
16. Cory, *The Rise of South Africa Vol. II*, p. 303.
17. Ibid., p. 305.
18. Ibid., p. 313 (footnote).
19. Ibid., p. 314.
20. John Laband, *The Land Wars* (Cape Town: Penguin, 2020), p. 158.
21. Andre du Toit, 'Experiments with Truth and Justice in South Africa: Stockenström, Gandhi and the TRC', *Journal of Southern African Studies*, Vol. 31, No. 2 (June 2005), p. 424.
22. Mostert, *Frontiers*, p. 516.
23. Millar, *Plantagenet in South Africa*, p. 123.
24. J.L. Dracopoli, *Sir Andries Stockenstrom, 1792–1864*: The Origins of the Racial Conflict in South Africa (A.A. Balkema, 1969), p. 41.
25. Cory, *The Rise of South Africa Vol. II*, p. 254.
26. Ibid., p. 277.
27. Kirsten McKenzie, *Imperial Underworld: An Escaped Convict and the Transformation of the British Colonial Order* (Cambridge: Cambridge University Press, 2016), p. 226.
28. Thomas Pringle, *Thomas Pringle in South Africa 1820–1826*, ed. John Wahl (Cape Town: Longman, 1970), p. 100.
29. Cory, *The Rise of South Africa Vol. II*, p. 279.
30. Randolph Vigne, *Thomas Pringle: South African Pioneer, Poet and Abolitionist* (Woodbridge: James Curry, 2012), p. 117.
31. John Fairbairn to Thomas Pringle, 2 March 1823, quoted in Jane Meiring, *Thomas Pringle: His Life and Times* (Cape Town: Balkema, 1968), p. 80.
32. Peires, 'The British and the Cape 1814–1834', p. 477.
33. Cory, *The Rise of South Africa Vol. II*, p 284.
34. Pringle, *Thomas Pringle in South Africa 1820–1826*, p. 93.
35. Meiring, *Thomas Pringle*, p. 85.
36. Pringle, *Thomas Pringle in South Africa 1820–1826*, p. 94.
37. Ibid., p. 95.
38. Ibid., p. 96.
39. Peires, 'The British and the Cape 1814–1834', p. 478.
40. McKenzie, *Imperial Underworld*, p. 153.
41. Ibid., p. 140.
42. *Records of the Cape Colony: Vol. XVII, Jan.–June, 1824*, p. 186.
43. McKenzie, *Imperial Underworld*, p. 148.
44. Ibid., p. 152.
45. Cory, *The Rise of South Africa Vol. II*, p. 266.
46. McKenzie, *Imperial Underworld*, p. 216.
47. Wendy Moore, 'Dr James Barry: A Woman Ahead of Her Time', *Guardian*, 10 November 2016 (https://www.theguardian.com/books/2016/nov/10/dr-james-barry-a-woman-ahead-of-her-time-review; accessed 24 October 2020).
48. McKenzie, *Imperial Underworld*, p. 78.

CHAPTER 4: CECIL JOHN RHODES (I)

1. Antony Thomas, *Rhodes: The Race for Africa* (Johannesburg: Jonathan Ball, 1996), p. 100.
2. Quoted in Thomas, *Rhodes*, p. 100.
3. Quoted in Brian Roberts, *Cecil Rhodes: Flawed Colossus* (London: Hamish Hamilton, 1987), p. 34.
4. Robert Turrell, *Capital and Labour on the Kimberley Diamond Fields, 1871–1890* (Cambridge: Cambridge University Press, 1987), p. 86.
5. Quoted in Thomas, *Rhodes*, p. 101.
6. Joseph Conrad, *Nostromo* (Everyman's Library edition, 1904), p. 58.
7. Robert I. Rotberg, *The Founder: Cecil Rhodes and the Pursuit of Power* (Cape Town: Oxford University Press, 1988), p. 125.
8. Roberts, *Cecil Rhodes*, p. 55.
9. Thomas, *Rhodes*, p. 132.
10. Quoted in William Plomer, *Cecil Rhodes* (London: Peter Davies Ltd, 1933), p. 51.
11. Ibid., p. 54.
12. Ibid., p. 60.
13. Thomas, *Rhodes*, p. 197.
14. Apollon Davidson, *Cecil Rhodes and His Time* (Moscow: Progress Press, 1988), p. 141.
15. Ibid., p. 142.
16. Joseph Conrad, *Heart of Darkness* (Amazon Classics edition), p. 5.
17. Quoted in Elizabeth Longford, *The Jameson Raid: Prelude to the Boer War* (Johannesburg: Jonathan Ball, 1982), p. 45.
18. Rotberg, *The Founder*, p. 443.

CHAPTER 5: PAUL KRUGER

1. Marjorie Juta, *The Pace of the Ox: A Life of Paul Kruger* (Cape Town: Human & Rousseau, 1975), p. xii.
2. Johannes Meintjes, *President Paul Kruger: A Biography* (London: Cassell, 1974), p. 21.
3. Martin Meredith, *Diamonds, Gold and War: The Making of South Africa* (London: Pocket Books, 2008), p. 77.
4. Ibid., p. 79.
5. Helga Kaye, *The Tycoon and the President: The Life and Times of Alois Hugo Nellmapius, 1847–1893* (Johannesburg: Macmillan South Africa, 1978), p. 40.
6. Ibid., p. 37.
7. J.S. Marais, *The Fall of Kruger's Republic* (Oxford: Clarendon Press, 1961), p. 23.
8. Richard Mendelsohn, *Sammy Marks: The Uncrowned King of the Transvaal* (Cape Town: David Philip, 1991), p. 20.
9. Kaye, *The Tycoon and the President*, pp. 37–8.
10. Mendelsohn, *Sammy Marks*, pp. 25–86.
11. Ibid., p. 87.
12. Ibid., p. 94.
13. Ibid., p. 31.

14. Charles van Onselen, *New Babylon New Nineveh: Everyday Life on the Witwatersrand 1886–1914* (Johannesburg: Jonathan Ball Publishers, 2001), p. 7.
15. Mendelsohn, *Sammy Marks*, p. 78.
16. Ibid., p. 78.
17. Kaye, *The Tycoon and the President*, pp. 50–53.
18. Ibid., p. 55.
19. Ibid., p. 54–8.
20. Ibid., p. 64.
21. Charles van Onselen, *The Cowboy Capitalist: John Hays Hammond, the American West and the Jameson Raid* (Cape Town: Jonathan Ball, 2017), p. 26.
22. C.T. Gordon, *The Growth of Boer Opposition to Kruger (1890–1895)* (Cape Town: Oxford University Press, 1970), p. 46.
23. Ibid., p. 47.
24. J.P. Fitzpatrick, *The Transvaal from Within: A Private Record of Public Affairs* (London: William Heinemann, 1899), p. 72.
25. Gordon, *The Growth of Boer Opposition to Kruger*, p. 47.
26. Ibid., p. 47.
27. Ibid., p. 49.
28. Ibid.
29. Email correspondence with Carel van der Merwe, 23 November 2020.
30. Robert Ardrey, *African Genesis: A Personal Investigation into the Animal Origins and Nature of Man* (Kindle edition, 2014).
31. Gordon, *The Growth of Boer Opposition to Kruger*, p. 50.
32. Paul Kruger, *The Memoirs of Paul Kruger: Four Times President of the South African Republic* (London: T. Fisher Unwin, 1902), p. 235.
33. Gordon, *The Growth of Boer Opposition to Kruger*, p. 210.
34. The Press, 18 March 1893.
35. Gordon, *The Growth of Boer Opposition to Kruger*, p. 219.
36. Ibid., p. 220.
37. Fitzpatrick, *The Transvaal from Within*, p. 72.
38. Gordon, *The Growth of Boer Opposition to Kruger*, p. 53.
39. Email correspondence with Richard Mendelsohn, 27 August 2020.
40. Marais, *The Fall of Kruger's Republic*, p. 31.
41. Meredith, *Diamonds, Gold and War*, p. 293.
42. Ibid., p. 76.
43. Ibid., pp. 276–7.
44. *Land en Volk*, 29 December 1892.
45. Gordon, *The Growth of Boer Opposition to Kruger*, p. 102.
46. Van Onselen, *New Babylon New Nineveh*, pp. 7–67.
47. Ibid., p. 56.
48. David Harrison, *The White Tribe of Africa: South Africa in Perspective* (Johannesburg: Macmillan South Africa, 1986), p. 23.
49. Fitzpatrick, *The Transvaal from Within*, p. 321.

50. Ibid., p. 70.
51. Meredith, *Diamonds, Gold and War*, p. 297.
52. Fitzpatrick, *The Transvaal from Within*, p. 70.
53. Paul Kruger, session of the Volksraad.
54. Fitzpatrick, *The Transvaal from Within*, p. 321.
55. SouthAfrica.co.za, 'The Selati Rail Scandal in the Kruger' (available at http://southafrica
    .co.za/selati-rail-scandal-in-the-kruger.html; accessed 16 October 2020).
56. Mendelsohn, *Sammy Marks*, pp. 90–1.
57. Bertha Goudvis, *South African Odyssey: The Autobiography of Bertha Goudvis*, ed. Marcia
    Leveson (Johannesburg: Picador Africa, 2011), pp. 93–6.

CHAPTER 6: CECIL JOHN RHODES (II)

1. Roberts, *Cecil Rhodes*, p. 149.
2. Phyllis Lewsen, *John X. Merriman: Paradoxical South African Statesman* (Johannesburg:
   Ad. Donker, 1982), p. 98.
3. Rotberg, *The Founder*, p. 275.
4. T.R.H. Davenport, *The Afrikaner Bond: The History of a South African Political Party,
   1880–1911* (Cape Town: Oxford University Press, 1966), p. 133.
5. J.G. Lockhart and C.M. Woodhouse, *Rhodes* (London: Hodder and Stoughton, 1963),
   p. 200.
6. James Rose Innes, *Selected Correspondence* (1884–1902), p. 82.
7. Mordechai Tamarkin, *Cecil Rhodes and the Cape Afrikaners: The Imperial Colossus
   and the Colonial Parish Pump* (London: Frank Cass, 1996), p. 119.
8. James Rose Innes, *Chief Justice of South Africa, 1914–27: Autobiography* (Cape Town:
   Oxford University Press, 1949), p. 87.
9. Rotberg, *The Founder*, p. 344.
10. Ibid., pp. 371–2.
11. Rose Innes, *Selected Correspondence (1884–1902)*, pp. 100–1.
12. Ibid., pp. 102–3.
13. Paul Walters and Jeremy Fogg, 'Olive Schreiner in Rhodesia: An Episode in a Biography',
    English in Africa, Vol. 34, No. 2 (2007), p. 108, footnote 31.
14. Olive Schreiner letter to Rebecca Schreiner, May 1896 (available at https://www
    .oliveschreiner.org/vre?view=collections&colid=132&letterid=4; accessed
    25 October 2020).
15. Gerald Shaw, *Some Beginnings: The Cape Times 1876–1910* (Cape Town: Oxford
    University Press, 1975), p. 37.
16. Rotberg, *The Founder*, p. 347.
17. John Xavier Merriman, *Selections from the Correspondence of J.X. Merriman: 1890–1898*,
    ed. Phyllis Lewsen (Cape Town: Van Riebeeck Society, 1963), p. 138.
18. Shaw, *Some Beginnings*, p. 37.
19. See Dean Allen, *Empire, War and Cricket in South Africa: Logan of Matjiesfontein*
    (Cape Town: Zebra Press, 2015), p. 124.
20. Longford, *The Jameson Raid*, p. 59.

21. Wikipedia, 'Jameson Raid' (available at https://en.wikipedia.org/wiki/Jameson_Raid; accessed 24 October 2020).

22. Mendelsohn, *Sammy Marks*, p. 102.

23. Lewsen, *J.X. Merriman*, p. 198.

24. Quoted in Eric A. Walker, 'The Franchise in Southern Africa', *Cambridge Historical Journal*, Vol. 11, No. 1 (1953), p. 97.

25. See Western Cape Archives KAB, CSC2/1/1/355/14, Exhibit No. VII, p. 17.

26. Rotberg, *The Founder*, p. 365.

27. Thomas, *Rhodes*, p. 310.

28. Frank Sykes, *With Plumer in Matabeleland* (Westminster: Archibald Constable and Co., 1897), p. 27.

29. See National Library, 'Burton Collection', Letter from Jan Hendrik Hofmeyr to Burton dated 19 September 1898.

30. *Decisions of the Supreme Court of the Cape of Good Hope Vol. XVI During the Year 1899* (J.C. Juta and Co., 1901), p. 5.

31. All quotes and documents can be found in Western Cape Archives KAB, CSC2/1/1/355/14 in evidence under Examination of the Honourable Cecil John Rhodes, M.L.A., pp. 1–12.

32. *Decisions of the Supreme Court of the Cape of Good Hope Vol. XVI During the Year 1899*, pp. 16–17.

CHAPTER 7: THE BROEDERBOND

1. Hertzog speech as quoted in Charles Bloomberg, *Christian-Nationalism and the Rise of the Afrikaner Broederbond in South Africa, 1918–48* (London: Macmillan Press, 1990).

2. Bloomberg, *Christian-Nationalism and the Rise of the Afrikaner Broederbond in South Africa*, p. 108.

3. Max du Preez, 'Introduction', in Ivor Wilkins and Hans Strydom, *The Super-Afrikaners: Inside the Afrikaner Broederbond* (Johannesburg: Jonathan Ball, 2012), p. xiv.

4. Bloomberg, *Christian-Nationalism and the Rise of the Afrikaner Broederbond in South Africa*, p. xix.

5. Ibid., p. 206.

6. David Welsh, *The Rise and Fall of Apartheid* (Johannesburg: Jonathan Ball, 2009), p. 9.

7. Allister Sparks, *The Mind of South Africa: The Story of the Rise and Fall of Apartheid* (London: Heinemann, 1990), pp. 163–4.

8. Quoted in Bloomberg, *Christian-Nationalism and the Rise of the Afrikaner Broederbond in South Africa*, p. 115.

9. Bloomberg, *Christian-Nationalism and the Rise of the Afrikaner Broederbond in South Africa*, p. 116.

10. Christoph Marx, *The Oxwagon Sentinel: Radical Afrikaner Nationalism and the History of the Ossewabrandwag* (Berlin: Lit Verlag, 2008), p. 528.

11. J.H.P. Serfontein, *Brotherhood of Power: An Exposé of the Secret Afrikaner Broederbond* (London: Rex Collings Ltd, 1979), p. 64.

12. David Harrison, *The White Tribe of Africa: South Africa in Perspective* (Johannesburg: Southern Book Publishers, 1987), p. 137.

13. Serfontein, *Brotherhood of Power*, p. 64.
14. Harrison, *The White Tribe of Africa*, p. 109.
15. Wilkins and Strydom, *The Super-Afrikaners*, p. 123.
16. Bloomberg, *Christian-Nationalism and the Rise of the Afrikaner Broederbond in South Africa*, p. 214.
17. Wilkins and Strydom, *The Super-Afrikaners*, p. 428.
18. These figures are taken from Brian Bunting, *The Rise of the South African Reich* (London: International Defence and Aid Fund for South Africa, 1986).
19. Bunting, *The Rise of the South African Reich*, p. 386.
20. Ibid., p. 386.
21. Quoted in Wilkins and Strydom, *The Super-Afrikaners*, p. 128.
22. Wilkins and Strydom, *The Super-Afrikaners*, p. 320.
23. Serfontein, *Brotherhood of Power*, p. 90.
24. Serfontein, *Brotherhood of Power*, Annexure E, p. 213, quoted in *Rand Daily Mail*, 22 November 1963.
25. Serfontein, *Brotherhood of Power*, p. 92.
26. Ibid., p. 95.
27. Wilkins and Strydom, *The Super-Afrikaners*, p. 337.
28. Ibid., p. 338.
29. 'Top SA Broker Sought Legal Action', *Sunday Express*, 14 September 1980.
30. Allister Sparks, *The Sword and the Pen: Six Decades on the Political Frontier* (Johannesburg: Jonathan Ball, 2016), Kindle edition.
31. Hennie van Vuuren, *Apartheid Grand Corruption: Assessing the Scale of Crimes of Profit in South Africa from 1976 to 1994* (Pretoria: Institute for Security Studies, 2006), p. 34.
32. 'The Man Who Smeared Dr Diederichs', *Sunday Times*, 1 March 1981.
33. Helen Zille in *Rand Daily Mail*, 1978, quoted in Van Vuuren, *Apartheid Grand Corruption*.

CHAPTER 8: THE INFORMATION SCANDAL

1. Sparks, *The Sword and the Pen*.
2. Mervyn Rees and Christopher Day, *Muldergate: The Story of the Info Scandal* (Johannesburg: Macmillan, 1980), p. 10.
3. Harrison, *The White Tribe of Africa*, p. 229.
4. Rees and Day, *Muldergate*, pp. 172–3.
5. Galen Hull, 'South Africa's Propaganda War: A Bibliographic Essay', *African Studies Review*, Vol. 22, No. 3 (1979), p. 92.
6. Ron Nixon, *Selling Apartheid: South Africa's Global Propaganda War* (London: Pluto Press, 2016), Kindle edition.
7. Max du Preez, *Louis Luyt: Unauthorised* (Cape Town: Zebra Press, 2001), p. 154.
8. Chris McGreal, 'Anti-Mandela Ruling an Error, Court Finds', *Guardian*, 11 September 1999 (available at https://www.theguardian.com/world/1999/sep/11/nelsonmandela; accessed 26 October 2020).
9. Joshua Haasbroek, 'A Historical Perspective of the Information Scandal' (MA Thesis, University of the Free State, Bloemfontein, 2016), p. 103.

10. Sparks, *The Sword and the Pen*.

11. Rees and Day, *Muldergate*, p. 99.

12. Ibid., p. 118.

13. Ibid., p. 116.

14. Rex Gibson, 'Obituary: Eschel Rhoodie', *Independent*, 28 July 1993 (available at https://www.independent.co.uk/news/people/obituary-eschel-rhoodie-1487534.html; accessed 26 October 2020).

15. 'South African Premier Vorster on Angola, 11 February 1976', AP Archive (available at https://www.youtube.com/watch?v=UrBFXTKb_Xc).

16. Nixon, *Selling Apartheid*.

17. Rees and Day, *Muldergate*, p. 190.

18. Wikipedia, 'Golden Rendezvous' (available at https://en.wikipedia.org/wiki/Golden _Rendezvous#cite_note-7).

19. Bart Mills, 'The Celluloid Scandal', *The Spectator*, 25 November 1978 (available at http://archive.spectator.co.uk/article/25th-november-1978/8/the-celluloid -scandal).

20. Ed Gibbs, 'Winnie – Review', *Guardian*, 21 September 2011 (available at https:// www.theguardian.com/film/2011/sep/21/winnie-mandela-toronto-film-festival -review).

21. Quoted in Joshua Haasbroek, *Hansard*, 8 May–16 June 1978, Part 74, Col. 6499–6500.

22. Rees and Day, *Muldergate*, p. 95.

23. Sparks, *The Sword and the Pen*.

24. Rees and Day, *Muldergate*, p. 128.

25. Sparks, *The Sword and the Pen*.

CHAPTER 9: THE SMIT MURDERS

1. Mary Braid, 'Obituary: Hendrik van den Bergh', *Independent*, 21 August 1997 (available at https://www.independent.co.uk/news/people/obituary-hendrik-van-den-bergh-1246509. html; accessed 22 October 2020).

2. Authors' interview with James Myburgh, 18 May 2018.

3. Ibid.

4. Chris Karsten, *Unsolved: No Answers to Heinous South African Crimes* (Cape Town: Human & Rousseau, 2007), p. 88.

5. Hennie van Vuuren, *Apartheid Guns and Money: A Tale of Profit* (London: Hurst & Company, 2018), p. 61.

6. Ibid., p. 63.

7. James Myburgh, 'The Smit Murders Reexamined', *Politicsweb*, 7 June 2010 (available at https://www.politicsweb.co.za/news-and-analysis/the-smit-murders-reexamined; accessed 22 October 2020).

8. Braid, 'Obituary'.

9. 'Eschel Rhoodie Talks about "South Africa's Biggest Secret"', *Noseweek*, No. 2, 1 July 1993 (available at https://www.noseweek.co.za/article/174/ESCHEL-RHOODIE-TALKS-ABOUT-; accessed 2 October 2020).

10. Roy Allen, 'Roy Allen on the Smit Murders', *Politicsweb*, 3 September 2013 (available at https://www.politicsweb.co.za/opinion/roy-allen-on-the-smit-murders; accessed 22 October 2020).

11. Joe Trento, 'CIA Helped Chile Recruit Cuban Killers', *Sunday News Journal*, 24 February 1980.

12. Ibid.

13. 'New Claims Made About Who Killed Robert Smit', *IOL*, 22 November 2012 (available at https://www.iol.co.za/capetimes/palazzolo-files/new-claims-made-about-who-killed -robert-smit-1428897; accessed 22 October 2020).

14. Liza Smit with Raquel Lewis, *I Am Liza Smit* (Johannesburg: Jacana, 2018).

15. Karsten, *Unsolved*, p. 96.

16. Van Vuuren, *Apartheid Guns and Money*, pp. 64–5.

17. Myburgh, 'The Smit Murders Reexamined'.

18. *Noseweek*, No. 132, 1 October 2010.

19. Ibid.

20. R.W. Johnson, *South Africa's Brave New World: The Beloved Country Since the End of Apartheid* (London: Allen Lane, 2009), p. 25.

21. 'Eschel Rhoodie Talks about "South Africa's Biggest Secret"', *Noseweek*.

22. Ibid.

23. Ibid.

24. Ibid.

25. Sparks, *The Sword and the Pen*.

26. Ephesians 6:11–12.

27. Gelofteland, 'Die Broederbond in die Afrikaner-Politiek (7)' (available at https:// gelofteland.org/index.php/suid-afrika/271-ab-in-die-afrikanerpolitiek/5891-die -broederbond-in-die-afrikaner-politiek-7; accessed 22 October 2020).

28. Sparks, *The Sword and the Pen*.

CHAPTER 10: THE BROTHERS MATANZIMA

1. Barry Streek and Richard Wicksteed, *Render unto Kaiser: A Transkei Dossier* (Johannesburg: Ravan Press, 1981), p. 118.

2. Patrick Laurence, *The Transkei: South Africa's Politics of Partition* (Johannesburg: Ravan Press, 1976), p. 23.

3. J.B. Peires, 'The Implosion of Transkei and Ciskei', *African Affairs*, Vol. 91, No. 364 (July 1992), p. 367.

4. Authors' interview with Roger Southall, 12 June 2020.

5. Streek and Wicksteed, *Render unto Kaiser*, p. 113.

6. *The World*, 17 January 1964.

7. *Umthunywa*, 28 March 1964.

8. Authors' interview with Bantu Holomisa, 17 May 2020.

9. Kaizer D. Matanzima, *Independence My Way* (Pretoria: Foreign Affairs Association), p. 1.

10. Streek and Wicksteed, *Render unto Kaiser*, p. 114.

11. Nelson Mandela, *Long Walk to Freedom* (London: Abacus, 1995), p. 271.

12. SA History, 'Kaiser Daliwonga Matanzima' (available at https://www.sahistory.org.za/people/kaiser-daliwonga-matanzima; accessed 22 October 2020).

13. Streek and Wicksteed, *Render unto Kaiser*, p. 115.

14. Matanzima, *Independence My Way*, p. 11.

15. Laurence, *The Transkei*, p. 15.

16. Roger Southall, *South Africa's Transkei: The Political Economy of an 'Independent' Bantustan* (New York: Monthly Review Press, 1983), p. 60.

17. Streek and Wicksteed, *Render unto Kaiser*, p. 112.

18. Ibid., p. 234.

19. SA History, 'Paramount Chief Sabata Dalindyebo' (available at https://www.sahistory.org.za/people/paramount-chief-sabata-dalindyebo; accessed 22 October 2020).

20. Authors' interview with Roger Southall, 12 June 2020.

21. Edward A. Gargan, 'At a Burial of African, Bitterness', *New York Times*, 21 April 1986.

22. Eric Naki, *Bantu Holomisa: The Game Changer* (Johannesburg: Picador Africa, 2017), p. 133.

23. Streek and Wicksteed, *Render unto Kaiser*, p. 237.

24. Ibid., p. 239.

25. Ibid., p. 237.

26. Ibid., p. 240.

27. Ibid., p. 142.

28. Ibid., p. 265.

29. Ibid., pp. 267–8.

30. Mandela, *Long Walk to Freedom*, p. 272.

31. Streek and Wicksteed, *Render unto Kaiser*, p. 270.

32. Authors' interview with Bantu Holomisa, 17 May 2020.

33. Peires, 'The Implosion of Transkei and Ciskei', pp. 367–8.

34. Streek and Wicksteed, *Render unto Kaiser*, p. 113.

35. Ibid., pp. 130–31.

36. Peires, 'The Implosion of Transkei and Ciskei', p. 367.

37. Ibid., p. 368.

38. Naki, *Bantu Holomisa*, p. 78.

39. Ibid., p. 78.

40. Peires, 'The Implosion of Transkei and Ciskei', p. 369.

41. Carole Cooper et al., *Race Relations Survey: 1987/88* (Johannesburg: South African Institute of Race Relations, 1988), p. 629.

42. Peires, 'The Implosion of Transkei and Ciskei', p. 368.

43. Ibid., p. 368.

44. *Weekly Mail*, 25 September 1987.

45. Ibid.

46. Ibid.

47. Compiled from *Weekly Mail*, 25 September 1987, and Cooper et al., *Race Relations Survey*.

48. Authors' interview with Bantu Holomisa, 17 May 2020.

49. Naki, *Bantu Holomisa*, p. 83.

50. Ibid., p. 97.

51. Cooper et al., *Race Relations Survey: 1987/88*, p. 81.

52. Ibid., p. 83.

53. Ibid.

54. Ibid., p. 85.

CHAPTER 11: LUCAS MANGOPE

1. Michael Lawrence and Andrew Manson, 'The "Dog of the Boers": The Rise and Fall of Mangope in Bophuthatswana', *Journal of Southern African Studies*, Vol. 20, No. 3, Special Issue: Ethnicity and Identity in Southern Africa (September 1994), p. 451.

2. Peris Sean Jones, 'Mmabatho, "Mother of the People": Identity and Development in an "Independent" Bantustan, Bophuthatswana, 1975–1994' (PhD thesis, University of Loughborough, 1997), p. 121.

3. Andrew Manson and Bernard Mbenga, 'The Richest Tribe in Africa: Platinum-Mining and the Bafokeng in South Africa's North West Province, 1965–1999', *Journal of Southern African Studies*, Vol. 29, No. 1 (March 2003), p. 27.

4. Lawrence and Manson, 'The "Dog of the Boers"', p. 451.

5. Ibid., p. 454.

6. Email correspondence with Andrew Manson, 18 August 2020.

7. Jeffrey J. Sallaz, *The Labor of Luck: Casino Capitalism in the United States and South Africa* (Oakland: University of California Press, 2009), p. 134.

8. Nicola Sarah van der Merwe, 'Gambling in the Bophuthatswana Sun: Sun City and the Political Economy of a Bantustan Casino: 1965–1994' (M.A. Thesis, University of the Witwatersrand, Johannesburg, 2017), p. 11.

9. Ibid., p. 35.

10. *Time*, 'King Sol', 12 September 1983 (available at http://content.time.com/time/subscriber/article/0,33009,926196-1,00.html; accessed 23 October 2020).

11. Ibid.

12. Van der Merwe, 'Gambling in the Bophuthatswana Sun', pp. 30–31.

13. Songfacts, 'Sun City by Artists United Against Apartheid' (available at https://www.songfacts.com/facts/artists-united-against-apartheid/sun-city; accessed 23 October 2020).

14. Van der Merwe, 'Gambling in the Bophuthatswana Sun', p. 113.

15. Alan Cowell, 'South African Whites Seek Black TV', *New York Times*, 1 August 1984 (available at https://www.nytimes.com/1984/08/01/arts/south-africa-whites-seek-black-tv.html; accessed 26 October 2020).

16. Rokas M. Tracevskis, 'Kaunas' Most Colorful Son Buried', *Baltic Times*, 11 November 2009 (available at https://www.baltictimes.com/news/articles/23848/; accessed 23 October 2020).

17. Arianna Lissoni, 'Africa's "Little Israel": Bophuthatswana's Not-So-Secret Ties with Israel', *South African Review of Sociology*, Vol. 42, No. 3, 2011, p. 83.

18. Sasha Polakow-Suransky, *The Unspoken Alliance: Israel's Secret Relationship with Apartheid South Africa* (New York: Vintage Books, 2011), p. 157.

19. Lissoni, 'Africa's "Little Israel"', p. 84.

20. Ibid., p. 85.
21. Ibid., p. 85.
22. Authors' interview with Andrew Manson, 29 June 2020.
23. R.T. Naylor, *Economic Warfare: Sanctions, Embargo Busting, and Their Human Cost* (Boston: Northeastern University Press, 2001), p. 170.
24. Jones, 'Mmabatho, "Mother of the People"', p. 288.
25. Ibid., p. 289.
26. John Seiler, 'Transforming Mangope's Bophuthatswana: Towards Democracy in the North West Province' (unpublished manuscript, 1999).
27. Brenden Seery, 'Knowing Mangope's Truth', *Citizen*, 22 January 2018 (available at https://citizen.co.za/news/opinion/1789886/knowing-mangopes-truth/; accessed 23 October 2020).
28. Black Sash, *Grasping the Prickly Pear: The Bophuthatswana Story* (Johannesburg: Black Sash Publications, 1990), p. 10.
29. Lissoni, 'Africa's "Little Israel"', p. 87.
30. Black Sash, *Grasping the Prickly Pear*, p. 19.
31. John Battersby, 'South Africa Quells Coup Attempt in a Homeland', *New York Times*, 11 February 1988.
32. Nancy J. Jacobs, 'The Great Bophuthatswana Donkey Massacre: Discourse on the Ass and the Politics of Class and Grass', *American Historical Review*, Vol. 106, No. 2 (April 2001), p. 499.
33. Ibid., p. 487.
34. Ibid., p. 500.
35. Bill Keller, 'Homeland, Apartheid's Child, Is Defying Change', *New York Times*, 28 November 1993 (available at https://www.nytimes.com/1993/11/28/world/homeland-apartheid-s-child-is-defying-change.html; accessed 26 October 2020).
36. Keith B. Richburg, 'Behold the Land of Bop – A Figment of Apartheid That Won't Go Away', *Washington Post*, 16 September 1993 (available at https://www.washingtonpost.com/archive/politics/1993/09/16/behold-the-land-of-bop-a-figment-of-apartheid-that-wont-go-away/96533335-19a7-4324-8c80-54f8135576a0/; accessed 28 October 2020).
37. Lawrence and Manson, 'The "Dog of the Boers"', p. 457.
38. Ibid., p. 458.
39. Keller, 'Homeland, Apartheid's Child, Is Defying Change'.
40. Liz Sly, 'Homeland a Throwback to the Old S. Africa', *Chicago Tribune*, 5 September 1993 (available at https://www.chicagotribune.com/news/ct-xpm-1993-09-05-9309050286-story.html; accessed 26 October 2020).
41. Wikipedia, '1994 Bophuthatswana Crisis' (available at https://en.wikipedia.org/wiki/1994_Bophuthatswana_crisis; accessed 23 October 2020).
42. 'In the Matter between the State and Lucas Manyane Mangope: Judgment in the High Court of South Africa (Bophuthatswana Provincial Division) Mmabatho, 20 July 1988'. Judgment on sentence was given in the same High Court on 21 August 1998.
43. Authors' interview with Andrew Manson, 29 June 2020.

44. John Seiler and Brendan Seery, 'The Skweyiya Commission: Lessons for a Democratic South Africa', *Indicator SA*, Vol. 13, No. 1 (Summer 1995), pp. 13–20.

45. Manson and Mbenga, 'The Richest Tribe in Africa', p. 46.

46. Sun International, 'Sol Kerzner' (available at https://www.suninternational.com/stories/people/sol-kerzner/; accessed 23 October 2020).

47. Van der Merwe, 'Gambling in the Bophuthatswana Sun', p. 117.

CHAPTER 12: WOUTER BASSON

1. Republic of South Africa, *Report of the Commission of Inquiry into the Department of Development Aid* (Pretoria: Republic of South Africa, 1991).

2. Michael T. Klare, 'Evading the Embargo: Illicit U.S. Arms Transfers to South Africa', *Journal of International Affairs*, Vol. 35, No. 1 (1981), pp. 15–28.

3. 'Dear Reader: Robert Smit's Deadly Bombshell!!', *Noseweek*, No. 32, 1 October 2010 (available at https://www.noseweek.co.za/article/2338/Dear-Reader-Robert-Smits-deadly-bombshell!!; accessed 26 October 2020).

4. Van Vuuren, *Apartheid Guns and Money*, Kindle edition.

5. Martin Welz, 'Monstrous Hatchlings', *Noseweek*, No. 132, 1 October 2010 (available at https://www. noseweek.co.za/article/2336/Monstrous-hatchlings; accessed 23 October 2020).

6. Marléne Burger and Chandré Gould, *Secrets and Lies: Wouter Basson and South Africa's Chemical and Biological Warfare Programme* (Cape Town: Zebra Press, 2012), Kindle edition.

7. Ibid.

8. Chandré Gould and Peter Folb, *Project Coast: Apartheid's Chemical and Biological Warfare Programme* (Geneva: United Nations Institute for Disarmament Research, 2002), p. 59.

9. PBS, Interview Dr Dan Goosen (https://www.pbs.org/wgbh/pages/frontline/shows/ plague/sa/goosen.htmlhttps://www.pbs.org/wgbh/pages/frontline/shows/plague/sa/goosen.html; accessed 23 October 2020).

10. Stephen Burgess and Helen Purkitt, 'The Secret Program: South Africa's Chemical and Biological Weapons', in *The War Next Time: Countering Rogue States and Terrorists Armed with Chemical and Biological Weapons*, ed. Barry R. Schneider and Jim A. Davis (USAF Counterproliferation Center, 2004), p. 54.

11. 'The Apartheid Regime's Sinister Chemical Warfare Programme (2000)', Journeyman Pictures (available at https://www.youtube.com/watch?v=yaAOMzGFCuU&t=682s; accessed 23 October 2020).

12. William Finnegan, 'The Poison Keeper', *New Yorker*, 8 January 2001 (available at https://www.newyorker.com/magazine/2001/01/15/the-poison-keeper; accessed 23 October 2020).

13. Truth and Reconciliation Commission, 'Chemical and Biological Warfare Hearing', 7 July 1998 (available at https://www.justice.gov.za/trc/special/cbw/cbw16.htm; accessed 23 October 2020).

14. Burgess and Purkitt, 'The Secret Program', p. 33.

15. See Burger and Gould, *Secrets and Lies*, Kindle edition.

16. Burger and Gould, *Secrets and Lies*, Kindle edition.

17. Staff reporter, 'Nats Were in Bed with Mafia Boss', *Mail & Guardian*, 5 February 1999

(available at https://mg.co.za/article/1999-02-05-nats-were-in-bed-with-mafia-boss/; accessed 23 October 2020).

18. Quoted in Constanze Bauer, 'Public Sector Corruption and its Control in South Africa', in Hope and Chikulo, *Corruption and Development in Africa*, p. 202.

19. Ibid., p. 223.

20. Ibid., p. 224.

21. June Goodwin and Ben Schiff, *Heart of Whiteness* (New York: Scribner, 1995), p. 144.

22. Republic of South Africa, *Report of the Commission of Inquiry into the Department of Development Aid*, 1991.

23. Quoted in Bauer, 'Public Sector Corruption and its Control in South Africa', p. 43.

24. Bauer, 'Public Sector Corruption and its Control in South Africa', p. 227.

25. '"From Murder, Corruption and Mismanagement to Democracy, Justice and Good Government": African National Congress Briefing Document to Submit on Corruption and Murder', 18 June 1992 (available at http://www.historicalpapers.wits.ac.za/ inventories/inv_pdfo/ AG1977/AG1977-A3-11-4-2-001-jpeg.pdf; accessed 23 October 2020).

CHAPTER 13: JACOB ZUMA

1. 'Letter to Lover Spells Trouble for Winnie', *Independent*, 7 September 1992 (available at https://www.independent.co.uk/news/world/letter-to-lover-spells-trouble-for-winnie -1549863.html; accessed 9 November 2020).

2. Suzanne Daley, 'South Africa Scandal over "Sarafina" Spotlights Corruption in the A.N.C.', *New York Times*, 8 October 1996 (https://www.nytimes.com/1996/10/08/world/south-africa -scandal-over-sarafina-spotlights-corruption-in-the-anc.html; accessed 9 November).

3. See Gareth van Onselen, 'Dlamini-Zuma and Sarafina II: The Original Nkandla', *Business Day Live*, 8 April 2016 (available at http://sa-monitor.com/dlamini-zuma-sarafina-ii -original-nkandla-bdlive-8-april-2016/; accessed 9 November 2020); Tom Lodge, 'Political Corruption in South Africa', *African Affairs*, Vol. 97, No. 387 (1998), pp. 157–87.

4. See Bauer, 'Public Sector Corruption and its Control in South Africa', p. 228.

5. See Jonathan Hyslop, 'Political Corruption: Before and After Apartheid', *Journal of Southern African Studies*, Vol. 31, No. 4 (2005), pp. 773–89; 'For Whom the Road Tolls', Noseweek, No. 47, 1 July 2003 (available at https://www.noseweek.co.za/article/136/FOR-WHOM-THE -ROAD-TOLLS; accessed 9 November 2020).

6. Wikipedia, 'Allan Boesak' (available at https://en.wikipedia.org/wiki/Allan_Boesak; accessed 9 November 2020); Chris McGreal, 'Boesak Took Cash Meant for Black Children', *Guardian*, 18 March 1999 (available at https://www.theguardian.com/world/1999/mar/18/ chrismcgreal; accessed 9 November 2020).

7. See Lodge, 'Political Corruption in South Africa', pp. 157–87; *News24*, 'Abe Williams Walks Free', 25 September 2001 (available at https://www.news24.com/News24/Abe-Williams -walks-free-20010925; accessed 5 November 2020).

8. Wikipedia, 'Tony Yengeni' (available at https://en.wikipedia.org/wiki/Tony_Yengeni; accessed 5 November 2020).

9. See Wikipedia, 'Schabir Shaik' (available at https://en.wikipedia.org/wiki/Schabir_Shaik; accessed 5 November 2020).

10. 'Scandal Rattles South Africa's Elite', *Guardian*, 9 November 2006 (available at https://www.theguardian.com/world/2006/nov/09/worlddispatch.southafrica; accessed 1 December 2020).

11. Wikipedia, 'Jackie Selebi' (available at https://en.wikipedia.org/wiki/Jackie_Selebi; accessed 5 November 2020); Bill Corcoran, 'Police Chief Tipped Off Drug Dealer, S Africa Trial Told', *Irish Times*, 9 October 2009 (available at https://www.irishtimes.com/news/police-chief-tipped-off-drug-dealer-s-africa-trial-told-1.753614; accessed 9 November 2020).

12. See Wikipedia, 'Bosasa' (available at https://en.wikipedia.org/wiki/Bosasa; accessed 5 November 2020).

13. Andisiwe Makinana, '"The ANC and Its Leaders Stand Accused of Corruption" – Ramaphosa in Heartfelt Call to ANC to Change Its Ways', *TimesLive*, 23 August 2020 (available at https:// www.timeslive.co.za/politics/2020-08-23-the-anc-and-its-leaders-stand-accused-of-corruption-ramaphosa-in-heartfelt-call-to-anc-to-change-its-ways/; accessed 9 November 2020).

14. Jacques Pauw, *The President's Keepers: Those Keeping Zuma in Power and out of Prison* (Cape Town: Tafelberg, 2017), Kindle edition.

15. See Pauw, *The President's Keepers*, and Adriaan Basson and Pieter du Toit, *Enemy of the People: How Jacob Zuma Stole South Africa and How the People Fought Back* (Johannesburg: Jonathan Ball, 2017), Kindle edition.

16. Hyslop, 'Political Corruption', p. 787.

17. Paul Holden and Hennie van Vuuren, *The Devil in the Detail: How the Arms Deal Changed Everything* (Johannesburg: Jonathan Ball, 2011), p. 273.

18. Govan Whittles, 'Zuma Pays Back the Money – But Where did he get the R7.8 Million?', *Mail & Guardian*, 12 September 2016 (available at https://mg.co.za/article/2016-09-12-zuma-pays-back-the-money-but-where-did-he-get-the-r78-million/; accessed 9 November 2020).

19. Theal, *Willem Adriaan van der Stel and Other Historical Sketches*, p. 249.

20. Pauw, *The President's Keepers*, Kindle edition.

21. Letter from Sir Richard Plasket in *Records of the Cape Colony: Vol XXIII Nov–Dec, 1825*.

22. Welsh, *The Rise and Fall of Apartheid*, p. 455.

23. Email correspondence with Andrew Feinstein, 20 October 2020.

24. Fouché, p. 231.

25. Gordon, *The Growth of Boer Opposition to Kruger*, p. 219.

PICTURE CREDITS

p. 1: Icswart / Shutterstock.com

p. 3: Rijksmuseum, Wikipedia Commons

p. 9: RKD – Netherlands Institute for Art History

p. 11: Cape Town Archives Repository / Nick Dall

p. 16: Cape Town Archives Repository

p. 21: Cape Town Archives Repository / Desmond Louw

p. 27: (both): Cape Town Archives Repository, E2820 and E313

p. 31: Cape Town Archives Repository, M139

p. 33: Cape Town Archives Repository

p. 35: Lady Anne Barnard, *South Africa a Century Ago (1797–1801)*, ed. H.J. Anderson
    (Cape Town: Maskew Miller Ltd, 1924), p. 110

p. 40: Cape Town Archives Repository

p. 46: Cape Town Archives Repository AG15693

p. 48: Cape Town Archives Repository / Nick Dall

p. 51: Cape Town Archives Repository M383

p. 57: Cape Town Archives Repository E3864

p. 58: Cape Town Archives Repository CA2509

p. 62: Cape Town Archives Repository

p. 66: Cape Town Archives Repository M448

p. 72: Cape Town Archives Repository M447

p. 73: Cape Town Archives Repository E8559

p. 79: Wikipedia Commons

p. 86: Supplied

p. 90: Supplied

p. 91: Cape Town Archives Repository

p. 92: Supplied

p. 95: Lantern slide of President Paul Kruger. Photographer and date unknown. Library of
    Parliament, South Africa

p. 99: Supplied by Richard Mendelsohn

p. 101: Sam Kemp, *Black Frontiers* (London: Harrap & Co., 1932), p. 10

p. 102: Cape Town Archives Repository

p. 109: National Archives Repository, Pretoria / Zabeth Botha

p. 118: Thomas Pakenham, *The Boer War* (Johannesburg: Jonathan Ball, 1979), p. 310

p. 120: *Punch*

p. 121: Supplied

p. 127: Leslie Ward, Wikipedia Commons

p. 133: *Illustrated London News*, 25 February 1896

p. 134: *Punch*

p. 137: Cape Town Archives Repository

p. 138: Olive Schreiner, *Trooper Peter Halket of Mashonaland* (London: T. Fisher Unwin, 1897), frontispiece

p. 139: Cape Town Archives Repository

p. 142: Cape Town Archives Repository

p. 151: Supplied

p. 152: National Archives Repository, Pretoria / Zabeth Botha

p. 154: Wikipedia Commons

p. 157: Supplied

p. 163: Supplied

p. 169: SABC Archive

p. 171: National Archives Repository, Pretoria / Zabeth Botha

p. 175: Supplied by Martin Welz

p. 179: National Archives Repository, Pretoria / Zabeth Botha

p. 181: National Archives Repository, Pretoria / Zabeth Botha

p. 185: National Afrikaans Literary Museum and Research Centre

p. 190: Tony Grogan Cartoon Collection (BC1460), UCT Libraries Special Collections

p. 201: *Rand Daily Mail*, 3 Nov 1978, p. 1 (online NewsBank)

p. 203: Gallo Images / Beeld Archives

p. 204: Gallo Images / Beeld Archives

p. 207: National Archives Repository, Pretoria / Zabeth Botha

p. 213: Vita Palestrant

p. 215: National Archives Repository, Pretoria / Zabeth Botha

p. 218: National Archives Repository, Pretoria / Zabeth Botha

p. 221: *Contact* magazine, 27 December 1962 / Disa Archives

p. 225: Harvey Campion, *The New Transkei* (Johannesburg: Valiant, 1976), p. 69

p. 231: National Archives Repository, Pretoria / Zabeth Botha

p. 235: *Weekly Mail* / *Mail & Guardian*

p. 239: Supplied

p. 241: Supplied

p. 243: National Archives Repository, Pretoria / Zabeth Botha

p. 245: National Archives Repository, Pretoria / Zabeth Botha

p. 246: Supplied

p. 257: National Archives Repository, Pretoria / Zabeth Botha

p. 259: Supplied

p. 263: Anna Zieminiski / AFP via Getty Images

p. 264: National Archives Repository, Pretoria / Zabeth Botha

p. 267: National Archives Repository, Pretoria / Zabeth Botha

p. 274: © Zapiro

p. 279: National Archives Repository, Pretoria / Zabeth Botha

p. 285: Shutterstock.com

p. 291: © Zapiro

p. 295: Discott, CC BY-SA 4.0 via Wikimedia Commons

p. 302: Matthew Blackman

p. 307: Supplied by the authors

GLOSSARY

boet: brother
braaibroodjie: South African braai staple; toasted cheese
chinas: friends
Die koeël is nie deur die kerk nie: The case is not closed
Engelse Gevaar: English Peril
gatvol: fed up
impis: armed division of Zulu warriors
induna: headman
koekie: cookie
landdrost: magistrate at the Cape
maatjies: mates
mielieboers: mielie or corn farmers
moering: beating
nogal: moreover
onbehoorlik: improper
ossewa: ox wagon
rooinekke: pejorative term for Englishmen (literally, rednecks)
Randlords: 1800s entrepreneurs who controlled the gold and diamond mining
    enterprises in South Africa, particularly on the Witwatersrand
secunde: second in command at the Cape
skelm: crook
Swart Gevaar: Black Peril
toestand: (in a) state
tjommies: friends
trekboers: nomadic farmers
Uitlanders: foreigners
Vaderland: Fatherland
veldskoen: leather shoes typically worn by farmers
verkramptes: conservatives
verligtes: enlightened moderates
volksstaat: homeland or people's republic/state
vrye burghers: Free Burghers; early settlers and 'free citizens' of the Cape

ABBREVIATIONS

ANC: African National Congress
AWB: Afrikaner Weerstandsbeweging
BDF: Bophuthatswana Defence Force
BOSS: Bureau of State Security
BSAC: British South Africa Company
CBW: chemical and biological weapons
CCB: Civil Cooperation Bureau
COSAG: Concerned South Africans Group
DET: Department of Education and Training
DG: director general
DP: Democratic Party
EFF: Economic Freedom Fighters
FNLA: National Front for the Liberation of Angola
IMF: International Monetary Fund
JZ: Jacob Zuma
MP: Member of Parliament
MPLA: People's Movement for the Liberation of Angola
NGK: Nederduitse Gereformeerde Kerk
NP: National Party
NPA: National Prosecuting Authority
OB: Ossewabrandwag
PM: prime minister
SAAN: South African Associated Newspapers
SABC: South African Broadcasting Corporation
SADF: South African Defence Force
SARFU: South African Rugby Football Union
SARS: South African Revenue Service
SSC: State Security Council
TDF: Transkei Defence Force
TRC: Truth and Reconciliation Commission
UCDP: United Christian Democratic Party
UCT: University of Cape Town
UNIBO: University of Bophuthatswana
UNITA: National Union for the Total Independence of Angola
VOC: Dutch East India Company
ZAR: Zuid-Afrikaansche Republiek

INDEX